Accidentally on Purpose

Accidentally on Purpose

A ONE-NIGHT STAND,

MY UNPLANNED PARENTHOOD,

AND LOVING THE

BEST MISTAKE I EVER MADE

MARY F. POLS

An Imprint of HarperCollinsPublishers

HarperCollins books may be purchased for educational, business, or sales promotional use. For information, please write: Special Markets Department, HarperCollins Publishers, 10 East 53rd Street, New York, NY 10022.

The events and experiences described in this memoir are true and have been faithfully rendered as I have remembered them. Conversations recounted come from my keen recollection of them; they are not written to represent word-for-word documentation. Some names, identifying details, and circumstances have been changed to protect the privacy of those involved.

Portion of "The Winter Hexagon" reprinted with permission from the Edward Pols Estate. The poem originally appeared in *The Sewanee Review* and is included in *Remembrance of Things to Come*, published by Bowdoin College (2007).

FIRST EDITION

Designed by Gretchen Achilles

Library of Congress Cataloging-in-Publication Data is available upon request.

ISBN: 978-0-06-125692-9

08 09 10 11 12   ID/RRD   10 9 8 7 6 5 4 3 2 1

FOR EILEEN SINNOTT POLS AND EDWARD POLS

The day returns, but nevermore
Returns the traveler to the shore.
And the tide rises, the tide falls.

—HENRY WADSWORTH LONGFELLOW

Contents

Accidentally on Purpose

PART I

Then

CHAPTER 1

The Trojan on the Floor

I STOOD IN A BACKYARD hung with streamers, trying to talk myself into a good mood while I waited for my hamburger to cook. This was my friend Dave's fortieth birthday party. I ought to be cheerful. There were balloons, for God's sake, and a homemade cake, and I was surrounded by plenty of people I loved and others I liked and others I imagined I'd like if I knew them. But while it wasn't even my fortieth birthday—not for ten months anyway—I felt each and every one of Dave's years. I was almost middle-aged. Ancient. The damp, foggy wind that is the specialty of a San Francisco summer whipped through my hair, and I could have sworn it whispered *Spinster* in my ear.

The passage of time was evident on all our faces and bodies. There was the former playboy novelist, grown thick around the middle; his boyish good looks were finally going to seed. He looked happy, though, chasing his young son around the backyard. An old flame of mine, the one we thought would never settle down, stood with his arm wrapped protectively around his vastly pregnant wife. My friend Kir joked about her crow's-feet, yet her oldest daughter stood nearly level with her shoulder, green-eyed and beautiful. Milestones seemed far less traumatic when you were bringing new life to the party.

The hamburgers were still raw in the middle. The cute orthopedic surgeon my friends had promised would be there had been called into surgery and wouldn't be coming. I went inside to the bathroom and stared into the mirror. My hair was frizzy and the gray was showing, although, sadly, not in a glamorous Emmylou Harris kind of way. I felt so left behind. I was the same person I'd been for the last fifteen years. I could be counted on to be fun, wry, and sarcastic. But I was also chronically lonely, sick of myself, sick of my sad stories, and even sick of my funny stories. I contemplated going home to soak in my sorrows. I'd put Kieslowski's *Blue* in the DVD player and break out my bottle of Irish whiskey. The cats would comfort me. The wind whistled up through the cracked bathroom window to add a fresh taunt: *Cliché*, it hissed.

I decided to go to Liza's house instead. She'd recently separated from her husband, Hugh, and he had their two young sons for the weekend. Liza and her brother John would cheer me up. I'd known them for more than half my life. As college students, we'd worked together at a funky old summer resort in Maine, the kind of family-style place that liked to hire waitresses and busboys from liberal arts schools with names the guests recognized. Twenty years later, there wasn't much we didn't know about one another.

We made pasta and discussed our various romantic plights. John thoughtfully stroked his goatee and nodded sympathetically. He was single, but Liza and I assumed it was only a matter of time for him. He sold wine, bought French soap, baked bread, and was *nice*. He was a catch. Not for me—he was practically my surrogate brother—but for someone, someone lucky.

I found myself prowling the house after dinner. I wanted to wash away the gloom of birthdays and the absent orthopedic surgeon. Usually it was easy to persuade Liza to set out on an evening's adventure. Up until the last few years, she had been fairly demure. Always elegant, but hidden away in baggy jeans. All that changed when she and Hugh moved to San Francisco. Her jeans got lower and tighter as her spirits grew higher and the marital bonds looser. Now that she and Hugh were apart, John had moved into their flat to keep Liza company.

"Just one beer," Liza had said finally, shrugging into a suede coat.

When we got to Finnegan's Wake, she flatly refused to advance past the first empty barstools. She was wearing a kerchief over her impeccably maintained blond highlights. She looked as though she'd rather be scrubbing the tub than going out for a pint.

"I'm Hagrid," she kept saying. Her older son was deep into Harry Potter. "I don't want to be seen."

So John and I perched at the end of the bar with her. The walls were brown and there was a pool table, and that was about the extent of the decor, the perfect blank slate for an evening. If we didn't run into someone we already knew at Finnegan's, we could usually count on making some new friends. A doughy middle-aged guy on the adjacent barstool had instantly perked up at the sight of us. But between Liza's charwoman headgear and John's barely suppressed yawns, I doubted it would be a late night.

I looked out the window. A guy in a baseball cap smoking a cigarette caught my eye. Cute, I thought. Really cute. Young, though. Maybe thirty-five, probably younger.

The cute guy flicked his cigarette to the ground and walked into the bar. He sat down beside us, taking a coaster off the top of a half-drunk beer. He knew the doughy guy, who had been attempting to engage Liza in conversation from the moment she sat down. This often happened when we were out. When it came to men, it was almost as if Liza emitted one of those whistles that only dogs can hear.

She sat up straighter in the presence of the cute guy. He had an infectious smile and wide, sexy eyes. Within minutes Liza had got him to lift off his green A's cap, revealing short, dark blond hair and a receding hairline. I could tell she was doing age calculations in her head based on the hairline. I was doing them too. She asked his name. It was Matt.

"Now, how old are you, Mr. Matt?" she asked. "Because we're quite old."

She was the only woman I knew who consistently lied upward about her age. Since she looked younger than she was to begin with, this usually produced expressions of astonishment and then a cheering round of compliments.

"I'm twenty-nine," Matt said. She winced, and I looked away. Twenty-nine was unacceptable. My last serious boyfriend had been five years younger than I, and that experience had produced no desire to dip into the youthful dating pool again.

But there we were, sitting next to each other at the bar, so we continued talking. The movie of *At Play in the Fields of the Lord* was on the bar television right behind us, and it launched us onto the topic of Peter Matthiessen. Matt didn't want to even glance at the screen because he planned to read Matthiessen next. In the ensuing discussion of literature, I thought, *Certainly this guy can't be a cretin.* At some point during this conversation, we looked into each other's eyes, and suddenly in my mind there was a *maybe*.

What I always loved about the hookup in the less complicated days—the days before the wretched biological clock intervened—was the sharp sense of recognition you had when you met a man's eyes and realized that not only were you going to sleep together, but he'd be the next person who would really matter to you. You just knew it. In recent years, that feeling had become less trustworthy. For whatever reason—his baggage, your baggage—it just wasn't as simple as it used to be. So even though I felt that electric surge when I met Matt's eyes, I decided to let it go.

Yet even a hint of that feeling is sometimes enough, because it makes you remember hope. By that I don't mean generic, theoretical hope, the kind that makes you tell yourself, "I'm a good and kind person; of course I'll find someone someday"; I mean active, palpable hope—the kind that resonates in your gut and makes you realize how pale theoretical hope looks in comparison. The first kind of hope is the fuel that gets you out of the house on a Friday night; the second is the kind that replenishes a depleted tank.

Liza went out to smoke a cigarette and left us there together. John was gamely talking to the doughy guy.

"Do you want to go out sometime?" Matt asked me. I smiled rue-fully and told him I was too old for him.

"Why?" he asked.

I didn't really have an answer. I could have told him about that last younger man, the one who actually *sucked his thumb*, but I re-frained. Matt wasn't even in his thirties yet. A boy toy, not someone I could really date. Liza came back to the bar before we'd resolved the matter. John had already slipped away, too tired to stay any longer. Soon it was closing time, and Liza asked Matt if he wanted to come back to her house with us.

We opened a bottle of port, smoked some pot, and watched Liza get drunker. Eventually she collapsed on the couch next to Matt, nestling her head against his shoulder. He had his arm around her, and I watched his fingers move on her upper arm. I turned away, fig-uring that the spark I'd seen in his eyes wasn't meant exclusively for me. I pushed aside the disappointment. But when Liza announced her intention to fall asleep in his armpit, he seemed alarmed and told her she should go to bed.

Together we helped her weave her way up the stairs, and then we went back to the couch. A minute later, he was kissing me. Two minutes later, he was on top of me, grinding his hips against mine. Three minutes later, I realized all of this would be better naked.

"I'm coming home with you," I said.

Matt's apartment was less than two blocks away from Liza's, so there wasn't much time to contemplate the wisdom of what I was about to do. However, he did give me pause as we stepped onto Cole Street together. He wanted me to know that his apartment wasn't much to look at.

"I've got to get a new place," he said.

Just as long as there's a *bed*, I thought. Hell, I'd be fine with an easy chair.

"But not until I get a J-O-B," he added.

My slightly stupefied brain cells put the letters together. My first thought was *Why is he* spelling *job?* The second was *Good God, why doesn't he have one?* The third was that I still wanted it to be adorable Matt who saved me from my unwanted celibacy. The last guy I'd considered sleeping with was forty-six and a fixture on Nerve. com's online dating service. He owned a home in the city that he was fixing up and also a lake house somewhere up near Mt. Shasta. He was what my mother would have called "a good catch." He most certainly had a job. He also had a big wide ass. I had taken one look at it in his pants and dreaded seeing it on its way to my bathroom, nude.

Running my hands over Matt's later in the night, I felt many things, none of them dread. Maybe just a little sadness during my internal debate about the wisdom of all this: "I should probably stop sleeping with beautiful young guys," the sensible me told myself. "But I *like* sleeping with beautiful young guys," I said back. "Yes, but it's not the path to settling down," Sensible Mary said. "Look, this could be the last beautiful guy who wants to sleep with you," I told her. "So just stifle yourself."

And there was bliss as well. Although it was not getting any easier to strip off my clothes in front of a man, especially after three weeks of shirking yoga while enjoying a Safeway two-for-one special on salt and vinegar potato chips, Matt made it painless. "You're beautiful," he murmured into my ear, pulling his T-shirt over his head in that peculiar one-handed way boys have. "You're awesome."

Awesome? God, I thought, please don't call me dude.

Then I tossed such concerns to the four winds. I was coming up on a full year without having slept with anyone. After that, celibacy starts to seem less like a misfortune that might end at any moment and more like a habit you can't shake. Yes, the pillows under my picky, thread-count–obsessed head were foam and only half covered with ratty navy blue cases, but I managed to effectively block that out. I knew my head would survive the night and that some other woman, or more likely, a girl, would have to deal with his bad bedding issues. In the meantime, I had his smooth slim body, his tenderness, and his insistent penis, which he kept rubbing against me, even after we'd had sex and I was sleepily, deliciously satisfied. He hadn't come yet and I wasn't sure he would. But I was too tired to ponder the mysteries of the male orgasm.

"Have you ever read *Lonesome Dove*?" I asked, figuring him for a fan. I can tell those guys from a mile away. My list of former lovers was filled with the kind of romantic, smart souls who warmed to Larry McMurtry.

"Twice," he said, into my neck. "I finished it and reread it right away."

"Good," I said. "I was going to tell you I'd give you a poke in the morning, but I had to make sure you'd get the reference first."

Matt had stacks of books next to his bed, many I'd read, some I'd been meaning to read, some I hadn't heard of but that looked compelling. He also had a pile of lacrosse sticks in the corner and an array of baseball caps on top of every post of his bed frame. If those were the accoutrements of the boy he still was, the books seemed like the accoutrements of the man he would become.

In the morning, I snuck into the bathroom, feeling chagrined at my situation. I'd been in nicer Porta-Potties, and in the light of day, the rest of Matt's place was revealed to be more of a boardinghouse than an apartment, with no living room and locks on all the individual bedroom doors. It seemed ridiculous for a grown woman to be there, an embarrassment. But when I got back to his bed, there he was again, whispering that he'd wanted me right away in the bar, making me feel desirable. This time, he came too.

When I picked my scattered clothes up off the floor and joked about making the Walk of Shame back to Liza's place, he laughed and said, "How is that supposed to make me feel?" I felt a twinge of guilt because, of course, I *was* using him. If I'd been twenty-nine as well, I wouldn't have left. We'd have gone out to breakfast and I'd probably have fallen madly in love. I looked at him, sprawled on the bed, naked and relentlessly lovely, and bent down to kiss him good-bye.

At my feet, I noticed the Trojan, still neatly sealed in its wrapper. The night before, I'd asked him if he had a condom and he'd dutifully gone and gotten one. But then he'd gone in and out of hardness, the way that guys do when they're nervous and shy with you. Or drunk. Putting a condom on a man with an iffy erection is like trying to catch a butterfly with a torn net; it may simply flutter off and be gone for good. Directness is usually my forte, but I once had a boyfriend who had struggled mightily the first time we slept together. When I mentioned, months later, that I'd debated cracking a joke to relieve the tension that first time, he looked at me and said, "If you had, that would have been the last time you'd ever have seen me." So after telling Matt to fetch the condom, I'd never insisted he put it on, not even in the morning, when shyness and alcohol had clearly ceased to be an issue.

But now that orange wrapper practically pulsated up at me through the dim morning light. Unsafe sex. My good cheer waned as I mentally skimmed over the risks, the soup to nuts of HIV and STDs. My married friends would be appalled. They always want to know if you used a condom, like schoolteachers checking your penmanship. I gave myself a chiding, then decided to be optimistic. He seemed totally straight, fairly innocent, and definitely not an IV drug user.

I never once gave any thought to pregnancy. I was a thirty-nine-year-old woman. What chance did I have of still having an eager, ready egg on the one night in eleven months that I'd had sex?

CHAPTER 2

The Magic Wand

ABOUT THREE WEEKS LATER, I had dinner plans with my friends April and Laura. I prepared for that night as I had for countless others, striving for casual yet sexy, with a sleeveless top under a suede jacket, and cowboy boots to make me feel tough.

I looked in the mirror. Still reasonably pretty. Not in a beachy way, but in an Irish kind of way, with dark hair, pale skin, green eyes. I am tall enough and long-legged enough to do jeans and boots well, although I have not looked good in a bikini since I was six.

That orthopedic surgeon who was supposed to be at Dave's birthday party was someone I'd just met. Since smart, attractive newcomers to my social circle were scarce, my interest had been piqued and I'd made inquiries. But when he hadn't shown up at Dave's, part of me had thought he probably wouldn't have returned the interest anyway. My self-confidence was ebbing. The scarlet A on my chest stood for Available, and at thirty-nine, I'd been wearing it long enough for it to feel like an apology. I had begun to suppose that when men looked at me, they presumed that there was something wrong with me. Why else would I still be alone?

I had been with what seemed like a wide variety of men, and clearly none had been right for me. A couple weren't smart enough. Some weren't ready to settle down. One was gay and still in the closet. Then there were the liars, the cheats. One who lived with someone else but moaned to me about how much more fascinating I was until he had me completely wrapped around his little finger. Then of course he let go, flinging me a mile into emotional cement.

But as rational as the reasons for these relationship mishaps were on an individual basis, collectively they took on the stench of failure, and the only consistent factor in the equation was *me*. Perhaps I was too bitchy, angry, bitter, controlling? Not needy or clingy anymore, but what about acerbic? I make my living as a movie critic, and maybe whatever it was in my nature that made me want to be a critic was off-putting to men. Ninety percent of my hate mail at work came from the opposite sex. "Bitch," they'd say. "Why don't you just keep your opinions to yourself?"

Certainly I'm opinionated and proud of it. But I'm also smart, affectionate, kind. I have a good job. On a mercenary level, I can get you into any movie at least three days before it opens. For free. The only catches are I'll be taking notes in the dark—and I won't want to talk about the film on the way home.

I am completely truthful. I have never cheated on anyone, nor would I. While it is true that I have two cats, the universal symbol of spinsterhood, I also love dogs. Dogs love me. I come from a family of six, so I work well in chaos. I am social. I can cook. I can make, and have made, lobster rolls for forty people in an afternoon. With fish chowder on the side. "You are such a catch," my friend Karen said once, using a tortilla chip to scoop up the ceviche I'd just made for her. "I just don't understand how you're single." Crunch, crunch. Scoop. "It doesn't make sense."

There was no point in dwelling on any of that right now. "Just a nice quiet night with the girls," I told my reflection. I put lipstick on, then wiped most of it off. It was hardly going to be a wild evening. Both April and Laura were still bruised from their last encounters, April with a younger boyfriend who turned out to be a jerk, and Laura with an ex-husband who left her for another woman shortly after Laura gave birth to their first child (a guy who, incidentally, immediately impregnated the other woman).

I felt that familiar female surge of guilt as we dug into a shared plate of fried calamari. I'd worn my loosest jeans that night because I was bloated and premenstrual. *This isn't going to help*, I thought, dipping another one into the aioli. *Blimp*.

Where was my period, anyway? It seemed as though I'd been mentally preparing for it for days. Actually a week. And then some. April and Laura were chatting away. I started in on my second vodka gimlet and realized that I was drinking with less relish than usual. Technically maybe I was, what, a day late? Maybe two? But God, my boobs were so sore. I tried not to be obvious as I pressed the sides of my arms against them. Really sore.

During a lull in the conversation, I put the glass down on the table.

"I'm a little worried that I might be pregnant," I said. "Just a little worried."

April's big blue eyes got bigger. Laura sat back in her chair.

"Who?" April asked. She sounded baffled, understandably. For all she knew, it had been a year since I'd had a boyfriend.

"This young guy," I said. "I met him at Finnegan's Wake."

I gave them the short version, until April, also a journalist, who specializes in health and science stories, started grilling me on when I'd had my last period, precisely what date I'd had sex with Matt, etc. She gave me a deadly serious look.

"I think after dinner we need to go get an EPT," she said. "You can do it at the bar."

We were headed to a bar in the Mission District, a retro place where the waitresses wear vintage dresses and they still let people smoke. I couldn't quite fathom the image of myself squatting over a stick in the tiny bathroom, with some drunken guy pounding on the door.

"If I'm pregnant, I don't want to find out at the Lone Palm," I said. "I'll do one tomorrow morning."

"If you're pregnant, what are you going to do?" Laura asked.

I leaned back in my seat. I felt far away. The noise in the crowded restaurant receded. The door opened and two couples walked in, bringing a breeze with them that reached all the way to our table, brushing across my cheeks.

"I guess I'll become a single mother," I said.

It sounded absurdly blasé yet terrifyingly true.

WHEN I BECAME A WOMAN of a certain age, that is, around thirty-five, my female friends began floating the suggestion of single motherhood to me. "Have you ever thought about doing it on your own?" they'd say, a wineglass in one hand, their brows slightly furrowed with concern over my future. Their cell phones would be close by, because a night out with the girls when you are thirty-five or older typically means that back home, a husband is bumbling through babysitting duties and will almost certainly require coaching at some point.

I'd drink deeply from my own glass and eye the hostess, who certainly looked as though she could use some help in the kitchen, right this minute. "I'll be back," I'd say. "I think Kir needs help cleaning that fish."

I didn't want to hear a sales pitch for single motherhood from a married woman. What did she know about it? Moreover, the question pissed me off, implying as it did that my romantic situation had been declared hopeless. I might think it was worth waiting for the right man, but my friends had clearly given up on that possibility. What they had—the smart, loving, outdoorsy husbands; the houses; the cooing babies; the adorable toddlers; the winsome five-year-olds; the minivans; the Christmas card postcards of perfection—all of it was out of my reach. They were suggesting that I resort to something I doubted they would ever have seriously contemplated doing themselves.

I knew they had my best interests at heart, but it seemed as though they were recommending I go climb Everest without an oxygen tank. It was obvious from observing them that motherhood was hard as hell. At my monthly book club, half the mothers in the room would be bursting into tears over sleep deprivation or some trauma involving a negligent nanny. The other half would be vague as to what it was we'd read; they'd blame their dulled memories on breast-feeding hormones. One friend with an infant couldn't cope with the strains of motherhood at all; she retreated into the garage and sat on the washing machine doing bong hits between diaper changes. And they all had husbands. With jobs. And nice houses. Why would I ever want to undertake this on my own? First I wanted a husband. With a job. And a nice house. Or even just a starter cottage with one bedroom.

If I did get stuck listening to their sales pitch for sperm banks and/or Chinese orphans, I listened with a skeptical ear. Sure, their friend from graduate school had become a single mother and was as happy as a clam, but that was *her*, not me. I was barely making ends meet on my own. Journalism is not a profitable business, at least not for reporters and feature writers. I didn't see how I could support a baby.

We tend to be united in fear, but divided in bravery. We look for excuses for why we can't do what someone else does. I suppose to these kindly women, I looked like a natural candidate for single motherhood, a semi-artsy Bay Area resident who did yoga, voted left, and wore jeans to work. But what they didn't know about me was that I was not interested in a nontraditional life. Beyond the financial constraints of doing it on my own, I longed for partnership with a wonderful man, marriage, and *then* family. Somewhere in the bottom of a box in my closet I had a pair of photos I'd ripped out of the *Washington Post* Sunday magazine almost twenty years ago, photos of a dark-haired model on a beach, wearing a slim-fitting lace wedding dress, which I'd thought would be just the kind of dress I'd like to wear to my wedding.

So when I said to April and Laura that I guessed that, if I was pregnant, I'd become a single mother, what I was really thinking was: *Jesus, Mary, and Joseph, what fool just uttered those words?*

· · ·

IT WAS AFTER MIDNIGHT when I sped down Guerrero from the Lone Palm. Since our night together, all Matt and I had done was go to a movie, but he'd made it into my cell phone directory. He might be too young and absent a J-O-B, but I'd be lying if I said I didn't want to sleep with him again. Plus, I figured, if I was going to find out I was pregnant in the morning, I wanted to lay eyes on the father of my child at least once more. It seemed only proper to call. Civilized. He answered.

"What if I picked you up and brought you home to my place?" I asked. "I'll bring you back in the morning."

"Okay," he said, agreeably.

At my place I noticed two things about him. The first was that my cats liked him and that he seemed to like them. The second was that we had very little to say to each other. He seemed so young and unformed that I would have believed him if he'd told me he was still in college. He'd been unemployed for an appallingly long time, temping sporadically for three years.

Nonetheless, he was still adorable. I was grateful when he lunged again, ending the stilted conversation. I'd no intention of telling him anything about the possibility that I was pregnant. I just wanted to see and smell and taste him again. Rolling around with him in my bed was just the diversion I needed.

In the morning, I dropped him off at his place and went straight to Liza's house. She and John were just getting up. I sketched out the scenario for her, and she immediately grabbed her coat.

"Let's go buy a test," she said. "Just get it over with."

Shopping for a pregnancy test when you are thirty-nine and unwed can make you feel like a teenager, a criminal, and a fool. The pregnancy tests at Cala Foods on Haight Street were actually locked up, along with the condoms, baby formula, and other items a desperate person might prefer to shoplift rather than pay for. They had only generic tests, none of the recognizable names, and this wasn't something I wanted to scrimp on. But I also wanted to get it over with. The line at the checkout was long. Matt lived just around the corner. What if he walked in? It would be poor form to have sex with someone and then be caught buying a pregnancy test the next morning.

We walked back to Liza's flat, me clutching the see-through plastic supermarket bag as I anxiously scanned the sidewalks for Matt. As soon as we reached the sanctuary of her steps, I scurried up them and headed for her green-tiled master bathroom.

"Do you want me to come with you?" she called up after me.

"No," I said. "That's okay."

I read the directions twice and got myself into position. Was that enough pee? I wondered. Did I hit the right spot? I set the magic, life-altering wand down on the edge of Liza's sink to wait and retreated to the edge of the tub. I inspected myself in her scary magnifying mirror. I pulled out her tweezers and yanked a few offending hairs. I looked at her collection of beauty products, more lotion than one woman could use in five years. I tried not to look at the stick. I should have found a magazine to read. Even *Elle Décor*—all Liza ever seemed to have around the place—would have provided some distraction. I checked my cell phone. It had been two minutes. I resolved to wait three more. What the fuck was I going to do if it was positive? How would I feel if it was negative?

It came to me then: disappointed. I'd be disappointed if the test was negative. In the stressful, fractious, vomit-filled months to come, I would continually return to those two or three minutes for reassurance. Just then my heart knew what it wanted.

I paced between the shower and the toilet for another minute, then took a peek. I checked the directions again. Plus did mean positive, right? It had to. You plus one. But sometimes these things are counterintuitive. I scrabbled at the box and held it far away from me; my glasses were downstairs.

I was pregnant. I walked into the kitchen with the stick in my hand. John looked up from his tea. His big brown eyes were bleary and even his goatee looked disheveled. "Oh geez Louise," he said. "No way." Liza fastened her eyes on mine for a long beat, then came to put her arms around me.

"Maybe we should go get another test," I said. "This one is generic. And it looked like it had been sitting in that case for a long time."

"You sure you don't want to sit and have a cup of tea first?" Liza said.

I shook my head. It was very important to establish beyond a shadow of a doubt what I already knew to be true. We went to a yuppie health store up the street, one of those places that look like the play stores we had as kids, with neat bins of couscous and brewer's yeast and mysterious wheat-colored potions. I plunked down my debit card for a double test with a brand name I recognized. This one promised results *before I'd even missed my period.* Did I have enough money in my checking account to buy the test? How pathetic was that? The walk back to Liza's house went directly past Matt's apartment. We crossed the street, as if proximity to him might make me more pregnant.

Of course the results were just the same. We stared at one another all over again. Then I started to cry.

"I'm never going to be alone again," I choked out.

"Oh sweetie," John said helplessly.

"Yes you will," Liza said, brushing the hair off my forehead. "Don't worry, you will definitely get some alone time. Not as much, but there will be some. I'll babysit. John will babysit."

"You don't understand," I said. "I don't *want* to be alone. And now I won't be. It's good. I'm going to have a family after all. A small one, but a real family."

CHAPTER 3

Where I Came From

I'D BEEN PREGNANT BEFORE, and it was an unmitigated disaster. I was twenty-one and living in Florence, Italy, fulfilling a longstanding dream to study abroad. I was staying with an Italian family, struggling to learn the language and find my way around town. At first I thought I had a urinary tract infection; my college boyfriend and I had been reunited for a week before I'd left the country, and we'd had a lot of sex. I'd been using the contraceptive sponge, and the whole experience had been a bit of a nightmare. One time I couldn't get it out, and he'd had to fish around inside me to find it. Maybe we took it out too early. I don't know. But there I was, five or six weeks into the semester, feeling miserable, and an Italian doctor was pronouncing me "gravidanza."

I'd gone to the central post office in Florence, the only place I knew where I could make an international call. Armed with handfuls of Italian coins, I'd called the boyfriend first, to break the news and discuss our options, and then my parents in Maine. Fortunately, my mother answered the phone. I absolutely couldn't stand to tell my father. I expected that I was going to break both of their hearts, but as a rule, my mother was far more tolerant of our mistakes. There were six of us and therefore plenty of mistakes.

My mother didn't miss a beat. "I'll help you raise it," she said.

She had been raising children since the late 1940s. I was the youngest, and there was a seventeen-year spread between me and the oldest, my brother Adrian, the only one of us who hadn't been a "mistake." My parents grew up Catholic. They didn't have a problem so much with *using* birth control, just a problem with making it work. "I've had a child for every kind of birth control I've tried," my mother would say. After Adrian came three girls, Cynthia, Elizabeth (whom we called Wib), and Alison. Then my mother had a bit of break for five years, before my brother Benet was born. I was the ultimate mistake, arriving three years after Benet and just before my mother turned forty-four.

She loved babies, but we'd shortchanged her in the grandchild department. By 1985, when I was in Italy, she had only two grandchildren. Here she was saying she was ready for more, regardless of the circumstances. Or maybe she was pro-choice only in theory.

I put my head against the wall of the phone booth. That fall in Florence was ceaselessly hot and I was sweaty and uncomfortable. The phones were equipped with a clock, telling you how much time you had left before the money ran out. I watched my lire disappear and wondered how much my crisis was going to end up costing all of us.

"I don't think I'm going to keep it," I told her. "But I think I have to come home."

Perhaps my fears were ungrounded, but I was afraid to have an abortion in such a Catholic country. I was ashamed and afraid and I hated having to tell my parents, but I needed their help. Within a few days, they had me on a train to Milan and then on a flight home to Maine. My father was waiting on the tarmac for me, a blanket under his arm—as if I were an invalid. Benet was standing awkwardly by his side, curly-haired, brown-eyed, skinny in his Bruce Springsteen–style jean jacket. We always stood up for each other, but usually I was defending him. I could tell from the look on his face that failing out of college or getting caught with a pipe in the pocket of your down parka was nothing compared with having to leave your study abroad program because you were pregnant. I had trumped all the mistakes of my five siblings in one fell swoop.

I had never felt like such a failure. For a few more days, we were trapped together in the old white clapboard house where I'd grown up, me trying to throw up as quietly as I could while I waited for my scheduled abortion. In the meantime, there was my father, a small man who held his head high, sobbing quietly at the breakfast table, imploring me to do it fast if I had to do it, telling me it would be less of a sin the sooner I did it. I had never seen him cry before. I couldn't go back to Italy. I lost a semester of school. I have no idea how much my mistake cost my parents, either monetarily or emotionally, but it crushed me. I'd failed as a daughter and I'd failed as the mother of the child I could have had.

How I would have liked to call my mother on that June morning in San Francisco almost twenty years later, to hear her say that she would help me raise the baby, and this time, to be able to say, "Thank you, yes, I'd love that." But I was grateful she still knew my name. She had dementia. The first signs of it had started when I was in my mid-twenties. Now she lived in a nursing home. I longed for her, but she had no strength to offer me, no reassurances, no solace. She had five grandchildren by then, including two new ones, Benet's little girls, but all she could do was watch them, smiling. When she held them, there was something tentative about her embrace, as if she thought she was not to be trusted with a baby in her arms.

As for my father, he was in his eighties now, and thin as an old cat, but he still strode purposefully through the streets of our hometown, the way he had for the last five decades. He was as sharp as ever, which is partly why I wasn't ready to share this news with him; he wasn't likely to take it well.

Instead I called my sister Alison, who lives just around the corner from my parents' house. Eight years older than I am, she is the soul of efficiency and the ultimate dispenser of sound advice. She will not have to sleep on it or get back to you or check with someone else before she can answer. She does not mince words.

"Wait," she said. "Who have you slept with?"

I told her about my evening at Finnegan's Wake. She fell silent. I heard her microwave beeping. She was warming coffee. Clearly she needed caffeine to help her process.

"I can't say that I'm not happy for you on some level," she said.

I'd always had the sense that Alison disapproved of me. Our older siblings tended to regard both Benet and me as spoiled, the pets, the ones who got the benefit of my parents' gradual mellowing. I'd tormented her as a child, listening in on her teenaged love affairs, poking around her bureau, teasing her about anything and everything. As we'd gotten older, she and I had grown closer, but I'd never been able to shake something my oldest sister Cynthia had once told me: "Alison thinks you're flighty."

Nothing about Alison was flighty. The rest of the girls in the family had soft, rounded features and dark, messy hair, but she had my father's strong nose and honey-colored hair, so straight and obedient you could swear you still saw the brush marks in it. Wouldn't she think getting pregnant during a one-night stand was the ultimate demonstration of flightiness? So I probed.

"What do you mean?"

"You've wanted a baby for a while."

Well, this was true—but in a fairly quiet way, at least lately. After I turned thirty-five it had started to feel unseemly to talk about it. What if it never happened? In a few more years I'd become the sad woman who wanted something everyone knew she couldn't have. My desires would no longer be appropriate, like a schoolgirl kilt on a gray-haired matron. I'd even tried to talk myself out of wanting kids, taking careful note of how much trouble my friends' children were. "So-and-so's kid punched a hole in the wall of their living room," I'd report to another childless friend. "Nine years old. Can you imagine?"

The fact that Alison was acknowledging my desire as something real and worthy suddenly made my predicament seem better. This was not a disaster the way it had been in 1985. This was something that made Alison happy for me. Moreover, Alison knew this territory. She'd split up with her husband so long ago that she'd practically raised their daughter, Katy, as a single mother. Katy was the oldest grandchild, in college now. She was my measuring stick. I had always kept track of my earlier, vanished opportunity for motherhood by counting back from however old Katy was. I could have had a child in college myself.

MY MOTHER HAD GONE back to school when I was still a little girl, working her way through Bowdoin College—where my father taught philosophy—taking one or two classes at a time until she'd emerged triumphant, diploma in hand, at the age of fifty-seven. When I'd gone off to North Carolina to attend Duke in the fall of 1982, she'd gone to Austin, Texas, to get her graduate degree in art history. Completing her education was her goal, but if she'd done so early in life, I know she would have gone on to have her own career, probably as an academic.

She had not been an active part of the feminist movement, but she was an admirer of the women who were, and she liked to remind me of my rights and of the opportunities available to me. She once sent me a postcard of a group of suffragettes being manhandled by the police. "I thought you'd appreciate these ladies," she wrote on the back. Or on another: "Have you seen *My Brilliant Career*? You really must." The messages she gave me, those that came from observing her life and those literally spelled out in letters and cards, weren't strident, but they were forceful.

My career choice, for example, could be traced directly to my mother. She never knew this, because by the time I made the change from being a news reporter to being a critic, her dementia was too advanced for it to register. But I felt the link. She had filled the house with the *New Yorker* for as long as I could remember, stacking up the old ones, wrapping twine around them, and pushing them under the crawl space below the entryway. She wrote notes to herself on the front in black ink, "V. good piece about Pentagon Papers," "Funny Talk of Town, p 16," just in case she might want to get back to them someday. As a nine-year-old, I wondered what she was talking about. The only things worthwhile in this magazine were the cartoons, the racing track column, and the movie reviews by some woman named Pauline Kael, who was funny and wrote in such a clear, direct way that most of the time I knew exactly what she meant, even though it would have been highly unusual for me to have seen anything she'd written about.

Trips to the movie theater were few and far between but always in the company of my mother. "Revolting," my father would say. "Sitting with strangers, watching nonsense while your feet soak in sticky soda spills." Her tastes ran far more to *Alice Doesn't Live Here Anymore* than to *Jaws*. Bowdoin had movie night on the campus every month or so, and she'd drag us along occasionally. Perhaps she took Benet and me to Laurence Olivier's *Richard III* for purposes of edification, although it could have had something to do with her refusal to ever pay for a babysitter. We were convinced she was trying to bore us to death. But I was more than content watching movies with her at home, hearing her gentle laughter all the way through *It Happened One Night* or her admiring sighs as Fred spun Ginger across the dance floor. We watched *On the Beach* together, and I turned to her and said, "You look like Ava Gardner." That made her smile.

As she sowed the seeds that would someday become my profession, she also passed on the craving for family. Not marriage necessarily, although in my twenties, I often opened letters from her to find they included clippings of marriage announcements of anyone from my hometown she thought I was even vaguely acquainted with. The examples set by my siblings weren't sterling: Out of six marriages, only two had lasted. Yet my mother instilled in me the desire to be part of a whole.

Some members of big families want to escape their crowded, claustrophobic surroundings. If you wanted to be alone in our household, climbing an apple tree or hiding in the upstairs bathroom (the only room with a nonpickable lock) was your best bet. But I never had that desire. Joining this big family last, I already felt I'd missed out on a lot of history, and I didn't want to miss any more. By the mid-1970s, when Benet and I were the only kids still left at home, I viewed Christmas attendance as a must for all my older siblings.

"What about Ade?" I demanded of my mother as we were making up the beds together. "Why isn't he coming home for Christmas?" Cynthia had come the day before and was probably now over in the reading room at the Bowdoin Library. Wib would be coming that night from Smith, unfortunately accompanied by her boyfriend, Sean, who had a most disturbing red beard. Alison lived a few blocks away. Benet was outside, drilling a hockey puck against the side of the barn, leaving black marks against the white shingles. My father would come home from his office soon and be annoyed about this, making Benet want to hit even more hockey pucks against the wall. Or against our unmovable father, who thought hockey was not nearly as nice a winter sport as squash.

"Adrian is staying in Charlottesville," my mother said, stuffing a pillow into a case. "He has to work." She sighed. I could tell she was sad too. We'd been party-planning for weeks, shopping the sale racks at Jordan Marsh together, ironing napkins and tablecloths, and debating our menus. (Roast beef or turkey for Christmas dinner? How many pans of Yorkshire pudding would we need?)

Adrian was so much older than I that I barely knew him, but I always wanted him there. I assumed he had to be lonely without us, because I imagined that I would be desperately lonely if I were away. Also, he could be counted on to raise a family occasion to the highest level of insanity. He'd arrive in a cloud of bluster with some girlfriend in tow, either too young or too old, too loud or too quiet, and proceed to drive my father to fits.

"So I'm in the middle of getting fellatio when this guy walks in," he bellowed at one memorable holiday dinner. The legs on my father's chair shrieked as he backed up from the table and stalked out of the room to go poke at the fire.

"What's fellatio?" I asked, looking around the table at my siblings, half of them aghast, half of them laughing. Even Benet seemed in on the joke. My mother sat at the head of the table, twirling her wineglass between her long fingers, shaking with laughter.

"You don't know what fellatio is, little girl?" Adrian said, bending toward me with an almost courtly gesture. "Well, let me tell you . . ."

"Adrian," my mother said. "Silenzio per favore."

I loved the sprawl of us, the noise of us, the way we filled a house. There was comfort in numbers, more of everything: more jokes, more drama, more presents under the Christmas tree, more people to play with, more siblings to give me quarters to be quiet during dinner. Whether by chance or circumstance, the books I read all seemed to be about big families. From the Pevensies of C. S. Lewis to the sailing Walker family of Arthur Ransome's *Swallows and Amazons* series, I kept getting the message that large families were somehow magical. You needed four for true excitement, I'd tell myself, and here we were, with six.

I certainly never thought I'd have six of my own. But I do remember thinking it would be nice to have three or four children. As soon as I could do simple math, I fixated on what life would be like in the year 2000, a date that hung in the future like a giant punctuation mark. I'd be thirty-six and, I believed, already a mother several times over. Given my mother's fecundity, maybe later when I was the ripe old age of forty, I'd throw another one into the mix, just for fun.

But here I was, ten months from being forty. A little more than eight months away from being a first-time parent. With a man I had spent less than twenty-four hours with, half of them sleeping.

"I'VE GOT TO TELL MATT," I said.

It was late afternoon on the Day of the Magic Wand. I'd told both Alison and Benet. Even my boss knew. Katharine Hepburn had just died, and Karen, not just my editor but also a close friend, had called to tell me I had to come in to work, to write an appreciation. "I just can't," I had told her. "I just did an EPT and I'm pregnant. There is no way I can think about Katharine Hepburn right now."

Hugh, Liza's estranged husband, had been informed. She'd called and asked him to come over and take care of the kids while we brainstormed our way through the drama. I'd been a bridesmaid at their wedding ten years ago, but I didn't really know Hugh until he and Liza moved to San Francisco five years before. Liza had been itching to get out of Maine, and so he'd found a job as the chief financial officer for an old Bay Area company. Now he was definitely part of my West Coast family, and the fact that they were separated hadn't changed that.

Hugh shook his head at my situation.

"How old is he? Twenty-nine?" he said. "He's going to freak out. Wait for a few weeks, until you're really sure what you're going to do."

Hugh had a tendency to think the worst of other men.

"Mary needs the information," Liza said. "She's got to know what he thinks."

"He's going to think, *I'm fucked*," Hugh said. "He's going to think, *Why the hell didn't I use a condom?* and *How fast can I get out of town?* How is that going to be helpful to her?"

"That's what *you'd* think," Liza said. She tended to think the worst of Hugh. "Not all guys are like you." She slid the cork out of a bottle of wine and poured herself a glass. "Thank God."

"Please," I said. "No fighting. Not right now."

I couldn't imagine waiting two long weeks to tell Matt. I'm an information gatherer by trade, and if he was going to tell me to get lost and never darken his door again, I needed to be able to start processing that information as soon as possible. He might get on a Greyhound and leave town. He didn't have a job, after all. He had nothing tying him to the Bay Area beyond enjoying the place. But my gut told me that he wouldn't leave town and that he wouldn't tell me to beat it. He seemed too decent for that.

Decency aside, however, there was no getting around how skimpy our relationship was. Make that our acquaintance. We'd spent exactly two nights together, a drunken one-night stand followed by a booty call, with a press screening of *The Incredible Hulk* in between, a night that had ended with him getting out of the car and bidding me good night with not so much as a handshake. I wasn't sure Matt knew my last name (or cared to), and here I was, heading off to what would be our fourth meeting, to break the news that I was having his baby.

Morally, I felt Matt had a right to know that I was carrying his

child, despite any temptation to keep it to myself and ensure to-
tal control over the situation—meaning no interference, no scary
custody claims down the road. But the even bigger moral issue was
denying my child the right to know his or her father. I'd be making
the assumption, based on a few fleeting encounters, that the child's
father wasn't worthy of being a part of its life. Who was I to make
that judgment? If Matt had been someone I'd slept with but hadn't
liked at all—and honestly, there were a couple like that in my past—
I might have felt differently. But I doubt it. Already I had started
thinking for two, and I felt my child deserved the chance to have a
relationship with his or her father.

"I think it's better if she goes to him with a game plan," Hugh
said.

"She can't have a game plan without knowing what he's going to
say," Liza said.

"Her game plan should have nothing to do with him," Hugh
said.

They could bicker all night. I'd been watching them do it for
years now.

"You know what, guys?" I said. "I'm going to sleep on it."

"That's good," Liza said. "You go home, you get into bed with the
kitties, and you just think about it. What do you have to do tomorrow?"

"I've got a screening in the afternoon," I said. "And I should write
a review in the morning." I wanted to do nothing. I wanted to call
in sick. But movies come out every week, whether you want them
to or not. It was summer blockbuster season, and I was seeing at
least five films a week and usually reviewing three. My daily calendar was marked up in multiple colors of ink indicating screenings,
interviews, deadlines. I often felt like a waitress in a diner that never
closed: you'd serve a meal, clean up, reset the tables, and people
would sit right back down and expect another meal. I never felt
caught up, and there were no opportunities to coast.

But I never, ever got tired of going to the movies. I got tired
of *getting* there: running an obstacle course of traffic, parking, and

dodging pedestrians to get to San Francisco on time (critics don't pick what time they go to the movies; we get usually one or two opportunities to see a film at a special screening, and if you miss the beginning, you're screwed). But once I slide into my seat and the lights go down, I am completely content.

If I use the word "mindless" in a review, it's usually an insult. But on the day after I found I was pregnant, I was thrilled when I realized I was seeing *Legally Blonde 2: Red White and Blonde*. Mindless was just what I needed. For ninety minutes, I could shut my brain off and stop outlining the conversation I was going to have with Matt. This wasn't like those state-of-the-relationship conversations I'd had in the past. There was no template. I needed to blurt out the news and see what happened.

WHEN THE MOVIE WAS OVER, I went to Liza's for a final pep talk. Then I hit Matt's number on my cell phone. He picked up right away.

"Hi Matt," I said. "It's Mary. There's something I'd like to talk to you about. Can I come over?"

There was a pause. But not a long one.

"Sure," he said, sounding more cheerful than cautious. *You should be cautious*, I thought. *I'm about to change your life. Maybe wreck it.*

I felt sick walking up his steps. His sexy grin of a few days before was replaced with something much milder; friendly concern perhaps. He held the gate open for me. His place looked even worse in the afternoon light. His room smelled. The lacrosse sticks in the corner were no longer cute; they were frightening symbols of his boydom, his utter lack of readiness to be a dad. I sat on his bed. He sat in a vinyl desk chair and put his elbows on his knees. His hands were together, almost in a prayer position, and he looked at me seriously and with sympathy, but without obvious fear.

"What's up?" he said.

I slid to the floor. I needed to be closer to the earth, to be on the most solid ground I could find. I put my hand against my forehead and looked down at his filthy filthy rug.

"I'm really sorry to tell you this," I began. "I know that you probably expected that I was on the pill or something, but the thing is, I wasn't on the pill and now I'm pregnant. I mean, I'm pretty sure I'm pregnant. I haven't been to the doctor yet, but I've taken a couple of tests."

I took a quick look at him. He didn't look alarmed. He hadn't moved. The rest of it came out of me in a rush.

"So, I think I told you, I'm thirty-nine. Which means this could be my last chance to have a baby. I can't even believe that I got pregnant, and so easily. I expected that if I ever actually tried to get pregnant at this point, it would take months and months, if it would even happen at all. So I just can't believe this. But I think I'm going to have this baby. Your baby."

His expression still hadn't changed. Probably shock.

"So I'll do it on my own, and I'll take care of the baby on my own, but I did want to see what you thought and offer you the opportunity to be part of the baby's life, if that's what you want."

He slumped back in his chair.

"So, how do you feel about babies?" I asked him. I'd run out of things to say.

"Well," he said quietly. "Everyone wants a child."

No, I thought, *no they don't. But how wonderful that you think that way. Your apartment is disgusting, you don't have a job, and you appear to have no obvious assets except for a beautiful smile. Yet you apparently believe that everyone wants a child, from which I'm going to extrapolate that you want one.*

That afternoon, there was nothing sexual between us. We lay on the bed together, his arm behind my head, but it was purely about comfort. He wanted to know how I felt about baptism. We talked about last names. My estimation of him shot upward when he told me he'd always assumed he'd marry a feminist, and that she'd keep her last name and that maybe they'd let the girls have her last name and the boys his. Telling him had gone as well as I could possibly have expected it to go. The conversation seemed in some ways bizarrely couple-like, practically cozy.

"Did you realize that we both have green eyes?" he asked.

I'd thought until then that his eyes were light brown. This was the kind of basic information I ought to have known about him before we conceived a child together. This self-rebuke—How could I? What was I thinking? Why wasn't I thinking?—was a constant refrain of mine that whole first year. But at the same time, his question about our eye color indicated that he was speculating about our child, less than an hour after having had his world rocked. That had to be a good sign. And as he'd said, "Everyone wants a child."

For the next eight months, I would clutch that remarkably simple but potent statement to me like a talisman. "This was his first reaction," I'd tell people. "It's going to be okay."

CHAPTER 4

Chasing High Tides

BECAUSE OF HOW FAR NORTH MAINE IS, and some complicated science involving the Gulf of Maine and the Bay of Fundy, the tides are extreme. Depending on the cycle of the moon, there could easily be a ten-foot difference between low and high tides. If you're out on a boat, you wouldn't notice it, but if you're in a small cove, the difference can be shocking. The landscapes laid bare by the departing tides were whole new worlds, raw and messy worlds. I always had an aversion to these naked demarcations of land and sea.

None of this matters on a sandy beach, but Maine has only thirty miles of those—the rest is rockbound. When we planned our family outings, we always consulted the tide chart before leaving the house. But there were plenty of times when a hot afternoon in town and a high tide at the shore did not correspond, and then we'd navigate punishingly sharp-edged rocks and pebbly beaches that bruised our feet. There were fields of sea grass and clutching tendrils of black and yellow seaweed to face. You might have to walk the length of a football field before getting to water deep enough to plunge into. Dozens of hermit crabs scuttled in the shallows, indignant at your very presence, ready to nip at your toes. Worse still were the mudflats that sucked balefully at your feet, leaving clots of gray muck on your ankles.

At high tide, none of that mattered. It was all under there, but when you were floating above the sea grass and the rocks, they were harmless. The mudflats held warmth from the last low tide, and so swimming over them was pleasant. "I'm in a warm patch," I'd shout to Benet when we swam together as kids. "I'm making a warm patch," he'd say, treading water, his bony shoulders sticking out, his mop of brown hair still dry. We never put our heads under.

The sea greeted you at high tide, came right to you, offered itself. If I could have, I'd have built a wall around my favorite swimming places, to trap the water forever. High tides were just *better*. They were what we showed the tourists; try finding a pictorial calendar of Maine that revels in the muck of our seaweed-shrouded shores. A low tide might illustrate the gloomy months when we were all waiting for the weather to change, March or November, but you'd never flip to July's photograph and see mudflats.

As I grew up, I thought that the right relationship would be like a high tide that would never ebb. Each time things didn't work out with a boyfriend, I felt myself like a low tide: exposed, messy, vulnerable. When you put a boat in the water at low tide, the trailer wheels leave ugly scars in the mud. High tide will whisk that ugliness away. A soul mate would do the same for me, curing all past ills, smoothing over my rough edges. Or so I believed.

I saw no beauty in low tide. Nor in being alone. I knew life thrived in tide pools, but it didn't interest me much. It didn't look the way I wanted it to look. In my adult life, I went about my business, waiting for a change in gravitational pull that would somehow make me whole.

TO THAT END, or perhaps simply by nature, I have always been romantically tenacious. Only once has a man said, "I love you" first to me; I have volunteered it every other time. I could offer at least a half-dozen mortifying examples of how this tenacity has not necessarily served me well, but those are stories I am, thankfully, no longer interested in. Peter will suffice as an example of my dogged persistence in the face of incontrovertible evidence that my true love was an asshole.

I'd met him in Washington, D.C., where I'd moved a few months after college. I was sharing a house in Mt. Pleasant with a group of young journalists. He was a teacher, handsome, well-educated, convinced of his own worth. He lived in a shared house too, filled with guys that were just as handsome and just as smart, as if their individual magnetic properties had pulled them into friendship. Peter's half brother was a well-known actor, and some of that glamour hung about his own chiseled features and long, lean frame. When I watched him ice-skate, I was practically paralyzed by his grace.

I was smitten. He seemed smitten, at least with the sex. When the cherry blossoms were in bloom, we drove to the Jefferson Memorial after midnight, determined to do it under the cherry trees. Our plan was foiled by someone with similar, solo plans, but we ended the night outside, on the lawn of the National Cathedral. I'd slept with only a few people before him, but he was the first I'd fallen for without reservation.

He had reservations about me, though. Maybe because he was testing his students during the day, he seemed determined to test me as well. If I liked T. C. Boyle's *World's End*, which I'd picked up at the bookstore because it had won some national award, then I was a fool. If I didn't like Marilynne Robinson's *Housekeeping*, I was another kind of fool. I left both books unopened, fearful I'd fail and be cast aside. But I didn't find the giving of these tests as appalling as I ought to; I thought it indicated he could teach me something. Until then, I was the best-read twenty-three-year-old I knew.

He once told me that I didn't challenge him. I can still see his narrow blue eyes as he delivered that line, waiting to see how I'd react to the condemnation. I should have gotten out of his bed, put my clothes on, and fled for good. Instead I stuck around. He broke up with me, not long after, the beginning of a long pattern of push me, pull me. Our status was so unclear that when he told me his final acceptance to the Peace Corps was contingent on his passing the "significant other" interview process, I had no idea what he was talking about. "They want to know if I'm going to be traumatized about leaving you," he said, his lips in my hair, his hand up my shirt. "Oh," I said. "Really?" So I was significant? "What did you tell them?" I asked.

"That I'll miss you, but that it wouldn't stop me from going," he said.

I believed that, eventually, he'd own up to feeling the same way about our relationship as I did. This misconception lasted all through the years he spent in the Peace Corps. I moved to San Francisco, a place I wanted to be, but that I secretly hoped would be cool enough to suit his standards when he came back. I pored over every letter he sent, looking for hints of his love in his accounts of latrine building. Meanwhile, I was interning at one of the city's alternative weeklies. I'd stood in front of a newspaper box on the street and known the thrill of seeing my name on a cover story for the first time. I decided to go to graduate school to study journalism. I felt as if I were on the right road, *my* road.

At the end of his assignment he'd called to ask me to come ride across the Sahara with him, on the back of his motorcycle. I had no money to get there, and the semester at Berkeley would be starting soon. Moreover, the mode of transport—me holding on for dear life, him making all the decisions—seemed too representative of our relationship, so I said no. But the invitation itself was enough to fuel my fantasy life. He was done with all this Peace Corps stuff, and whom did he want to see? Me. I was ready to clean out a drawer in my bureau for the Great White Adventurer upon his return.

He'd been home less than twenty-four hours when he called to ask if he could visit me the next day. I was at my parents' house in Maine at the time and he was at his mother's, a day's drive away.

He came to the front door. No one ever used the front door except for the mailman and people collecting for the American Cancer Society. The hug hello was awkward, off-kilter. I felt instantly aware of my body, the body he knew so well, and desperate to get him out of the house and into some environment that had possibilities.

"I was thinking we'd go to the beach," I said.

"Sounds great," he said, shrugging with studied nonchalance. "Are we going to have lobster?"

"Definitely," I said, picking up my bag.

We flirted at the beach. We flirted through our lobster dinner. Then we walked down to a dock and stood looking at the moon on the water, and maybe I shivered, and that made him reach out for me. "I missed you so much," he said, between kisses. "There hasn't been anyone else." I pulled back and looked at him quizzically. We'd been honest with each other, and I knew he hadn't been celibate in Africa. Nor had I in D.C. or California. "No one like you," he corrected himself.

Even if my father had caught us in the spare room that night, I don't think I would have cared—that's how happy I was. The next day Peter and I walked downtown, hand in hand, had lunch, and stopped at the Bowdoin campus on the way back. My father had been teaching there since 1949. I knew every corner of the campus; this was my territory and this was who I was, a philosophy professor's daughter from Maine. We sprawled on the grass together. I put my head on his thigh. I had never been happier in my adult life. The tide was in, the waters lapping around my shoulders. This gave meaning to all those hopes I'd been holding on to for four years.

He didn't touch me.

"I get the feeling this means a lot to you," he said.

"What do you mean?" I said, craning my neck to look up at him.

"This reunion," he said. "Or whatever it is."

I sat up. He was digging acorns out of the ground with a stick.

"*Whatever* it is?" I said. I wanted his cards on the table.

"You seem to believe that we belong together," he said, looking at me now. "Or something like that."

I was angry. Finally. I stared at him. I felt fierce, but very sure of myself.

"You asked me to come to the Sahara with you," I said levelly. "Then when you come back, I am the very first person you want to see. I am the person you can't keep your hands off of. You tell me there's been no one else like me in the last three years. I'm sorry,

Peter, but I'm not pretending all of this doesn't mean something anymore."

"It doesn't mean anything," he said.

"Really?" I said. "Nothing? I don't believe you. I think you love me."

He looked away. "I feel something for you," he said. "It's deep, but I don't understand it. I just know I don't want to end up with you."

All I had wanted since the first time he'd kissed me was to end up with him. That was the life I wanted. I had let him torture me. I had tortured myself. I had tried to make myself into someone he'd want.

I was standing up now and my hands were in tight balls at my side. I turned and walked away. Walked home across the browning grass of late summer, feeling the tide I thought I'd captured rush away, wondering, even now, as I peeked over my shoulder, if it could come back. All he had to do was get up and follow me. Which he did not do.

ELEVEN YEARS LATER, I was thirty-eight and less of an idiot, but no less romantically challenged. Moreover, the bad things that happened with men had become less significant for the kind of quivering mess they left me in than for the amount of my valuable reproductive time they had consumed. I no longer had four years to waste moping after anyone, not even Apollo himself. If you believed Sylvia Ann Hewlett, I did not have four *months* to waste. She was the author of *Creating a Life: Professional Women and the Quest for Children*, a book that came out in the spring of 2002 to much fanfare. Her premise was that women who had put career first, women who cared about success, women like *me*, tended to find themselves childless and unhappy in their late thirties, with little chance of saving themselves from this self-inflicted tragedy. Here's how the book opens: "There is a secret out there, a painful, well kept secret: At mid-life, between a third and half of all high-achieving women in America do not have children. A nationwide survey of high-earning career women conducted in January 2001 shows that 33 percent of them are childless at ages 40–55, a figure that rises to 42 percent in corporate America. By and large, these high-achieving women have not chosen to be childless. The vast majority yearns for children."

Except for the high-earning part, her accusatory finger seemed pointed directly at me. True, I didn't work in a "corporate" job (I owned one suit), and if the definition of high-achieving meant high-income, that wasn't me. But my career had always been of utmost importance to me. I didn't imagine ever quitting my job to stay home full-time with the children. So I felt a kinship with the ambitious women who worked as lawyers, investment bankers, stockbrokers, and such.

In my social circle, very few of my friends who were moms were also high achievers in the working world. Conversely, the high achievers I knew were mostly single, childless, and depressed about it. Hewlett's book, with its ominous, shaming tone, only reinforced that: "It behooves the next generation to pay attention. By doing so, twenty-something women might be able to avoid the cruel choices that dogged the footsteps of their older sisters."

I was indignant. Hadn't Susan Faludi debunked all this with *Backlash*? Weren't we beyond accusing career women of screwing up their chances of snaring a man and a family life? I found plenty of backlash against Hewlett on the Internet. But I still couldn't get those "cruel choices" out of my head. Had I made them, even unconsciously? Would I pay for them? Whenever a friend struggled with getting pregnant, I'd listen to the sad saga and worry for her. I'd hope that the ovulation kits would help or the Clomid would work or the in vitro fertilization would take. And always, I'd imagine myself in her shoes someday. It was no wonder Hewlett's book sent me into a cold sweat.

I didn't have to look far to find anecdotal evidence either. I had one forty-one-year-old friend who had just been told her eggs were shot and if she was going to have a second child, she'd have to hire an egg donor. "You better get on it, Mary," she warned me in her kitchen, pointing a serving spoon in the general direction of my empty womb. "I had no problem getting pregnant three years ago, and now look at me." Another friend had decided, after years of waiting for a good man, to try motherhood on her own. But going to a sperm bank hadn't worked, and she had given up artificial insemination for the expensive, invasive, full-court press of IVF. Her insurance would pay for three tries, and then she was on her own. I hated the thought of her need, unmet.

There was no doubt my clock was ticking. I thought maybe the batteries had even run out. I did math in my head all the time. "So, Mum was forty-three when she had you. You've got five years before you have to start feeling hopeless." Except that I needed to meet the guy, and get to know him a little, and pick out the invitations and the dress. Also, science tells us that it gets harder the later you start. My mother had been a baby-making machine. After five children, what was a sixth to her? "Just like a BM," she'd said to me once, cheerily describing the process of giving birth to her last child.

When I was thirty-six, my gynecologist had taken a look around during a pelvic and then casually mentioned that if I wanted to have children, I should do it sooner rather than later. "I'm not really in the right financial position," I told her. "That doesn't matter as much," she said. "If I were you and I was in a good relationship, I'd go ahead and worry about the financial stuff later. That tends to work itself out anyway." With each month that passed after that unhelpful nudge, I assumed I was compounding a bad situation. I felt like a company that had been already operating in the red for a couple of years, headed toward bankruptcy.

BUT I WAS NOT DESPERATE. I had standards for what I wanted and I had learned a few lessons about holding out for someone I could really count on. My last serious boyfriend had been an earnest young man I'd met at a Lucinda Williams concert. All our interests seemed to run parallel. He worked for a local politician I admired. He was trustworthy and kind. The only catch was that I was five years older than he was. That bothered him a lot and me a little, but nonetheless, within a year he'd bought *Mortgages for Dummies* and taken me home to meet his parents. There were a few bad signs, though, mostly over issues of power. "You've got to let me be the man," he complained one night after I'd insisted on driving home from a party because he had been drinking. "Who or what is this man you are speaking of?" I wanted to say. Because he looked very much like the boy to me, with his belligerent, semi-intoxicated expression, swaying forlornly at the end of the bed.

Then one night, when we were watching *ER*, I glanced over and Owen was sucking his thumb. "You're sucking your thumb," I said, incredulous. "Right here, in front of me." He took it out of his mouth and looked straight ahead, a strange, secretive smile on his face. He simply did not respond. Someone on the television screen was getting intubated by a new intern. Owen appeared rapt.

I tried to figure out what this habit meant for him and for me. A Web site called www.adultthumbsuckers.com told me that my boyfriend was far from alone and that I needed to be more open to his needs. "If your spouse or partner doesn't understand, then maybe they are not the right person for you," the Web site said. I went nuts trying to analyze him. What kind of mother/separation issues did this signify? Because I still imagined us getting married, I managed to keep my mouth shut for a full month before I spilled the beans to anyone.

"He does *what*?" my therapist asked. "Really?"

She blew her nose. I'd been seeing her for only a few weeks. Before the revelation of the thumb-sucking, Owen and I had had a few problems, and I was anxious to make sure that I didn't fuck this one up. My insurance company had sent me to her. That meant I got only eight sessions before they threw me to the wolves of self-pay reality. I think she had the same cold the whole time I was seeing her.

"Well, that's weird," she said. Then she looked guilty. We both knew therapists weren't supposed to make those kinds of judgments.

But once she'd put it out there, there was no going back. A professional had declared my boyfriend weird. I gave the relationship with Owen another couple of months, hoping he'd cease and desist, or at least engage in conversation about the issue. One weekend we went away together to Yosemite to cross-country ski. I agonized over how to bring it up. After a nice dinner, when we were lying in bed, I stepped out on a limb.

"When we have kids," I said, "I don't think you can suck your thumb in front of them. You know that, right?"

He nodded vigorously. I got up to go to the bathroom, and when I came back, he guiltily dropped the sheet, which he'd had up to his mouth, hiding the evidence. That was one of the first times I turned away from him sexually. Soon there were more. I couldn't get over what a turnoff it was to see a grown man sucking his thumb. Whenever we disagreed about anything, he'd plunge the thumb into his mouth, as if it were in retaliation for some perceived slight. He seemed to want to reclaim some power from me, an imbalance that he perhaps equated with my being older.

The final straw was when I went to Italy for a vacation with my family and realized during an idyllic moment floating down a canal in Venice that not only did I not miss him at all, but I was grateful he wasn't there with me. The night I got back, we broke up. I didn't have a single second of regret. For the first time ever, I'd been swimming at high tide, but I couldn't stop thinking about what lay just beneath the surface.

I'd learned an important lesson about my willingness, or lack thereof, to compromise in order to be with a man to have a family. I could have stayed with Owen, and if I had, I would have had house, husband, and, I don't doubt, within a few years, children. I knew people who had settled just to get that traditional family. I realized I wasn't actually capable of that.

BUT HERE I WAS, I was almost six weeks' pregnant by a stranger, and it seemed to everyone that it might be a good idea for us to get to know each other better. So on the Fourth of July I invited Matt to join all of us at Liza's. Hugh was there too; on holidays in particular, Liza and he tried to do family things together for the sake of their boys. Matt and I hadn't talked much lately, just a few conversations on the phone. He arrived, drank a few beers in quick succession, and requested a burger with just a bun and cheese, nothing else. "A slice of tomato, though, right?" I said. He shook his head. "Potato salad?" I said.

"What's in it?" he said, peering into the bowl. "Carrots?"

"And celery," I said. "A little red pepper. Some apple. That's what makes it so good."

He waved me off. "I'm not much for vegetables."

Liza was blasting Neil Young's "Harvest Moon" and singing along.

"Do you like Neil Young?" she asked Matt.

"Is that who this is?" he said. "I knew it was one of those old guys. Not really I guess. My stepfather likes him, though."

John was in mid-bite. His eyebrows went up, over the top of the burger. I averted my eyes. Common ground was proving scarce.

After dinner, Liza pressed Matt to try my brownies.

"This woman can *cook*, you know," she said. "You have no idea. Her whole family. They could open a restaurant."

"Liza," I said, giving her the look that said, *Tone it down, would you?* I felt like the potential bride in an arranged marriage, being hyped for the groom. Only it would have been a shotgun arranged marriage. Matt took a brownie and chewed thoughtfully. "It's good," he said. I was getting the impression he wasn't a rhapsodizer. "Well, I should get going," he said. "Thanks for the burger." He gave me a kiss on the cheek on his way out the door. "See you later."

"Whew," Liza said. "After that lovely family dinner I'm going to need to step out back."

She vanished to smoke. Hugh and I started the cleanup.

"He seems nice," he said encouragingly, stuffing discarded corn-cobs down the disposal.

"You think?" I said.

"Sure. He doesn't say much, though, does he?"

"No," I said, picking at a brownie. "Not much. It's kind of a weird situation, though."

Hugh laughed. "I'll say."

I handed him a stack of plates.

"So how old is he again?" he asked. "Twenty-nine? He seems younger, doesn't he?"

He did. He seemed younger and younger all the time. He worked references to episodes of *The Simpsons* into half the things he said. I couldn't believe I'd thought for a second he might be thirty-five. Hugh and I fell into a companionable silence.

"Poor boy," Liza said, coming back in from the laundry room. "He doesn't know what to think. And who can blame him?"

John was looking through Liza's CD collection. "He could have at least brought some beer," he chimed in.

"He said he's had only one temp gig in the last month," I said. "I don't think he has any money."

"Oh," John said. He stroked his beard thoughtfully. He loved that goatee. "Baby daddy better dust off that résumé."

"What does he want to do?" Hugh asked. Hugh knows how to succeed in business, and he's baffled by those who don't.

"I don't think he has a clue," I said. "He talks about getting into one of those training programs for stockbrokers, but I think he's too old for it."

"He did go to college, though, right?" Hugh asked.

"U Mass," I said. "On the five-year plan. Or maybe it was the six-year plan."

"Maybe he's a slow starter," John said.

"I hope he starts soon," I said. "I really don't want my baby to have an unemployed father."

Matt seemed so directionless. If you measured young adulthood by the mattress you buy post-college, for instance, he was way behind. He hadn't even gotten to the futon phase yet. Everything in his dreary little room came with the rent. I wondered if his stunted growth had something to do with his childhood. He'd had a rough time of it; his parents split up when he was five and he had desperately wanted his father to come back. Matt lived with his mother and saw his dad and stepmother only on vacations and weekends. His mom remarried when he was eighteen, and he'd gained a stepfather and a pair of younger stepsisters, but he didn't have much to say about his family. He warmed up when he was talking about the cats he and his mother had had, or their dog, but he volunteered very little. He asked less. He didn't seem curious about anything. He waited for me to start every discussion. His responses were those of a polite but only mildly interested stranger. He felt like a visitor to my life, except that, presumably, he was going to be around for a long, long time.

"Hey," John said. "I don't suppose we're still going to speed dating next week?"

"Jesus," I said, staring at him. "I forgot."

NEEDLESS TO SAY, despite my fortitude about dumping the thumb-sucker, by the end of my thirty-eighth year, I had grown quite worried about my future. Sometimes I actively tried not to worry, because people (married people, always married people) said to me, "Oh, when you stop worrying about it, *that's* when it is going to happen." I wish people would stop saying this to their single friends, because not only is it not true, it is inadvertently cruel. It makes you feel as though there might be a formula you could follow to find a happy ending. Or a map that could get you out of the outback of single life if you studied it hard enough.

At any rate, I'd started 2003 with a campaign to find a man and settle down. I was no longer going to leave anything up to fate. I was going to do all the things that had ever been suggested to me by those well-meaning friends eager to see me married. I vowed to try online dating and go on a Sierra Club singles hike, even though I had always pictured those hikes as being filled with a dozen pretty, outdoorsy women in their early thirties and two overweight guys in their fifties wearing Rolling Stones T-shirts. And I would take a class and meet new people, just like in that sweet Danish film *Italian for Beginners*, where various dysfunctional Danes found love in Italian class. I was going to approach this like looking for a job, with energy and enthusiasm.

When I started online dating, it was initially like stumbling into Whole Foods after a lifetime of shopping at Safeway. But its short-comings soon became apparent. Most men seemed to be treating it as an extension of the singles bar, and the impression I got was that they were more interested in expanding their dating pool than in having relationships. Yet they wanted women ten years younger than they, presumably for their fresher, more fertile eggs. I also couldn't get over my disgust at their physical criteria for women. Short was okay, but if you weighed more than 120 pounds, even the real toads weren't interested. All those coffee dates I'd gone on had proved in-teresting in an anthropological sense but far from fruitful. Most men seemed far better online than in person, and I found myself impa-tient with the lag time between e-mail conversations and finding out the bitter truth. One guy I'd gone out with twice had asked for a third date, then called the next night to tell me he had met someone else.

"When did you have time?" I sputtered indignantly before saying good-bye.

Speed dating, in contrast, had the allure of an up-front look at the guy and a chance to see if there was actual chemistry. Sure we'd be talking only for three minutes, but it seemed more efficient. How-ever, the proportion of thirty-nine-year-old women wanting to get into speed dating is quite a bit higher than that of men of the same age, and the company I'd contacted had no openings in the thirty-five to forty-two age bracket for months to come. I offered to bring John; they always needed more men. They booked me into the earli-est possible open session. I never dreamed I'd be seven weeks' preg-nant when our session finally rolled around.

"Christ, I hope I don't have to puke in the middle of this," I said to John as we approached the Bubble Lounge in downtown San Francisco. "And there'd better be snacks."

"And babes," John said, holding the door for me. "Ones who aren't pregnant."

The setting was inauspicious, dark and a little sleazy. This was the kind of "singles" place I usually avoided. I ordered a ginger ale and sat down at my appointed table, marked with the letter K.

The third guy to slither into the seat across from me was so nervous that he already had huge sweat marks showing on his blue oxford.

"Hi, K," he said. "That must stand for Kute."

"Actually," I said, "it stands for Knocked Up. That's me. Can you believe it? I'm just here browsing for a husband to go with my baby."

He laughed reflexively. Then he registered what I'd actually said. He bit his lip. He glanced longingly over at L's table. She looked normal. She looked Kute.

"I'm kidding!" I said. "K is for Kidder. That's me."

I behaved myself after that, and the guys weren't bad. A half dozen seemed like guys I wouldn't mind going out with again. An attractive, earthy geologist from Marin, divorced with two children, seemed incredibly nice. I started to warm to the prospect of going camping with him and his kids, forgetting for an hour or so that I was pregnant. At the end of the evening I turned in a scorecard indicating I'd happily see five or six men again.

The card looks not unlike an SAT form. Once you turn it in, you wait to see how everyone "grades" you. I'd done well enough, with a dozen men saying they'd like to see me again. The next evening, as I pored over their profiles, I was pleased to see that the geologist was also interested in me. But when I got into bed and turned off the light, I realized, of course, that I couldn't date any of these men. Yes, the geologist had baggage too, but who on earth wanted to date a pregnant woman? (Well, yes, Seal, but I am not, nor was I ever, Heidi Klum.) I lay in bed awake, wondering if maybe I was rushing into having this baby too soon. After all, now I knew I could still get pregnant. I could fall in love, get married, and start trying to have a child with my husband immediately. What if one of these men was the perfect person for me, and I wasn't going to be able to ride off into the sunset with him because I was having the bastard child of an unemployed twenty-nine-year-old?

When I woke the next morning I was an emotional wreck. I'd turned down my HMO's offer of prenatal counseling, but perhaps I needed it after all. When Matt and I spoke later that day, he was fretting about when to break the news to his parents. I told him to hold off. "I might not have this baby," I said. "I don't know if I can do this."

He was quiet for a while.

"Hello," I said, as aggressively as I could. "Are you still there?"

"I can't tell you what to do," he finally said. "But I'd rather you didn't have an abortion."

On this issue, Matt never wavered, not even for a minute. Many men would have jumped at the chance to take the classic easy route, offering to pay for an abortion or drive me to the clinic. That sort of volunteerism is cheap. You'll never convince me that the emotional toll of an abortion on a man is even one-tenth of what it is on a woman. Matt's reaction, which wasn't born out of religious or political impulse, touched me. It came from a true desire to have and know his child. When he had told me everyone wants to have a child, I'd thought, *Not everyone*. Not, for instance, my boyfriend from college. He'd paid. He'd driven me there. He'd held my hand in the waiting room. Then, when they'd called my name and I'd said, "I won't do this if you don't want me to," he'd said nothing.

I'd had a friend who had gotten pregnant by a very rich man a few years before. She didn't tell me she'd been pregnant until after she'd had the abortion. "I knew you'd cry and that would make me cry," she'd said. She was right, I would have cried. I also would have urged her not to do it. She longed for a child and she was crazy about this man. But he was in a longtime relationship he wasn't about to end for my friend. He'd have set up a trust fund for his child, in all likelihood, but he wasn't going to be part of some pretty package she might have had in her head. So she'd had the abortion. She was younger than I was, but even so, I'd thought, what a gamble. What if no one else came along? What if that was her only chance to be a mother? (Happily, it wasn't.)

As I reflected on my situation in comparison with hers, I realized that if money weren't an issue, I wouldn't be debating going ahead with this pregnancy. But money *was* an issue. I had very little, and Matt seemed to typically have about $5 on his person and no more in the bank. My impression was that he hadn't made a concerted effort to find or hold down a job in months, if not years. His father and stepmother had been sending him rent money regularly. I couldn't rely on him for money, and despite his quiet opposition to an abortion, I wasn't sure I could rely on him for any real help with the baby.

On the way in to see my pregnancy counselor, I stopped at the bathroom. Already I had to pee all the time. There was a cleaning lady in there replacing the toilet paper rolls. I looked at her and thought, *I bet you have three kids at home and two jobs. Yet here you are, surviving. What kind of weak and pathetic person am I to even question whether to have this baby?*

Minutes later, I was telling my counselor this. She was in her fifties, a quiet, low-key type, one of those born listeners who nod, but not so much that you cease to trust them. There was nothing remarkable about her. She was the perfect sounding board.

"Everyone's situation is different," she said. "That woman could have three children and two jobs and a lousy husband, but she might also have an extraordinary family network to provide her with day care. It doesn't sound like you'd have that. Your family is where?"

"All on the East Coast," I said. "My mother is in a nursing home and my dad is eighty-four. I do have sisters, but none of them are going to move out here."

I looked at her expectantly.

"Tell me some more of your concerns," she said.

She was wearing a cardigan to guard against the air conditioning chill, but I felt sweaty, partly from the walk to get here, partly from nerves, but mostly from the pregnancy hormones.

"I just wonder if I'm ever going to meet a man now," I said. "I've had enough trouble so far, and once I burden myself with someone else's child, who is going to want me then? I feel as though I might be throwing away a chance at real happiness. I know I'm going to be creating an incredibly difficult life for myself."

Before I knew it, I was telling her about Owen the thumb-sucker, and how once I caught him looking wistfully at a picture of me from when I was twenty-eight. I asked him why he had that look on his face. "You were so pretty," he said. "I wish I'd known you *then*."

"Have you considered the possibility that you might start meeting different kinds of men if you're a mother?" the counselor asked.

I'm sure I looked at her blankly. Like who?

"There are men who might be more attracted to you as a mother," she said. "Men who might be better to you and for you in the long run. No guarantees, of course, but it could happen. Your romantic life doesn't have to end just because you have a child."

"So are you saying I might actually attract a better caliber of man?" I asked. "More mature?"

She gave a little shrug, the kind they teach in therapy school, the kind that says, *I'm not going to spell it out for you, honey. Do some work here.*

Then we talked about money. I'd have to expect to pay at least $8 an hour for infant day care in the Bay Area, possibly up to $16, she said. She'd be happy to hook me up with a good agency to find someone with references, but I'd be looking at close to $1,300 in day care bills every month, at least for the first year of the baby's life. I got two paychecks a month, each about $1,600. I was sweating so much, my underwear was sticking to me.

"But there might be some creative solutions," she said. "Can you change your work schedule at all? Or ask Matt to stay home with the baby? It doesn't sound like he's very ambitious. Maybe he'd like that."

Asking Matt to be Mr. Mom was a possibility, although that would mean I'd end up being the breadwinner, which, given my salary, would be a bad state of affairs. Changing my work schedule might be an option too. One woman in my department worked Sunday through Thursday so that she could have the same days off as her husband. I could do something like that, ask Matt to take the baby on Sundays while I worked. That would be one less day of day care.

The counselor wanted to know how I felt about having an abortion.

"On some level, I can't really imagine it," I told her. "I know how it works and I've been through it before, but I told myself never, ever again, and to imagine breaking that vow and living with myself afterward is almost unfathomable. Even though I know it might be the most sensible thing, I know I'd have to be prepared for some serious depression."

I looked down at my hands. More and more they look like my mother's. I wonder when the age spots will arrive, when arthritis will bend my knuckles, twist my long fingers the way it twisted hers. Six children. It couldn't ever have been easy, but I think we made her happy.

"And I fear I would regret it for the rest of my life," I said. "I fear that I could take away my only opportunity to be a mother."

"These are good things to think about," she said. "I recommend you make a list."

"I have," I told her. "Pros and cons. They come out about even. At least mathematically."

"Sometimes five pros aren't worth as much as one con," she said. "And vice versa. Keep looking at your list."

I left the counseling session without having made a firm decision, but feeling better about my options. I did need to think creatively and I needed to stop my natural tendency to wallow in pessimism. I liked to think of that as Yankee practicality, as an ability to face the truth. But it was possible that it was merely a case of garden-variety negativity. I told the counselor I'd call her the next day if I needed to talk more.

That night, I stared at my pro and con list. I could shuffle things around all I wanted. I could hope that after an abortion another man would come along and we'd fall madly in love and he'd get me pregnant at just the right time. But could such hope be trusted?

• • •

ON THAT DAY when Peter had told me he didn't want to end up with me, my mother found me sobbing on the terrace. He had returned to the house long enough to throw his bag into his car and back out of the driveway with force that was both defiant and definitive.

I put my head in her lap and voiced the first real doubts I'd ever had about myself romantically, that there was something wrong with me, something missing, something that a really great guy like Peter needed to have in a partner.

"I don't know," she said, stroking my hair. "Didn't he tell you once that he didn't think you were challenging?"

"Yes," I sobbed, lifting my head to look at her. "I still don't know what he meant by that."

"I think what he meant was 'I'm terribly insecure, and anyone who is too nice to me falls under suspicion of being even more flawed than I am.'"

She was so soft. It was August and the grape arbor cast a green light on everything under it. The birds had been pecking at the grapes, even though they were far from ripe, and there were hard green nuggets rolling around her feet. She was wearing white canvas sneakers. They were the same kind she'd always had when I was a kid. Whenever we went swimming, she kept them on. That had been her solution to the discomforts of low tide.

"Moreover," she said. "I can't believe that anyone who actually knows you would say you aren't challenging. That's absurd."

I wish I could have believed my mother then. Or paid more attention to the lesson Peter had given me about hoping for the wrong thing. All that longing for a life with him had been fruitless and self-destructive. Nothing about us had boded well for a future. But I'd believed in the fantasy of him so deeply that I'd held a place in my heart for him for four long years. He'd been my ideal, and, as I looked back on that long-ago heartbreak, I couldn't see why. I could keep on that well-established path of longing, waiting for something or someone that suited whatever my ideal was at thirty-nine, which could, at forty-nine, seem equally appalling. What made me think any of those guys from speed dating would turn out to be anything special? How realistic was it to fantasize about a life that felt like high tide, when even nature couldn't hold on to that fullness for more than a minute?

I would have a complicated future ahead of me, one that looked nothing like what I had wanted. I was terrified. What was growing inside me was still smaller than a pea. But it was solid.

"A bird in the hand," I told myself. A bird I was lucky to have. A bird other women I knew were struggling to catch. How could I look them in the eye if I decided that this pregnancy was too inconvenient and daunting to go ahead with?

I believe passionately in a woman's right to choose, always have and always will. But it is one thing to have an abortion when you're a college kid with your whole career and life ahead of you. For someone in my position, in my late thirties, wanting a child, it ultimately seemed untenable. To know that for sure, I had to have this conversation with myself.

I picked up the list of pros and cons and tossed it into the recycling.

CHAPTER 5

Telling the Grinch

BOTH MY PARENTS were products of Catholic families, Catholic schools, and Catholic neighborhoods in Newark, New Jersey. They'd raised their first two children halfheartedly in the faith, moved to Maine, settled into the academic life, and then completely given up on the rest of us. Politically and socially, they didn't see eye to eye with the church. But they were a curious mix of modern sensibility and tradition, people who couldn't completely escape their upbringing. My mother believed in birth control—however badly she practiced it herself—but she'd still get misty-eyed over the pope. My father had once said, in all seriousness, that he always imagined his daughters would be virgins when they got married.

Like most mothers, mine was the parent who served as point person for matters relating to the children. She was the main instigator of phone calls and letters, the travel agent, and the procurer of all Christmas cheer. My father wasn't cheap—send him to the grocery store and he'd come back with multiple bags of Pepperidge Farm cookies, while we'd be lucky to get a paltry bag of Milanos out of her—but when we were kids, Christmas always sent him into a deep sulk. He'd hang around the outskirts of our festivities, looking aggravated, as if we were troublesome party guests he hoped would be leaving soon. It was also extraordinarily hard to pick out a present that pleased him. For this reason, Benet and I began calling him the Grinch at some point in the seventies, and because his grumpiness and propensity to fly off the handle were not limited to the holidays, it quickly became a year-round title. In matters of dispute between the Grinch and his offspring, my mother could generally be counted on to serve as our defense attorney. Whether this was because she actually was on our side or because she just wanted to be on the opposite side from him was not clear.

But as my mother had faded into dementia, my father had stepped into the breach and become both mother and father to us all. The two of us had always had a stormy relationship, fighting about everything from literature—he was a snob about anything post–Edith Wharton—to deodorant, which he didn't believe in. But we adored each other.

I knew that in telling him about my pregnancy, I couldn't hurt him any more than I had back in 1985. It did seem likely he'd be angry. And could I blame him? I knew what he wanted for me. It was the same thing I wanted for myself, or rather, what I *had* wanted. I could hardly expect him to make such a radical adjustment quickly.

My plan was to wait until I was twelve weeks' pregnant and out of the miscarriage zone. My doctor seemed pleased with my progress and told me she didn't see reason to worry, but for women my age, the miscarriage rates do start to go up. I figured I should wait until I was sure of my bombshell before I dropped it. I already had plans to go back to Maine for my annual August visit, and a few days after I arrived there, I'd pass that three-month milestone. I thought I'd tell him in the company of my siblings, in the warmest atmosphere I could imagine, perhaps after a day of kayaking in Casco Bay, over a bowl of fish chowder.

But the familial pressure was mounting. By mid-July, all my siblings knew except for Adrian, who has always had an unfortunate tendency to spill any beans that came his way. They were as nervous about Dad finding out as I was about telling him. I'd rouse myself from another round of vomiting to find another e-mail or phone call asking precisely when I'd break the news. Alison wanted to be able to get out of town in the aftermath. Wib thought Dad's feelings would be hurt once he realized that he was the last to know. There was general concern that the peaceful August interlude we all looked forward to would turn into a drama of epic proportions.

Finally, one Saturday morning late in the month, I just went ahead and called him.

"So," I said. "I have some news. It's big news, and it might seem initially like bad news, but really, it's not."

I recommended that he sit down. I sat down myself, and then immediately stood up.

"I'm going to have a baby," I said.

He was silent.

"That is, I'm pregnant," I said.

More silence.

"It's an accident, completely," I said. "But I'm happy about it. And the father is going to be involved, and he's actually sort of pleased about it himself. He's a very sweet guy."

And then it came.

"Is this young man going to marry you?"

He'd summoned up his thunder voice, a special tenor he'd reserved in my childhood for serious matters, such as threats of punishment. As in, "I'm going to come down on you like a ton of bricks, young lady." With all his children grown, he mostly called up the thunder voice now for business-related matters—for instance, recording his outgoing message on voice mail. This time, though, there was also something vulnerable in there, a tremor that gave me pause. The poor old man. Eighty-four years old and getting this kind of news.

The questions poured out after that, and with each response I gave, I winced a little more. By my father's standards, it all sounded so bad. No plans for a wedding, or even, for that matter, dating. No Ivy League graduate, no "good" family. (Not that we were in any sense a "good" family.) My child's father didn't even have a job. I barely knew him. I could still count on two hands the number of times I'd seen him in person. My one paltry offering was that Matt's family was Catholic. Never mind that Matt himself had no interest in religion. Neither did I. But my father held on to that like a life raft. I took it as a sign of how desperately my news had put him at sea.

In between questions, I offered this explanation. I was not getting any younger. I wanted to be a mother. I was dead certain that my life would feel incomplete if I did not have a child. This could be my last opportunity. As I tried to convince my father that it would be okay, I realized that I wasn't saying any of this just to placate him. It really was true, and I knew that I stood on the firmest of moral grounds. My father would join me there eventually, because he was a lover of firm moral ground. In Rumer Godden's *The Greengage Summer*, one of my favorite books as an adolescent, the young narrator describes believing that if you could see a person's bones, you'd know the quality of his character. Someone bad would have stained or darkened bones, and the truly good would have the purest, whitest bones. I knew what color my father's bones were.

BUT WHAT ABOUT MATT? What color were his bones? My first trip to the doctor with him had been a miserable occasion. It was about eight weeks into the pregnancy. He took the train across the Bay and walked up to my apartment, arriving sweaty and clutching a bottle of Mountain Dew. He looked terribly young.

We walked the few blocks to the medical center in silence. The first appointment was sort of a cattle call, a conference room full of grumpy, tired-looking women and their jittery husbands, all receiving the most basic of information about their pregnancies, from "Smoking is bad" to "Saltines might help." Matt and I sat side by side without touching. I passed pieces of paperwork to him and glanced over as he filled them out. So that's his address, I thought. That's his social security number. How could all these vital pieces of information be so alien to me? I turned away when I saw his pen hovering over the box for income level. That I was sure I wasn't ready to know.

I raised my hand to ask questions about cat litter. I knew all

about the don't-touch-it rule. Contact with cat feces during pregnancy can cause birth defects, and even miscarriage. But I wanted
specifics. What if I wore a mask over my mouth and nose? Would
gloves do the trick? The nurse who led our session didn't seem to
know what to make of my line of questioning. It must have seemed
to her that the obvious solution was to have the father of my child
change the cat litter for the next seven months. He was sitting right
there, looking perfectly able-bodied. I was embarrassed by the obvious lack of chivalry in whatever relationship we had, but I had to
ask the questions.

Our next stop was the lab, where I had blood drawn to start the
process of genetic testing. I'd already felt awful, but now I felt woozy
as well. The day was hot and unusually muggy. Afterward Matt and
I plodded down the sidewalk together, me feeling so fragile that I
clutched his arm like a little old lady.

"If you think I'm coming over to change your cat litter every
week, you better think again," he announced.

I hated him at that moment. I hated his face, I hated his hair, I
hated his clothes. He was still holding his bottle of Mountain Dew
and I hated it too. Who drank Mountain Dew besides sixteen-year-
old lacrosse players? And here he was telling me that the most important thing he'd taken away from our first medical visit was that,
yeah, our baby could be retarded if I dug around in a box full of cat
shit every couple of days, but that wasn't his problem. If I'd had a box
of cat litter in front of me, I would have tried to make him eat it.

At least that was half of my reaction. The other half was straight-
forward fear. I was going to need this Mountain Dew–swilling jackass. Instead of telling him off, the way I wanted to, I was going to
have to keep my mouth shut. I felt as if I were caught in a vise. Nothing seemed good, nothing seemed right.

A couple of weeks later I was so worn out from throwing up that
I called my HMO and asked for the advice nurse. I explained my misery, and she told me to come in to urgent care right away. Within two
hours, I was hooked up to an IV, being given fluids and—gloriously—
an antinausea medication called Phenergan. A nurse wrapped a heated

blanket around me and told me to close my eyes and rest. It was so blissfully what I needed, to be pampered, to be acknowledged as a person who was too sick to be left alone, that I sat there crying, but with a smile on my face. I left with a bottle of Phenergan in pill form, which I clung to for the rest of the pregnancy.

ONE AFTERNOON, my friend Sam called when I was in my new favorite position, curled up in bed. The news about my pregnancy was starting to spread. Sam is my dear friend Kir's husband, and father to her three children. He's one of the most direct people I know, and that's saying something, because most people who know me would say I'm the most direct person *they* know. So Sam and I share bluntness and an unwillingness to suffer fools. This means we've had a few fights in the course of our fifteen-year friendship. I know he loves me like a sister, but he's like no brother I've ever had. My brothers might pick *on* me, but they never pick me apart. Sam is like Dr. Phil, but more ruthless. I approached his call with some trepidation.

"Listen," Sam said. The S lingered. When he's insistent about something, he puts the emphasis on his Ssss, so that the conversation reverberates with a certain Ssssamness.

"I just want you to know that I think this is a great thing you're doing. Children are amazing, and I know you'll be an incredible mother."

I fiddled with the sheets and waited for the "but."

"But I hope you don't have some idea that you and this guy— what's his name?"

"Matt," I said, dully.

"Matt," he continued. "Right. I hope you don't have the idea that you are going to end up together. Because that would be the worst thing you could do for this baby. You can't count on this guy for a minute. You have to be prepared to do this completely on your own or you shouldn't do it."

I may have been guilty of putting some positive spin on the Matt situation with my friends, but I hadn't lied about him. Matt wasn't the person I'd imagined myself having a child with. I wasn't sure we had anything in common besides a fetus and a love of books.

"I'm not expecting him to be my boyfriend, Sam," I said. "But he says he's going to help take care of the baby, and that has been a factor in my decision. Maybe he'll bail somewhere down the line, and if he does, I'll cope."

Sam was just gathering steam. "You have to expect him to bail. You should *plan* on him bailing," he said.

I tried to shift the topic off Matt.

"Look Sam, almost all of my friends have already had children. They're going to be able to help me. I'll have a great support network. I have Kir. Kir knows *everything* about kids. I have Liza. I have Sara."

"That's true," he said, in the tone of an expert debater softening up his opponent before going in for the kill. "But none of them have had children like this. Everyone was married. You are going to be alone in this emotional landscape."

I started to cry. Alone in this emotional landscape. I pictured all the married mothers I knew standing under a peaceful, high canopy of redwood trees, cradling their babies and looking up, smiling. The towering height of the trees was reassuring; *Things have always been this way,* they seemed to say. Everybody in that landscape was wearing Patagonia. They looked comfortable and content.

Meanwhile over in *my* emotional landscape, I saw a lone figure, clutching a wailing baby on a blackened hillside. In my news reporting days, I covered a lot of wildfires. When the burn is fresh, but the immediate danger has passed, the firefighters often take reporters back into the fire zone. They drive you up into the hills, on roads that are the only man-made things that haven't been destroyed, and then they park and invite you to get out and walk among gray ashes, ravaged trees, and patches of smoldering earth. Secretly, I loved the theatricality of being backstage at a disaster, with its eerie sense of disruption and eloquent reminder that we are all very small, but I certainly didn't want to linger in this desolate landscape.

I was beyond being able to make Sam understand my point of

view. If I even had one. I was so at sea that for the first time in my life, I wasn't sure I had an opinion. I wept into the phone for another minute or two, figuring it wouldn't hurt for him to see how wretched he was making me feel. He had three kids. He couldn't just be happy for me, getting to have one?

"I'm sorry," I said, between sobs. "I just don't want to talk anymore."

I tossed the phone to the end of the bed. It landed next to McGee, my tiger-striped gray cat. He put his ears back and looked at it, then looked at me, offended. "Come here, Mr. McGee," I said, and put my hand out to him. He stood up to nuzzle me, and then plunked down next to my chest and started to purr. I tried to tell myself Sam was being ridiculous. Plenty of women had babies by themselves, and presumably they'd be in that emotional landscape with me.

But there was something in there I couldn't shake: his supposition that I would construct a fantasy around this whole thing whereby I ended up part of a couple. Sam didn't know me back when I was pining for Peter. But he did know the Mary who was capable of wanting the wrong things. As I lay there with my feline support network, I realized how much I craved my mother, wanted her to come and stroke my hair and tell me I'd never be alone in any stupid emotional landscape, because she would be there.

ALL THROUGH THOSE FIRST ELEVEN WEEKS of pregnancy, I couldn't wait to get to the Cove. On real maps of the Maine coast, this inlet is too small and insignificant to have a name, but on the map of my life, it is the ultimate destination, a beacon beckoning me every summer. In my mind, it deserves capitalization, for it is my happiest landscape. All the way across the country, trying to breathe through my never-ending desire to puke, I imagined myself floating on my back in the Cove, looking up at the pine trees against a radiant blue sky. I'd finally get my mind to stop chewing on itself. I could be serene, the way pregnant women are supposed to be. At the Cove, I might even start to enjoy the idea of being pregnant.

The drive from Brunswick takes only about a half hour, but if you're impatient, it seems a lot longer. The turnoff onto the dirt road that leads to the Cove comes up so suddenly you could blow right by it if you weren't paying attention. Then you'd end up at the lodge where John and Liza and I had all met, barely a quarter mile past the turnoff. Its dock, the place where I'd first kissed Peter when he came back from Africa, was just a short paddle by kayak from the Cove. Benet and Beth had gotten married on the lawn next to the lodge's saltwater pool. My oldest sister, Cynthia, had worked as a waitress there back in 1971. So much of my family's history had been written in this place.

"Was the Boathouse as dirty as ever when you arrived?" I asked Wib, stretching my hand out her car window and letting the wind hold it up.

"The usual," she answered. "Although it did seem as though someone might have passed a vacuum over the floor. No firewood, of course. There are some hideous new comforters on the upstairs beds. But otherwise, exactly the same."

I sighed with pleasure and then inhaled the ocean air. Exactly the same was exactly what I wanted. Our summer rental, our home away from home for a few weeks every August for the last decade, was in many ways extraordinarily uncomfortable. The oven was so uneven it burned everything, and the plumbing backed up at least once a summer. The mattresses were miserable, thirty years old if a day. The interior was too dark, because of the thicket of pine trees that leaned in on either side of the house. But we loved the Boathouse. It was our place.

We bumped down the road, past the tree where all the residents have posted their names on painted wooden boards. Liza and John's parents' sign "Bigelow" was shiny and new, just as neat and trim as their house. The Boathouse was at the end of the road, and they were our next-door neighbors.

"Oh my God, I wonder what Mrs. Bigelow is going to think of my future as an unwed mother?" I said as we drove by their place. "She's *such* a Catholic."

"Well she already knows about it," Wib said. "I believe one of her children already gave her a full report."

Liza, no doubt. I couldn't blame her for wanting to deflect some attention from her own difficulties. Her mother was of the opinion that Liza should just stay married, no matter how much Hugh annoyed her.

"Does she seem scandalized?"

"Less than I would have expected," Wib said. "But she did wring her hands a little."

We pulled into the turnout we used as a parking lot, and I climbed out of the car, shouldering my bag. A few yards down a pine-needle-strewn path, and there it was, the sliver of water and the rambling, wood-shingled building straddling it. It looks something like a pirate's ship. Local legend paints the Boathouse as an old speakeasy and smuggler's den. I believe the former and wish I could believe the latter, but both are certainly imaginable. It's built on stilts over a stream that empties out into the salty Cove. At low tide, only a freshwater trickle runs under the house; at high tide, the waters of Casco Bay slap against the bottom steps on the lowest porch. For an hour or two a day, the Cove turns into our personal swimming pool, which obligingly ceases to be frigid for a few weeks in late July and into August.

Wib's husband, Sean, walked out onto the footbridge to greet us. Three decades later, he still had the beard, although it was more gray than red now. It no longer disturbed me, but their teenaged son, Matthew, complained about it mightily. Sean was barefoot and, from the looks of his windblown hair, had just been sailing.

"Let me take that," he said, lifting my bag off my shoulder. "A lady in your delicate condition shouldn't be carrying anything."

He snickered. I ignored him. There was no way I could declare my pregnancy a joke-free zone. Adrian would be here in a couple of days, and then I'd probably be longing for some subtle snickers.

"How's the water?" I asked.

"Sublime," Wib said. "Rough on entry of course, but then just perfect."

"I'm going to get my suit on and get right out there," I said, stepping inside.

The door opens onto an enormous living room, with a galley kitchen, elevated just enough so that the cook can bark orders to the slackers on the couch who should be snipping green beans or piling logs into the great stone fireplace (even in August, the night breeze comes off the waters of Casco Bay with a chill). The biggest, heaviest picnic table I've ever seen sits adjacent to the kitchen, armed with two vicious benches that have left bruises on every shinbone in our family. Every year Wib brings more of her own china and kitchen equipment and leaves some of it there, as if by doing so, we could gain a claim on this place we fantasize about owning. I stepped out onto the screened-in porch, which overlooks the water. Because the bedrooms are so musty, we always sleep out here. Wib and Sean had already dragged out mattresses for themselves, Matthew, and me. Other family members would come and stay for a night here and there, and Benet might bring his older daughter, Isabella, down for a sleepover, but we were the main tenants.

I looked down at the water, which had a silvery glint. The sky was overcast, and the air was heavy. Swimming was nice on days like this; it made me feel more like a fish and the water could seem warmer. But my stomach was churning. I'd made Wib stop for fries at McDonald's on the way down, assuring her that salty food was just what I needed. As she joined me at the rail, I let out an enormous burp. The seals in the harbor probably thought their long-lost sister was in town.

"Yikes," she said. "Do you need a Tums?"

I bent over, resting my elbows on the railing, which was cut from a tree trunk. "Tums suck," I said. "They do nothing for me."

I tried to breathe. "I'll be right back," I said, running for the bathroom.

• • •

I DID SWIM THAT VACATION, between bouts of morning sickness, which in my case was really morning, noon, and night sickness. My father, who came down for dinner and a kayak ride most days, was completely distressed by how much throwing up I was doing.

"It's perfectly normal," I said, returning from the bathroom yet again, fish chowder safely out of my system, teeth brushed for the fifth time that day. They were all staring at me. Without insulation, sound carries easily at the Boathouse. Dad was shaking his head.

"Gross me out the door," Adrian said, getting up to fill his soup bowl again. "Girl, you've got it bad."

I was getting the feeling he was right. Not every pregnant woman throws up, but even the ones that do usually ease off around the twelfth week. I was at thirteen weeks, and there was no sign that it was easing up. I was trying not to take the Phenergan every day, because it seemed better to avoid drugs as much as possible. But surely, I asked my father, his own wife, who bore him six children, had done some vomiting?

"Never," he said.

"Oh, I'd hear her in there every time she was pregnant," Adrian said. "Wib. Alison, Benet, and then Mary. Don't forget, my room was right next to the bathroom. She'd be in there, singing away to the porcelain throne. Blah. Bhleck. Barf." He laughed. Matthew gazed at him with admiration. For a fifteen-year-old boy, having Adrian around must have been like having Evel Knievel in the house. Only instead of leaping rows of cars, he flew in the face of proper customs and conventions.

Dad, on the other hand, looked pained. "In any event," he began, which meant, *Will you all be quiet for a cursed minute?* "You should watch what you eat, Mary. I think you're making yourself sick by eating an inappropriate diet. Seafood! And those hot dogs, for heaven's sake!"

Alison had already spoken to Wib about the hot dogs. I liked them steamed, on a steamed bun, with yellow mustard and ketchup and then a dollop of sauerkraut. It was a Boathouse tradition, and I didn't want to stop, especially when there was so little else that I craved. "You've got to tell her to stop," Alison told Wib, who duti-fully passed it on. "There's listeria in hot dogs." "I cook them," I'd said. "Well done."

That night I didn't feel like defending myself. The room felt fogged in with disapproval, so I went out to the porch and lay down on my mattress. Throwing up was not my fault, but being pregnant certainly was. My emotional landscape was crowded with people that evening, but I felt very alone in it.

I knew my father harbored suspicions about my pregnancy. That somehow, I planned it. We already had that conversation once, and I had assured him there was no way I would do this to myself on purpose.

"Not even accidentally on purpose?" he'd asked.

"I can see why you might think that," I'd replied. "But would I choose Matt as the father?"

My niece Katy came out to the porch and knelt beside me. She stroked my hair. "I feel so alone," I sobbed, and she patted me some more. "Don't worry," she crooned. "It's going to be all right."

Would it? I was reading *Sister Carrie*, one of those great Ameri-can novels I'd always felt I *should* read, and I was horrified at the fate of the fictional George Hurstwood, who ran away with the beautiful young Carrie, fell on financial hard times, and never again found lasting or gainful employment. I began to fear Matt might be a mod-ern-day Hurstwood, lacking the drive and self-confidence to get a job. I could be dragged down by him. I did not want to co-parent with George Hurstwood.

My tears subsided, not because I felt better, but because I'd sim-ply run out of steam for the night.

"Can I get you anything?" Katy asked softly.

"Some Honey Nut Cheerios?" I said. "With milk?"

The next day my father handed me a small brown paper bag. "These might help, dearie," he said. I opened it up and found a pack-age of lemon drops and a box of German peppermints.

"Thanks, Babbo," I said, smiling at him and using our other, kinder pet name for him.

He patted me on the shoulder. "Do try to lay off the lobster and hot dogs, though."

I WENT TO SEE MY MOTHER at her nursing home. We sat together in the garden, she in her wheelchair, me in a folding chair next to her. All the other inmates, as my father called them, were inside, including the scary lady who liked to play wheelchair derby. Once she'd followed me into my mother's room and trapped me in a corner, charging forward every time I tried to get around her. Still, I found her less disconcerting than the old woman who shrieked, "I love you" at anyone who came to visit.

My mother's gray hair was hanging lankly in her face. She was wearing a Texas Longhorns' shirt and sweatpants. It appeared that my father had started buying her shoes that were identical to his, blocky pieces of stiff leather that looked like something from the Gulag. She was slowly making her way through an ice cream cup, the kind we had in grade school, the kind that always tastes a little freezer burned.

"So Mumma," I said to her. "I'm going to have a baby."

She stared off into the distance. "Why would you want to do that?" she said.

I felt stung, although, of course, this is not what my mother would have said if her mind were intact. She would have cheered me on, told me that husbands were unnecessary. "Simply accoutrements," she might have said.

She went back to waiting for something or someone she could no longer identify. Her whole existence was about waiting. She was waiting for the end of life, and for so long, I'd been waiting for the beginning. The one that had suddenly changed shape and was growing inside me now, nothing like any fantasy I'd ever had. I kissed my mother good-bye, dodged the old man who waited by the locked-down door, like a cat trying to make a surreptitious exit, and drove back to the Boathouse.

I went for a solitary swim, pulling myself up on the rocks on the far side of the Cove. The tide was on its way out, and I could see the remnants of the old boat ramp jutting out of the water in front of the Boathouse.

The house actually has a name, something quainter, but everyone we know calls it the Boathouse because that's precisely what it is. Underneath the living room is a cavernous space, home now to bats rather than boats, a few old broken oars, and bags of charcoal from summers gone by. I'd gotten in the habit, every summer, of going downstairs to drag open the sliding door and indulge my romantic side. I have long had the idea that someday I will exchange wedding vows in front of this door just as dusk is falling. Vines and flowers will be wrapped around the supporting beams, candles will be flickering in the evening breeze, and across the water, turning navy blue now in the twilight, the lights of a nearby inn will appear, the windows shining a buttery yellow invitation out into the coming night. I'll be clinking champagne glasses with my new husband, who will of course understand exactly why this place appeals to me so much.

My sisters never thought much of this scenario. "I don't think they'd want us burning candles," Wib said when I told her about it. "This whole place could go up in minutes. And where would everyone *sit*? What about getting Mum down those stairs?"

Alison shuddered. She is the lone member of the family who is immune to the Boathouse's charms. "I like sun," she always says, when we try to coax her to leave her house in town and drive down to see us, and we can't argue. The Boathouse is surrounded by tall trees, and if you want the sun, you have to swim to it. When the water is brutally cold we lie on the Bigelows' dock, getting warm enough to brave the swim back.

I could hear strange thumps coming from the lower floor of the Boathouse. Matthew must be down there. I hadn't ventured into the room yet that summer. Nor would I. Any smell could set my stomach churning, but the truth was I did not want to visit the place I had always imagined would set the stage for the perfect life I knew I wasn't going to have now.

The door slid open, and Matthew appeared in it, holding a hock-ey stick. He was indeed the source of the thumping.

"How's the water?" he shouted across at me.

"A little colder than yesterday," I yelled back. "But not too bad."

"How many times have you puked today?" he said.

"Just once," I said.

"We should have lobster then," he said. "To celebrate."

Matthew could eat three lobsters in one sitting. He was an ex-pensive teenager.

"Let's," I said. I sank back on my elbows, admiring the way my belly protruded in my wet suit. I hadn't exactly found the serenity I had hoped for in Maine, but I was getting the sense that serene preg-nancies were just another fantasy.

RIGHT AFTER I GOT BACK from Maine, Matt called with encourag-ing news. He'd landed a temp job that seemed likely to last at least for a couple of months.

"They said they've got a lot of work for me," he said, sounding positively jubilant. "They showed me this room of files they want reorganized. I could be here awhile."

The company, a bond trader, had its offices down in San Francis-co's Ferry Building.

"It's a killer view," he said. "You can watch the ferries coming in. I can see Oakland. If you were driving across the bridge, I'd practically be able to see you."

I'd never heard him so upbeat.

"That's great," I said. "I'm really glad."

"Anyhoo," he said. "I'm off to get a burrito."

I looked at the phone, bemused.

"Anyhoo?" I said. "Does your mother say that?"

"No," he said. "Homer."

"Who?" I said.

"Homer Simpson," he said.

"Right," I said. "Okay, well enjoy your burrito. And I'm really happy for you."

I hung up the phone smiling and went back to looking through the mail that had accumulated in my absence. There was a big box from Amazon. I opened it up and found a stack of pregnancy books. Hip mommas, thinking mommas, hot mommas, and even a guidebook for mommas on a budget. Then there was a big, beautiful, glossy coffee-table book about pregnancy. I looked for a note in the box. "Thought these might come in handy," it said. "I'm so excited for you. Love, Sara." Sara was one of my oldest friends. We'd met interning at an alternative weekly, gone to journalism school together, and then worked at the same paper in Southern California. Sara was strong and brave and a feminist. I could have imagined her having a child on her own, that is, before she married our friend Mark and had two children with him. Theirs was an emotional landscape I envied. I opened the coffee-table book and started looking at the pictures. Cells dividing, microscopic egg sacs, and then the tiny fetuses. They were so fragile, so delicate, so amazing.

I looked at the note again. When I'd told Sara about the whole emotional landscape conversation with Sam, she'd clucked sympathetically and told me not to take Sam too seriously. "He's the most bombastic man in the world!" she'd said. But she knew that I wouldn't be able to stop myself from taking it to heart, and this was her way of saying, *I'm here*. I never doubted that my friends would rally around me. But I felt bolstered by Sara's care package.

The first winter after a wildfire is tough. The rain pounds the naked ground, and without trees and shrubs to anchor the wet earth, whole hills might give way. I'd seen the wreckage of mud slides. But I had also seen what happens in the spring. With their larger, overhanging competitors out of the way, the grasses and flowers rebound with ferocity. Seedpods cracked by the flames, their contents lifted by the hot winds, spread farther than ever before. Once, I followed a park ranger as he walked through a burn area in the Santa Monica Mountains, showing me how varied the blooms were after the fresh start of a fire. He tramped off the path and cupped a dark brown flower with a yellow center in his hand. "This is a chocolate lily," he said. "They're usually pretty uncommon around here. But we've been seeing quite a few of them. It's amazing what turns up after a fire."

Maybe I'd find some chocolate lilies in my new landscape.

CHAPTER 6

Living with Boys

EACH TIME I VISITED my gynecologist the contradictions of my luck pulled at me. "Looking good," she'd say, looking at the ultrasound image. "*Such* a strong heartbeat," and I'd hear the beautiful sound of that heartbeat, like a galloping horse running toward me. I'd feel overwhelmed with gratitude, knowing how hard it was for so many women, first to get pregnant, then to stay that way. Here I was, with this baby I hadn't planned, and he or she was doing everything just right.

But in the waiting room, I was often the only woman alone; all the other women had a man with them, a man who had his hand on her knee, proud, possessive, soothing. After that depressing first trip to the doctor, I had decided that Matt wouldn't accompany me on any prenatal visits; there was too much pretense about it. Moreover, his passivity, the way he just sat like a lump, drove me insane. He was the absolute opposite of me.

"You're one of those people who always sat at the front of the class, aren't you?" he said to me.

"No," I snapped. "I sat in the back when I was in school. Or the middle. Don't make me sound like Tracy Flick."

"Who's Tracy Flick?"

Our points of reference were always off. I felt as though I needed a crash course in Homer and Bart Simpson in order to speak his language.

"The girl from *Election*, Reese Witherspoon's character," I said. "She was an uptight overachiever. And as it happens, now that I am an adult, when there is information I need or want, yes, I do sit in the front, so that I can increase my chances of getting that information."

I was lecturing. Something about Matt's cluelessness inspired this tone of voice from me, which sounded suspiciously like my father's. But I did believe in asking questions, lots of them. Being a journalist had taught me that being a shrinking violet didn't get you anywhere. Sometimes you had to humble yourself and ask the obvious question, the one that might make other reporters turn and look at you—thinking, *Duh!*—because the chances were quite high that none of us actually knew anything. The other lesson I learned was not to take no for an answer. Not until the person I was asking had shut the door, locked it, and gone to bed.

Matt had spent his whole life sitting in the back row. He was honest about his academic failings, telling me he had earned such bad grades in high school that he had no chance of getting into the colleges he'd imagined himself going to. He admitted that he'd deliberately done badly in school, figuring he'd distinguish himself by remarkable failure rather than the success he was scared to hope for. "I remember my mother pounding on the table every night, trying to get me to do my homework," he told me. "And I'd just look out the window until she got worn out." He went to a community college, applied himself just enough to transfer to U Mass, then slacked off for the rest of his academic career. The thing he'd been good at was lacrosse. I knew enough to know that even if he'd only sat the bench on the U Mass men's lacrosse team, he had to have had talent. Normally skills involving helmets and shin pads would have meant nothing to me. I had survived being the second to last picked for volleyball, kickball, and every other elementary and junior high school gym sport (the girl in leg braces was generally last). But Matt was so far from my dream co-parent that I was grasping at straws. While talking to Wib, I offered up the tidbit that the father of my child had demonstrated considerable prowess on the lacrosse field.

"What position?" she asked. Her son played lacrosse, so she knew the sport.

"Goalie," I said.

"That's *good*," she said, with as much enthusiasm as if I'd told her Matt had majored in quantum physics at MIT. She is an encouraging person by nature. "That means he's got to be good under pressure. Coolheaded."

"Really?" I said. "God, I hope so."

AFTER I SCHEDULED my amnio appointment, I decided to break my rule and have Matt come with me. I needed him; I wasn't allowed to go home alone after it, and none of my friends was available. Amnios are recommended for women over thirty-five, but I also really wanted to know the sex of the baby. Ultrasounds weren't definitive on this topic; my friend Kir had spent her entire third pregnancy assuming, wrongly, that she was having a girl based on what the ultrasound technician had told her. I wanted a girl more than anything. I actively did *not* want a boy. I'd recently heard a guest on an NPR program discussing how difficult it was for boys born to single mothers to grow up without strong male role models. I'd spent ten minutes sobbing in the car over that one. Moreover, my observations, limited though they were, had led me to believe that if I had a boy, he had a better than average chance of being a gun-toting, Game Boy–playing, Ritalin-popping beast. Boys weren't supposed to be verbal, so I expected if I had a boy, he wouldn't say much of anything until he was three, and at thirteen he'd stop communicating entirely, except to greet everything I said with a grunt of contempt. Then I'd have to deal with wet dreams. I also assumed that a boy would be just like Matt. I pictured myself pounding on the kitchen table while his eyes drifted away from his homework and toward the window. "You're just like your father," I'd be snarling at my teenaged son. "I never should have gone home with him!"

In the unlikely event that destiny, having tampered with all my plans for myself to date, would have also robbed me of a companion in dollhouse decorating, I wanted to be prepared. Not that I'd be putting a baby boy out on the mountainside for the coyotes. But I didn't want to have a look of dismay on my face if and when they said, "It's a boy!"

Matt took my hand as I lay on the table. The gesture reminded me of being on a field trip in elementary school when the teacher makes you hold hands. The nurse let me see the baby on the ultrasound screen for a minute; then she turned it away so that I wouldn't see the needle making its long descent into my womb. But Matt watched on another screen, while I watched his face. He was rapt. I realized this was his first glimpse of the life inside me, and I was gratified by the pleasure on his face.

WHEN I'D TOLD MATT I was definitely going to go ahead with the pregnancy, I said I wanted us to live together for the baby's first year. The fearful part of me was imagining being alone all night, every night, with an infant's mysterious needs. I also thought it would be better for Matt. He could escape his vile hovel and start living like a grown-up. I reasoned this arrangement would be better for the baby, who would then get to bond with both parents on an equal level. Also, I didn't want my child to grow up thinking of Daddy as the person who lived in a dump.

On the day that he'd said, without stopping to think about it, that he wanted to be involved in our child's life, he'd made me feel that we could be a team, and though I'd question it later on, I was proceeding as if we were just that. When I wasn't quaking over the challenges I'd set for myself, I was sure I could help him get his shit together. I was older, wiser, and prided myself on being a problem solver. Matt needed a makeover. Improved living conditions would be just the tip of the iceberg.

"I think it would be good for all of us," I told him one night on the phone. But I knew even as I said it that this might not sound like such a great offer to Matt, who was clearly trying to keep as much physical distance between us as possible. Since my announcement, his half of the sexual current between us had evaporated completely. He'd started treating me like a sister. He'd actually called me "sport" the week before.

"I think I could make a nice home for us," I had added, to fill the silence on the line. "I have plenty of furniture. You'd just need a bed. We'd get a three-bedroom apartment. Or two, and you could have one and the baby and I would take the other."

"That sounds like a sitcom," he'd said dubiously. "What if I'm seeing someone or you're seeing someone?"

Did this guy have any social graces?

"That's what you're worried about?" I said. "Your sex life?"

I wasn't anticipating doing a lot of dating in my infant's first year of life. I couldn't look beyond that time frame, because to look farther into the future was too overwhelming. To start considering Matt's future sex life was even more daunting. I suddenly pictured myself with the roommate from hell. I'd be pacing the halls in the middle of the night with my precious baby girl, who would be howling with displeasure, while behind Matt's door, some pretty young thing would be howling with pleasure. I could only imagine our breakfast conversations:

"You better have used a condom."

"We did."

"All three times?"

"*Yessss*," he'd say, pouring Froot Loops into a bowl. "Is there any milk?"

He'd eventually agreed to the arrangement, provided we'd make our home together in San Francisco. I hadn't lived in the city for years; it had been too expensive for me on my own. But there would be advantages to it. For one thing, I could just hop on a bus and get to my night screenings, instead of commuting by car. I'd also be close to Liza.

Nevertheless, as I'd gotten to know Matt's history, I'd become nervous about sharing a place with him. The longest he'd been at any company since he moved to the West Coast was four months. I had to consider the possibility that he might not be able to hold on to a job. I had no financial cushion at all. If I got stuck with the full rent for a two-bedroom in the city, I'd be bankrupt in two months. So I sat him down one day and told him I worried he'd be a rent risk. Sharing a place was no longer on the table. He was dejected at getting a lecture, but clearly relieved to be off the hook.

My prenatal counselor had suggested I consider living with another single mother. We could pool our resources for day care and rent. The prospect made me feel tragic; there I'd be in some sort of Berkeley commune, my dirty-faced brat hand in hand with the dirty-faced brat of another idiotically careless woman, a pot of black beans bubbling on the stove. But I knew I had to start asking the tough questions, start treating the possibilities for my future like a story I was reporting. I posted an ad on a Web site that matched single mothers. Then I went looking for local members of Single Mothers by Choice, a national group. There had to be a chapter in the East Bay, where cultural and social freedoms reigned supreme.

An officer in the local chapter called me back. Sasha's voice was breathy, her tone friendly. She was eager to listen, and when I got to the cat litter story, I could practically hear her nodding sympathetically. It felt good to spill my story to someone who might have some wisdom to offer. Or at least that's what I kept saying. "I was hoping you could offer me some wisdom." (Somewhere inside me, I could hear my mother's cynical voice responding: "Well, dearie, the first wisdom I'd offer is to use a condom in the future.")

Sasha sighed. "You're just like me," she said.

Oh, thank God. I wanted to be just like someone.

"The father of my child?" she said. "No job. Actually he's homeless. I got pregnant one night when I visited him in the homeless shelter. Kind of intentionally."

He'd seen his daughter exactly twice. Once they had bumped into him at a street fair. Another time he'd turned up at her parents' house demanding to see the child. Drunk. Even with his Baltimore accent, Mountain Dew in one hand and empty résumé in the other, Matt suddenly looked better to me. Yet Sasha recommended that I cut off all ties with him.

"Whatever you do, don't put his name on the birth certificate," she continued. "If you do that, then he's automatically entitled to visitation. If you leave it off, he's going to have to do DNA testing to prove that the baby is his, and it doesn't sound like he's the kind of guy that would want to spend money on that."

Single Mothers by Choice would help me, she said, but there was something I needed to know.

"Most of the women in the group have unknown donors," she said.

"What does that mean?"

"They used a sperm bank. And they have some issues with women who do know their donor. So there is kind of this faction, see? There are people like us in the group, just not that many."

There have been many times in my life when I didn't do something I should have done and then been dogged by guilt for not having behaved in the practical, sensible way. With this in mind, I told Sasha that I would come to the next meeting of the single mothers' group, even though the world of donors you weren't supposed to know and drunk homeless donors you did know sounded thoroughly unappealing. She also suggested my moving into an apartment near her that might be vacant in the next few months. "We could share child care!" she said brightly.

I drove by Sasha's place a few days later. The front yard was filled with the rubble of plastic toys. I decided I'd stop some other time. Then that weekend, I set out for my local library, where Sasha had told me the East Bay's Single Mothers by Choice group would be holding a meeting. I tried every door, peered in windows, and circled the whole building, but I never found them. Maybe, I thought, I'll just see how things go for now on my own. If I get desperate, I can always track them down. Then I went home and threw up.

WHEN I CALLED for the amnio results two weeks later, I was sitting at my dining room table, which also served as my home office. I had the computer on and was surfing the Net, not expecting to get a human being on the other end of the line. My genetic counselor was gleeful as she told me that, despite its advanced age, my egg had been in perfect condition. No genetic deformities detected, everything healthy and progressing well.

"And did you want to know the baby's sex?" she asked.

"Yes," I said, bracing myself.

"You're having a boy!" she said gaily.

"Oh," I said, and mumbled a few things before getting off the phone.

I had a hair appointment across town about fifteen minutes from then, so I made my whiny phone calls from the car. I started with Kir. She'd had two girls before she had her son, and it sometimes seemed as though she'd willed the first two pregnancies to turn out the way she wanted. I remembered Kir sobbing, in the last weeks of her third pregnancy, that perhaps this baby was a boy after all. Her supposition was that only a wretched boy could make her feel so physically ill. So I thought she'd understand my misery. Certainly she knew immediately what was going on. All I had to do was say amnio and sob into the phone.

"So it's a boy," she said flatly.

"Yes," I sobbed. "Couldn't I have this one thing go the way I wanted it to?"

Kir would have been justified in saying, "Get over yourself, you jackass," but she was kind enough not to. So was Wib, who listened quietly at the time. "When I heard you sobbing, I assumed Down syndrome," she said later. "Boy, was I pissed." I wish I had a picture of myself, sitting in the hairdresser's chair. There I was, bloated, my face puffy and red, my hair in need of a trim, with gray roots three inches long, wailing away. I was a pure portrait of misplaced, foolish woe.

BY OCTOBER, when I'd hit the five-month mark, I'd finally made the transition from looking merely fat to being obviously pregnant. This meant I had to do a lot more explaining, mostly to colleagues.

"I didn't know you were dating anyone," one of the more obnoxious critics said to me as I walked into a screening in a shirt that clung to my belly. "I wasn't," I said, trying to sound as cheerful as possible.

But with people who didn't know me, and therefore didn't have awkward questions, the pregnancy was a lovely conversation piece. One day, baby bump on proud display, I walked into a pristine, ultra-sleek hotel suite in San Francisco, where Jack Black sat waiting for me on an oversize leopard-skin footstool. He bounced over to shake my hand.

"So sorry, I know I'm a little bit late," I said. Two minutes to be precise.

"It looks like you've got a complicating factor there," he said, indicating my belly.

"I do, yes," I said, relieved he was being kind. It was mutually understood that celebrities would keep you waiting. But never vice versa. If he'd been huffy about it, the publicist could have told me to go home without my interview. The fact was I'd been late because I needed to stop in the bathroom to puke. But I didn't want to have to tell my boss that. Employers, even the most considerate ones, are quick to assume even the most aggressive woman in the office might be headed for the mommy track once she started throwing up on the job.

"I've got one of those too," he said.

"One of what?" I said.

He put his hand on his stomach, and I realized I had been clutching my belly. It was hard not to touch it all the time, because I still couldn't believe it was real.

"Mine's bigger," I said.

"I think mine's bigger," he said, wiggling those eyebrows at me. He lifted up his shirt to show off his hairy stomach. It was no contest.

"I win," I said.

"Mine's definitely softer, though," he said.

Celebrity interviews were the thing people always asked about at dinner parties, but I found them silly. If I admired the star in question, I felt particularly bad asking my questions, knowing chances were good they'd heard them all before, most likely that very day. I'd had a mild crush on Jack Black since *Shallow Hal*, but I'd long since abandoned hope that my interviewing skills would transcend the parameters of a celebrity tour—twenty closely monitored minutes in a hotel room—to net me either a shocking quote or a famous boyfriend. However, as I sat down for my chat with Jack Black, I discovered that this belly hanging in front of me gave me a new sense of freedom. For him, it seemed I was playing the role of the future mother, rather than a female reporter with an agenda. I felt different as well; the me that thought Jack Black was intimidatingly cool seemed a million miles away. It reminded me of the way I felt whenever I walked through Banana Republic these days, the relaxation of the complete outsider. Hmmm, so which kind of chinos will I be missing this season? Cropped? Who cares? Jack and I could talk about *anything*. We were just a pair of people with big bellies.

THE NEXT WEEKEND, Matt's mother, Katherine, and his stepfather, Charlie, came to San Francisco on what seemed to be a fact-finding mission. She'd made it clear to Matt that she was excited about a grandson, regardless of the circumstances. But I assumed they wanted to know, was I then, or would I ever be, a mean and nasty skank who would deny them visitation rights and raise the child poorly?

Part of me resented the fact that I was to be put through my paces at all. A small voice inside me said, wickedly, "If you hadn't told him, you'd never have to deal with quasi-in-laws you might not like." But I found it easier than I expected to suppress the voice. I was changing. There was not just a baby inside me but also a mother in me, waiting to be born. *I'm doing this for my child*, I thought as I circled in the Upper Haight, looking for parking. These people would be his family.

I met Matt on the street outside his step-aunt's house. The idea that he had an aunt in town should have been cheering—family, a potential babysitter, someone to bring over fruitcake at the holidays—except she was two years younger than I. On the other hand, it was true that she had all the trappings of maturity. She had a good job, was financially settled, and owned her own flat in a beautiful building. Her neighbors were Benjamin Bratt and Talisa Soto. I lived next door to a 7–Eleven. Sometimes I looked at her and thought, *Now you, you could be a single mother.*

Matt and I walked up the steps together. As I'd parked, I'd seen his mother standing in the doorway. She was tall and had short hair, dyed platinum blond. I tried to put myself in her shoes. How nervous she must be. How nervous I would be if my son pulled this kind of stunt on me someday. I knew I'd be extremely skeptical of whoever the mother was. I extended my hand over my protruding belly—I felt so pregnant at that moment—and smiled.

"Mom," Matt stammered from behind me. "This is, this is . . . the mother."

He'd forgotten my name. In my moment of empathy for his mother, I'd overlooked Matt, who was suffering his own case of nerves.

"Hi," I said. "I'm Mary." I felt far sorrier for him than I did for myself.

Like Matt, his mother seemed sweet, nice, and passive. We had wine and cheese while a football game blared from the television set. *Please don't let me die in childbirth*, I thought. *I don't want my son growing up in a house where life-changing encounters are conducted in front of the television.* Then we set out for a noisy Italian restaurant in North Beach, one that, appropriately enough, served family-style dinners. I took one bite from the enormous platter of garlicky pasta and reached for my Phenergan.

Matt had warned me his stepfather would probably grill me. "That's just how he is," he said. "And my mom is probably going to want to talk about the name."

I'd already decided on the baby's names. All three of them, including his surname, which would be mine. Every time the subject came up with Matt, I'd made it clear that it was not up for negotiation. Clean my cat litter once a week and I might listen. If I was going to be in charge of the bills, the rent, the health insurance, all of it, there was no way I'd be embracing the patriarchal naming system.

"So," I said. "Katherine, Matt tells me you have some questions about the baby's name?"

She blinked. Her eyes were big behind her glasses. Maybe shaped like Matt's, but brown. I kept going. Better to just get the controversial stuff on the table right away.

"I chose Dolan Edward Pols for a couple of reasons," I said. "My father's name is Edward, and so far, none of the grandchildren has his name. Dolan was *his* mother's maiden name, and I always liked the sound of it. She came from a big family, thirteen kids I think. Or maybe fifteen." I should have had my facts down, damn it. Every good salesman ought to. "Anyway, the Dolans were bookies."

"Irish bookies?" Charlie asked. He came from a big Irish family himself.

"Yes," I said, as enthusiastically as if he'd just won a prize. I was well aware I was displaying the subtlety of a freight train. But I was so anxious to establish the protective boundaries I thought I needed that I wasn't going to stop and reflect on any impression I was making beyond the most important: strength. "Irish bookies from New Jersey. They were a naughty bunch, apparently, and had very regular dealings with the Newark police, which embarrassed my father. But they were always very kind to him. He was the first person in his family to be accepted to college, and it was Harvard, so that meant a lot to them. They bought him a couple of nice suits, and one of them escorted him to Cambridge on an airplane, which in those days wasn't exactly common. Flying from New Jersey to Boston, that is. Plus, I like Dolan. It's different. I'm a little worried he'll go through school being called Dylan, but what can you do?"

Katherine was still steadily blinking at me. "That's a nice story," she said. Her voice was soft and sweet, almost southern-sounding. I wondered if there was something more she wanted to say. If there was, she didn't say it. Given my own mother's situation, I was acutely aware that I was meeting the only grandmother Dolan would ever know. Even though I wanted things to be on my terms, I wanted us to get along. When we parted on the street, there were good-bye kisses all around, vows to keep in touch, and offers to help in any way they could.

"That's my grandson you have in there," Katherine said, nodding toward my belly. "Take good care of him."

There was just one ominous note. Charlie, shaking my hand, said it had been a pleasure to meet me. Again there was an offer of help. "And later on, send that boy to us and I'll whip him into shape," he said. "We don't want him turning out like Matt."

Matt stood mutely by my side. He didn't seem fazed by what I saw as a pointed criticism. I had the sickening sense that Matt's family, who knew him so much better than I did, had their own set of reservations about him as a parent. But was he so used to being considered problematic that he didn't even react? Later, when I brought it up, he wouldn't even remember the comment. Maybe he dismissed it as a bad joke from a relentless kidder. But Charlie's words rang in my head. The mind always latches on to what it fears the most. Mine was a steel trap when it came to nuggets of negativity.

CHAPTER 7

Trailer Life

I NEEDED TO MOVE. I'd been in the same one-bedroom apartment in Oakland for six years. It was cute, with hardwood floors, pretty windows, and a tile fireplace, and the $1,000 rent wasn't too bad, compared with other Bay Area rentals. But every year, the landlord raised it as much as the law allowed. He was the sleaziest man I'd ever met. Every time the plumbing backed up, which was frequently, he threatened to have the plumber use "the special camera" that would reveal whether that was *my* tampon that had clogged the pipes or something equally offensive from one of the other tenants in the building. He was a chauvinist. He double-talked with such dexterity that even when I'd steeled myself to stand up to him, he'd wear me down just by repeating the same lies. He was the Karl Rove of landlords. I despised him.

As a woman on her own, I had loved my little home and my funky neighborhood, but I couldn't imagine bringing the baby home to either. The street was edgy. I'd come home one night to find a homeless woman sleeping on the landing next to my front door. I wasn't thrilled with her encampment but I didn't want to tell her to leave. She was there the next night as well, and I peeked out at her feeling all the requisite yuppie guilt. The third night, I came home around 2 A.M. to find her astride a man, in the full throes of ecstasy. I stepped over them, flew up the steps, and called the police. The bounds of my hospitality were not that broad.

I was on the ground floor, and the apartment above me had

been home to many tenants during the six years I'd lived there. The people with soft treads and cats never stayed long. The people with heavy boots and little dogs that barked and televisions that droned all night—they stayed forever. The last group were drug dealers with a pit bull and a set of grow lights in the attic.

The stasis that had kept me there seemed representative of this whole uncertain period in my life. I kept waiting for something to come along to spur me out of there: a boyfriend, a marriage, a new job, moving back to Maine. At long last, here it was. Only it wasn't someone who would alleviate the financial burden or invite me to share a mortgage. The baby simply needed a better home, and I was going to have to find him one. Buying was out of the question. Two-bedroom homes in the Bay Area were at least $700,000. Even if my father gave me some money and I cashed out my 401(k), the mortgage payments on the smallest of condos, a studio apartment even, would leave me with no wiggle room for day care. Or food.

I wasn't frugal by nature and I'd only finished paying off my graduate school loans the year before. I lived paycheck to paycheck and didn't even have the savings for a security deposit on a new rental. No single mother had surfaced from the ads I'd posted on Web sites for shared housing, at least not anyone I felt compatible with. What I needed was someone who would take me in for a month or two so that I could save some money for a security deposit. Plenty of my friends had houses, but they also had children and not that much square footage. Nor would they want to host my two middle-aged cats. Liza could have offered shelter, if John didn't already have squatter's rights on her spare room.

"And I don't know if he's ever going to leave," she hissed as we opened his door one day that fall. We were looking for a bottle of wine—John was a wine salesman and he always had samples—but it was so dark, smelly, and crowded with clutter, we both drew back at the entryway. "Good God," I said. "That's my brother," Liza said as she forged the sea of discarded clothing, rarely used photographic equipment, and stacks of cardboard boxes. "The messiest of my children. But I know there's half a case of that Sancerre in here."

She emerged triumphant a few minutes later, one bottle in hand, another tucked under her arm. "I'm calling these this month's rent," she said. "Are you going to have a glass? That's allowed, right?"

"I allow it on principle," I said. "I'm with the French on this. But I'd probably just throw it up." Between worrying and nausea, I hadn't been sleeping well, and the thought of anything that might knock me out was appealing. "On second thought, maybe just half a glass."

"We'll put an ice cube in it," Liza said. "Don't tell John. He'd be horrified." She got out her favorite glasses, the etched ones with the square bases. We'd drunk out of them the night I'd gotten pregnant. That night was so indelibly printed on my mind that I even knew exactly what shoes and underwear I'd had on.

"So what are we going to do with you?" she asked. "You could move in next door. The Hovel always has vacancies. I'd be able to help you all the time. And it's really quite sweet in there."

The Hovel was the apartment building two doors down from Liza's place. Her husband, Hugh, had been living there since they separated. It wasn't a hovel, but that's how he referred to it. He wasn't happy about being banished from their flat.

"I've been thinking about the trailer," I told her. "Kir and Sam's trailer."

She stared at me. "Arden's trailer? Oh, honey. That seems extreme."

Arden was Kir's dad. He was a poet, an outdoorsman, and a man who had decided long ago that work was not for him. He was magical, a broad, tall man with a voice so warm it could melt away anyone's bad mood. He was just the kind of father you wanted along on camping trips, on long car rides, at every holiday. He also had a sort of wanderlust that made him a challenge to house; sometimes he'd live with his former mother-in-law, sometimes he'd be on the road for weeks visiting friends. Kir wanted him to have a base, so she and Sam—the same Sam who had told me I'd be alone in that emotional landscape—bought him an Airstream trailer and installed it in their backyard in northern Marin. They parked it in a shady spot, and he settled right in. Then right around the time Kir was due to have her third child, she realized she hadn't seen her father since the night before. She went down to the Airstream and found him on the floor, dead of a heart attack.

The trailer had sat mostly empty since then, with only a few weekend visitors making use of it here and there. It would be small, particularly for the cats, but as I resigned myself to my new complicated life, it seemed like the only sensible solution. The romantic part of me liked the idea of living where Arden had lived; he was the kind of man who would have absolutely celebrated my having a child out of wedlock. He would have laughed off all the impracticalities. He was a man who knew that love mattered most, and he'd passed that on to Kir.

Liza was superstitious. She thought my habit of taking walks in the graveyard near my house was weird, and here I was, proposing to take up residence in a trailer where a man had died. She looked at me with a combination of dismay and concern.

"It would just be for a couple of months," I told her. "Until I've got some money together for a security deposit. I'll be looking for an apartment the whole time I'm there."

"*I'll* give you money for a security deposit," she said.

Kir had made the same offer when I'd asked about the trailer. I'd told her the same thing I told Liza: I didn't want to start borrowing before I even had the baby. I'd lived so long on the margins of fiscal responsibility that I had big fears about what it would be like once he arrived. I had to get a grip on my finances immediately. Borrowing didn't seem like the way to do it.

My goal was to spend two months in the trailer and move into my new place by January 1. The baby was due at the end of February. I told myself the two months would fly by, but it seemed like the ultimate lesson in humility: pregnant by a man I'd met in a bar and about to move into a trailer. Maybe there was an element of self-punishment in my decision, some sort of reflexive urge not just to swallow my bitter medicine, but to overdose on it. My father and family, the ones I feared would judge me the most, would have to see, through my willingness to embrace trailer living, that I was not going to become a burden to them.

KIR HAD DISCOVERED a desiccated rat carcass under the stove when she was getting the place ready for me, plus enough rat shit to indicate that this had not been the Airstream's lone rodent occupant. She'd tried her best to air the place out, but it still held the stale scent of Arden's Camel cigarettes, now mixed with a touch of dead rat. The day before I moved in, I went to Maiden Lane in San Francisco, where all the fanciest shops were, and walked into the Diptyque store. They sold French candles, the kind Liza always had in her house; she was the only person I knew who indulged in such extravagances. I sniffed candle after candle. They were heavenly. The shopgirl informed me, in her pretty accent, that they would burn for more than twenty heures. That might be enough to counter the eau de rat. I settled on one that smelled like the lilacs in my parents' backyard and put it on my credit card. It cost $48. The inherent contradiction of the act was insane, but I told myself no one needed to know.

That first night, I lit the candle and put my clothes away in the cubbyholes and cupboards over the bed. It was tidy and efficient. Like a boat, I kept telling myself. A land boat. Meanwhile, the cats prowled all 165 square feet of the place, then settled in front of the stove. There was a crack at the bottom, and they seemed fixated on it. I got down on my knees two or three times to see what was entrancing them but couldn't see anything. I turned to McGee. "Whatever it is, I'm counting on you to catch it," I said, kissing his gray head. He ignored me, green eyes trained on some treasure I dearly hoped would stay hidden.

A FEW WEEKS BEFORE, the baby had begun to move. Those little flutters still startled me. He seemed to stir more at night, when I was lying down, as if he were trying to get comfortable too. I ended up wedged in between both cats in the bed; with so few other perching options in the trailer, they'd taken up posts on either side of my legs. They wore indignant expressions all the time now, like passengers on a plane that's been rerouted or forced to circle over its destination.

"Hello, baby," I said on the third evening in our new home. "Are you going to settle down in there?"

I knew you were supposed to talk to your baby, so he'd know your voice. It's hard not to feel as though you're striking up a conversation with a stranger on an elevator, though. Maybe he'd prefer to be left alone so he could get back to sleep. What did he know in there of the uprooting his mother had just done, of this crazy way station we'd arrived at?

He. I was getting used to it. I wasn't quite ready to call him Dolan; it seemed presumptuous.

"I'm sorry I cried when I found out you were a boy," I said.

The day before, my friend Karen had asked how I was adjusting to the idea of a son. All along she'd been a strong lobbyist for a boy, probably because she had a very nice teenaged son.

"Didn't you ever want a boy?" she'd said. Her tone was wistful, as if she were sad on behalf of the whole sex I was rejecting. "They're so affectionate, so nice to their mothers. Sean is so sweet to me. And they're easy."

"No, I really didn't," I said. "I just wanted a girl."

But lying there in the dark with one hand on my belly and the other stroking McGee, I remembered how I used to look at a photograph of a boy with curly dark hair, thinking, *Yes please, I'd like one just like that.*

It was an old passport picture, belonging to a man named Michel. I don't know why he kept that photo taped to his refrigerator door, himself aged five or six, but I'd stare into it hungrily, imagining our little boy looking just like that.

Michel was from Argentina. I met him when we were both working for the *Los Angeles Times* in a suburban bureau so far from downtown that the people who worked there clung together for companionship. I'd taken the job not long after graduate school. Michel had been in the States for years, first for college, then working in Silicon Valley as a software engineer. He was starting a new career, and he was sweetly eager about it. When he didn't know what he was doing, he got flustered and cute, grateful for help. There was something safe and nonthreatening about him, a lack of aggression that made half the office assume he was gay. I thought he might be, too, but I found myself hoping he was just sensitive. I started inviting him to things.

"Hey, Michel," I said, taking a slight detour on my way back from the printer, a detour that led me right by his desk. "It's my birthday next week and I think we're going to have a margarita party on the beach. If you want to come."

"Really?" he said. He had such a nice, open face. A beaky nose. Green eyes. Curly dark hair, cut close to his head. "My birthday is coming up too. When's yours?"

"The seventeenth," I said. "When is yours?"

This wasn't an idle question.

"The twenty-fourth," he said. "Exactly a week after yours."

"Oh," I said. *Oh no.* I stood there looking at him. He was still smiling at me, not in an I'm-going-to-hit-on-you way, but with sweet sincerity.

"That's my ex-boyfriend's birthday," I said. Good Lord. Was I cursed? That was Peter's birthday. But not *just* him. "And my other ex-boyfriend, too. Although he was less significant." I was digging myself deeper. I might as well divulge everything. "And my college boyfriend, the one I was with for almost five years. His birthday is the day after yours."

"Wow," he said, laughing now. "That's pretty weird."

"I think I better uninvite you to my margarita party," I said. "I think maybe I should never speak to you again. I have some issues. Not to be neurotic. Although I guess that is neurotic." I was wishing I'd sent my document to the printer in the other corner of the office.

"What if I bring some really good tequila?" he said. "Would I be welcome then?"

We were friends for a couple of months before anything happened. I was determined that he was going to have to make the first move, in part because I genuinely feared the birthday hex, but also because I'd just been burned by my most recent boyfriend and I wanted to make sure Michel was both interested and available. One night, after we'd spent the day together hiking up near Santa Barbara, and the evening lying on the floor of his living room, drinking port, I pushed up onto my elbows and said it was time for me to go. He leaned over and kissed me. "You think you can lie there on my floor looking so beautiful and then say you are leaving?" he asked. "I think you should stay."

The high tide came rushing in, and I thought this time it might stay. He was a steadying influence, respectful and gentle. He took me rock climbing and I trusted his belay completely. He fed me pappadums warmed on his gas stove and made me rethink my previous objections to Indian food. I held him when he cried about the breakup of his parents' long marriage. He played the piano for me and showed me how to end a fight with laughter rather than tears. I found the French erotica under his bed and thumbed through it, wondering at his secret desires, the ones I wanted to understand. If I felt that I was more passionate about the relationship than he was, I dismissed it as being a fluke of personality; I was about the heart and he was about the head, but this struck me as a good combination. I wanted us to be together.

He'd had plenty of girlfriends. I probed about the last one. Why did they break up?

"It seems as though you were really into her," I said.

"Yes," he said. "I liked her a lot. But I think she was a little too into my package."

"Your *package*?" I said, puzzled.

"Yes," he said.

"You mean this?" I said, reaching over to demonstrate.

He laughed. I loved the way he snorted when he was taken over by mirth. Peter had never had much of a sense of humor. Peter hadn't thought I was funny at all.

"No, no, no," he said, still laughing, and waving his hands to indicate there was nothing anatomical about this package. "You know, the package of who I was: Jewish, Stanford, rock climber, pianist, software designer."

"Oh," I said. "I see. So she was shallow."

I was instantly struck with guilt. I liked his package, too. When you read the Vows pages in the *New York Times*, it always seemed as though couples brought résumés to a relationship. I liked Michel's. I approved of it. It looked nice next to mine. Diversity, then confluence in journalism. Was there something wrong with that?

We had talked vaguely of the future. His ambitions were very clear. He wanted to move back to the Bay Area, and get a job covering Silicon Valley for one of the big newspapers. I wanted to get back to the Bay Area too, although the job prospects weren't as good for me as they were for him. Every newspaper recruiter was hungry for tech writers.

When he found a job there first and relocated, we tried breaking up. He wasn't ready for a bigger commitment, and I told him I didn't think a halfhearted long-distance relationship was worth maintaining. Then I drove up to visit, on the pretense of seeing other friends. We'd just have lunch or dinner or something, I said, casually. He said I should come see his new apartment. After lunch, he played the piano for me. I stood leaning against the doorjamb, with my head on it, watching his hands.

"That's beautiful," I said. I was trying not to cry.

He got up, putting the lid down over the keys, and came toward me. He was careful that way, always paying attention to details. Neatness was important to him. Once, when we talked about living together, he'd said he was concerned that I was too messy. But on this day, he wasn't finding fault. He started kissing me. He undressed me in his living room, going down on his knees in front of me, pulling me down in front of the piano.

A few weeks later, on another weekend trip, we went to the beach. While we were lying in the warm sand, he told me I'd have to move up to San Francisco if we were going to make anything work.

Even an ultimatum sounded good to me. I told him I'd start looking for a new job right away.

"It's not as if I don't want to be back here myself," I said.

He nodded. "That's good," he said. "I don't want you to move here just for me."

I filed the equivocation away in my head and closed my eyes to enjoy the warmth of the sun. We'd work things out. I just had to get a job.

Later, when we went back to his apartment, I took a shower to get rid of the sand. Then I grabbed a green towel from the hook on the back of the door. I was wearing it when I stepped into his bedroom.

"So if I get a job up here, do you think we'll live together?" I asked. I was combing my hair.

He looked up at me and put his face in his hands in horror. "Oh no, the *towel*," he said.

"What?" I said. "Is it dirty?"

"It was just *cleaned*," he said.

"You wanted me to use a dirty one?" I said. I'd gone to college with three smallish striped towels, hand-me-downs from the family linen closet. For years, that was all I had, and I imagined that someday, when I was a real grown-up, I'd have a closet filled with stacks of fluffy towels, dried in a dryer, not hung out on a clothesline to get stiff and hard, the way ours always were at home. At thirty-one, as I was on that day with Michel, I still had the towels my mother had given me, but I also had at least a semblance of a real linen closet. One thing I was never stingy about was towels for guests.

"It was for my father," Michel said. "He's coming this week. I want him to have a fresh towel."

I felt stung, and went back into the bathroom to get dressed. I hung up the towel on the back of the door again.

"When it dries it's going to be pretty close to fresh," I told him.

"No," he said, clearly annoyed. "I'll have to go back to the Laundromat tomorrow."

The signs of trouble in a relationship can be so small that you feel idiotic recounting them to friends. "It's not that he isn't generous," I had told one friend after that weekend visit. "I think he's just not that generous toward *me*. In spirit that is." An incident involving a clean towel seemed insignificant on its own. But when I thought about the time I'd said to Michel, "Are you going to be okay with me wanting a dog someday?" and he'd responded, "I'd allow a dog if the children wanted one," the towel started to seem like part of a larger problem.

A few weeks later I called Michel to tell him I had an interview at a paper in the Bay Area and it looked promising. It would be only a lateral career move for me, but I was willing to do it. Michel reminded me he didn't want me to move for him. I pressed, and before I knew it, he was telling me he didn't see a future for us.

It was the lowest tide. I went into the bathroom and sat down on the floor to cry. In times of deep misery, I always end up crouched in the corner of a bathroom. I think this may be because as children, we were always told by my father, in the midst of whatever tantrum we were throwing, that we should go into the bathroom, wash our faces, and come out smiling. This meant I spent a great deal of time in my formative years gazing at my sobbing self in the mirror, marveling at the infeasibility of that puffy red face ever producing a smile again. Perhaps then, as an adult, I was just reverting. Or maybe the sheer messiness of the tear deluge called for proximity to absorbent materials and drains. Anyway, for nearly two hours that day, I stayed on the cold tile, wondering what I could have done differently, or better, that would have made Michel want to keep me in his life. I went for the interview anyway, got the job, took it, moved myself up to Oakland—choosing my apartment in part because Michel said he liked the breakfast place on my prospective block more than any other brunch spot in the whole Bay Area—and waited for him to change his mind. Once I'd made it easy for him, once he no longer chafed at the obligation, he would come back around, just as he had on the lovely day when he played the piano for me in his apartment. Only he never did. My hope evaporated so slowly that I caught traces of it in myself for years to come, like perfume trapped in the folds of a sweater you rarely wear.

I wiped the tears off my face. Thinking about Michel had sent me into self-pitying mode. Something stirred outside the trailer. Probably deer, I thought, sitting up to peek out the window. As soon as I lay back down, the baby fluttered again. I rolled onto my side. Instead of talking to him, this time, I tried to just *think* in his direction. *I'm so sorry, little man*, I said. *It's awful of me to have wanted the son of one man but to have had such a wretched attitude about the son of another.* Whether I approved or disapproved of the man, whether I liked or disliked his package, this little boy would be mine, mine to love.

AS DAVID BYRNE SAID, "This is not my beautiful life." Nor was the trailer my beautiful house.

"So you've only been peeing in there, right?" Kir asked. She was bent over, looking at the underside of the trailer.

My temporary residence had some plumbing issues. It also had some heating issues, involving the gas hookup. The stove was not working either, which might have had something to do with the rat carcass. But the plumbing issue was the most pressing.

Kir was preparing to unhook a piece of tubing from the trailer. But there were two, and neither was marked. We knew one was the intake and one the outtake, and the distinction would be a critical one.

"I think so," I said, standing at a careful distance. It was early morning. Kir had walked down from the house in her busy-mom costume, Adidas slides, yoga pants, and a rain jacket. I have often heard people debating whether Kir looks more like Jackie Kennedy or Julia Roberts. Both comparisons are fair, but hard to hold against her. For one thing, she never acts as though she thinks she looks that good, and for another, she's charmingly spastic. During graduate school she once spent an entire morning with a pair of old underwear hanging out the leg of the pants she had grabbed from the hamper.

The wastewater tank was covered in a layer of autumn leaves. Inside it, something very bad seemed to be happening, because there was hideous upheaval when I tried to flush the toilet. Sam, who knew about the inner workings of the Airstream, was in Korea on business.

The dogs, Whidbey and Goose, were running cheerful circles around the trailer. Their favorite pastime these days was harassing my cats by standing on their hind paws to bark into the trailer's narrow windows.

As Kir grabbed one of the valves I thought back to a day when we'd driven over Mt. Tam to Stinson Beach together in her tiny yellow Opel—this was in graduate school, long before kids or minivans— and I'd noticed that as we sped down the side of the mountain she seemed quieter than usual and intensely focused on shifting gears. As we roared up to the stop sign at the bottom, she'd yanked up the emergency brake. I'd given her a quizzical look, and she revealed that the brakes had gone out temporarily. Downshifting had kept her in control. The fact that she could keep this information to herself, remain calm, and pilot us safely down the mountain had instilled in me great confidence that Kir could get me out of most messes.

"I hope this is the right one," she said. "I think it is."

She carefully disconnected the tube.

I'd like to think I wasn't responsible for everything that came out of that tube, but the alternative is that whatever composed that torrid combination of fluids and solids had been in there for two years. Whatever it was, I watched it flow over Kir's bare feet with a combination of guilt and a desire to be far far away, throwing up in some very clean toilet bowl in a home with indoor plumbing. I'd been so optimistic and cheery about making this work, and I needed it to be all right, since I had nowhere else to go. But my heart had been sinking and my energy ebbing since I moved in. I was not myself; I was a creature carrying another creature, and I needed some creature comforts.

Kir quickly swapped the tubes and stopped the flow, holding everything as far away from herself as she possibly could. She looked up at me, grimly.

"Now you know how much I love you," she said.

KIR WAS THE FIRST of my friends in the Bay Area to have children, and thus my first experience with losing a friend to motherhood. Not that she wasn't still there, and not that I didn't adore her children. But things had changed. Whereas once we'd spoken on the phone for an hour several times a week, now her answering machine was always on, and she no longer picked up midway through a message. Her priorities had shifted, and I felt rejected and insignificant. And she was just the first friend to go down that path; the rest fell like dominos, until my most active friendships were with my few remaining single friends; and my boss, Karen, whose kids were teenagers; and Liza, of course, who was headed toward being single again.

Those first infants in our midst were greeted like gods and goddesses. We hosted showers, we oohed and aahed over sonograms. We attended naming ceremonies in droves, offered to babysit, and took countless photographs of the new parents proudly cradling their progeny.

Then suddenly, doors were shut. There were schedules to be observed, nap times to be guarded zealously, lost parental sleep to be grabbed in snatches during the day. Trips to Tahoe were a thing of the past, or rather, a thing to be shared only with other couples, other couples who had children. Playdates for Junior were more important than Mom's playdates with Mary. Moreover, the level at which we single people were allowed to participate had been capped by some mysterious force that seemed larger than our friends.

April, also single, once gamely sewed together a baby quilt for an expectant friend, from squares we'd all contributed. She made plans to deliver it at a weekly gathering held at one of the city's public basketball courts. She waited for an hour, then went home. The group, it turned out, had changed its plans and had gone to a more baby-friendly gathering place, but no one had bothered to tell April. Rarely a person to lose her cool, April was furious at the lack of respect all the new parents had shown her, at the implication that her time was no longer valued. I sympathized completely and felt secretly grateful to her for blowing her top; maybe this would make a difference in how we were treated.

It didn't, though. The arrival of children simply changes everything. Behind their backs, we thought of these busy new parents as self-centered. Behind our backs, they reassured themselves that *they* had their priorities straight and labeled us both ignorant *and* self-centered. In retrospect, we were both right.

So my time in the trailer was the first significant chunk of time I'd spent with Kir in years. She had a BA from Stanford and a master's from Berkeley, but her promising career in documentary film had been shunted aside after Teya was born and I had never understood why and how that had been so easy to give up. Seeing Kir's daily work as a mother was a revelation. Between getting the older kids ready for school, entertaining the youngest, getting him to day care for a few hours so that she could volunteer at the charter school the older ones attended, getting them all home, serving them dinner, and getting everyone to bed, she had barely any time for herself. As we folded mountains of laundry together at night, the fact that she had never had the time or energy to return my phone calls suddenly made sense.

The payoff also became clear to me. I did most of my writing in the outbuilding that served as Sam's office. I'd get the woodstove roaring, turn on my computer, and sit in front of his window, which looked out on their woodsy two-acre parcel. When the kids came home from school, I'd watch them play. Teya and Jensen would be deeply absorbed in something in the long grass. I'd poke my head out and ask what they were doing. "Talking to our fairy," they'd say, grinning up at me, gap-toothed, their faces fresh versions of their mother's and father's. Or I'd watch Kir bouncing on the trampoline with her little boy, in her jeans and down parka, looking like a teenager, albeit a very tired one. The kids would ask to see my cats, crowding into the trailer in a happy jumble, squatting to look under the bed and behind the toilet for Casco and McGee. They might request a tea party, and when the cookies and weak tea had been consumed, demand to do my dishes. I'd acquiesce, sitting on the couch two feet away, watching them earnestly at work. They were like fairies themselves, exhausting and exhilarating at the same time. I wondered, watching them, listening to them, whether my own child could possibly be as bewitching.

CHAPTER 8

Playing House

A LAWYER FRIEND had been giving me advice about the legal ramifications of having a child with someone I wasn't married to. I was wrestling with the idea of not putting Matt on the birth certificate. I wanted my child to know his father, but I didn't want a shared custody situation. Matt had seemed pleased by the news that the baby was a boy, but we weren't spending much time together. Nor had he proposed any solutions to any of my problems. They felt very much like *my* problems, not ours. He'd shown up when I asked for his help in moving to the trailer, but in comparison with all my guy friends, who treated my pregnant self like a precious orchid while they joked and jostled with one another, Matt had just seemed like the random guy someone had brought along. Significant, but random.

The worst part was that every time I made an effort to include him in the pregnancy, I felt rebuffed.

"No thanks," he'd said when I suggested he sign up on a Web site that sent weekly updates on the stages of fetal development. I found it fascinating and I thought he might too. "I've got enough reading material about pregnancy."

I'd given him a couple of the books friends had lent me. He'd barely looked at them when I'd handed them to him. It seemed as though he was holding me—or rather us—at a distance. One thing I couldn't handle was indifference. It felt like an insult to the baby.

When the lawyer asked me what Matt wanted out of our arrange-ment, I hadn't known what to say. "You've got to find out," he said. "Have a serious heart-to-heart."

So I asked him to meet me one night at a cafe near his apart-ment. I was terse on the phone and made it clear this was a Talk. Matt arrived late, just as I was midway through a plate of one of the few foods I was craving, a winter salad with apple and blue cheese. He seemed tense and nervous. We didn't exactly have pleasantries to exchange, so I cut to the chase.

"I'd like a clearer sense of what you want," I said. "Are you going to want shared custody?"

He sagged back in his chair and exhaled loudly. His face soft-ened.

"Phew," he said. "I'm so relieved."

"Relieved?" I asked. "Why would that question relieve you?"

"I thought when you called you were going to tell me you were cutting me out," he said. "You sounded mad."

Tears came rushing into my eyes. His relief was palpable; he wasn't bullshitting. He'd been overcome with worry that I was going to tell him to beat it. That meant so much to me. I don't know what I'd been seeing in him—perhaps numbness induced by terror—but a man couldn't be indifferent and have a reaction like that. How could I, even for a minute, tell this guy he wasn't going to have access to his child?

"I would never do that," I told him.

My own tears surprised me. I always assumed I could be ruthless in a crisis. Matt wasn't proving exactly good in these circumstances, but he wasn't out-and-out bad. *I have to give him more of a chance,* I realized. More of a chance than my natural inclination would have allowed for.

"But you haven't exactly been attentive," I continued. "Every time I've suggested something to you, whether it is reading a book about parenting or checking out a Web site about babies and preg-nancy, you scoff at the suggestion."

"It might seem like I'm scoffing, but I'm not," he said. "I was reading in one of those books that fathers are like a trimester behind in terms of understanding where the mothers are at."

Ending a sentence with a preposition. I stopped myself from saying anything. Quoting the books was good. At least that meant he'd been reading and not just watching reruns of *The Simpsons*.

"So I'm sort of in the first trimester now," he continued. "And I'm getting it. I know it's hard for you."

"So what do you want?" I said. "My big fear is that you are not going to be a part of this and then in a few years, when you have some girlfriend who makes you feel guilty about neglecting your child, you're going to come around and want to be part of his life. And you're going to try to take him away from me or share custody."

In California, as long as he was on the birth certificate and hadn't demonstrated some solid evidence of monstrosity, he would be entitled to have Dolan with him half the time. I didn't want my child going back and forth between households if I could possibly avoid it.

"Listen," he said. "I was raised by a single mother. I believe that a child's place is with his mother. But I want to be there, more than my own father was. That's important to me. I want to be helpful."

I'm sure I looked doubtful.

"Look," he said. "I know how to do this. This was my childhood. I'm well equipped for this. I understand it. You have to trust me."

He sounded so sincere. But when it came to a child, trust wasn't something you just handed over. "You're going to have to prove to me that you're trustworthy," I said. "I'm sorry, but I have to be careful."

"I will prove it to you," he said.

That talk in the cafe was a turning point for us. So was Thanksgiving. Matt's father, Miles, and stepmother, Frances, were coming for the whole week. Liza had generously invited all of them to her house for turkey, but they'd declined. They wanted to spend the holiday alone with Matt. I felt rejected without even having met them, but I wasn't anticipating much of a relationship with them. Miles had instructed his son not to sign anything and told Matt that I would have him over a financial barrel for the rest of his life. "Frances is very angry," his father had said. Probably because Frances had been helping fund Matt's three years in the Bay Area drifting aimlessly from one temp job to another. She must have been terrified she was going to have to take care of his child now as well.

Still, I wanted to meet them. With my parents in their eighties, Matt's parents, both sets of them, were going to matter to Dolan. We made plans for a dinner the night before Thanksgiving.

I'd put on a pair of velvet maternity pants and one of Kir's hand-me-downs, a capacious, brightly colored silk top. I actually felt pretty with my bump protruding in front of me. When I walked into the bar, I found them sharing a flight of wine. Miles's son might think red wine should be kept in the fridge, but clearly Miles didn't. Matt was dressed up, and he came to greet me, putting his arm around me warmly. He told me later there was a piece of paper in his pocket with my name written on it. He didn't want to forget this time.

We shook hands. Miles looked so much like Matt, I was surprised. I wondered if my son was going to look exactly like them. Their easy smiles were the same, and their voices were practically identical. Frances was dainty and pretty. If either of them felt angry or strange about the situation, I couldn't tell. I felt my antipathy fading.

"I know this is a really odd way to meet," I said as soon as we sat down at our table. "I want you to know that this is not the way I would ever have planned to have a child. But honestly, at my age, I'm lucky to have this opportunity at all."

"Well, we're happy to meet you," Miles said.

"If you have any questions about this unorthodox arrangement we're working on, just ask away," I said.

Frances was studying the menu. So was Matt. Miles nodded. "We will."

He cleared his throat. "Matt, what are you thinking of having?"

"What's pancetta?" Matt asked.

"It's like an Italian bacon," Miles said. "Terrible for the arteries, but delicious."

"What about this one, botta . . . arghh?" Matt asked. He was pointing to a pasta dish.

Frances and I both spoke at the same time.

"Dried . . ." she said.

"Fish roe," I finished.

I looked around the table. Our conversation might not be deep and meaningful, but at least it wasn't going to be unpleasant.

What struck me about Miles and Frances that night was how in love they seemed. They'd been together since Matt was about five, and it was evident that they still adored each other. He fussed over her—Did she like her sand dabs? Another glass of wine?—and she reveled in his attentiveness.

Matt was a different person altogether with them. For the first time, he seemed eager to please, to impress. One of my chief complaints about Matt had always been how little effort he expended, professionally and personally. But with Miles and Frances, he seemed curious about what they were doing, what they liked, why they liked it. He wanted to be involved.

I imagined him as a young boy, visiting his father and stepmother. He would have been wishing his father would come back home and make his heartbroken mother happy again. Already refusing to eat his vegetables, refusing to eat anything but a plain hamburger, writing on Frances's walls in indelible ink. Meanwhile their love would have been exclusionary without intent. As they talked of their lives together, I noticed the way Matt chimed in. "Wasn't that the place in that neighborhood you really loved?" he ask during a conversation about the bungalow they'd rented in Los Angeles twenty years before. "Was that when you switched jobs?" He seemed not to have experienced their life together so much as he'd simply heard about it.

My heart softened toward him. I felt a mixture of sympathy and empathy. I was picturing my own little boy, suffering his own pain over whatever situation Matt and I worked out. What if Dolan longed to be a part of his father's life and felt left out? And I hadn't done everything in my power to keep that from happening? I resolved to try harder to do what I could to make the gap between us smaller, and not just on Dolan's behalf. On that night, I started thinking of including Matt in our lives because of the boy he'd been; I didn't want him to feel excluded from another set of lives.

The thought of the drive back to Marin was too exhausting to contemplate. Matt offered me his bed and I took him up on it, thinking we would just sleep. I hated his room and loathed the idea of throwing up—as I knew I would—in a toilet shared by four messy, rootless guys.

We lay side by side, me in pajamas, him in sweatpants and a T-shirt. And at some point, we turned to each other. It had been about five months since we'd slept together. Sex with him was, as it had been before with him, exciting and fulfilling. But that bump between us made the connection more than physical; it was both a monument to our past sex and the ever expanding marker of our future relationship.

For the first time, I felt true tenderness toward him. And so we embarked on the next phase of this tentative relationship.

THE RAIN CAME DOWN in endless sheets that fall, hitting the roof of the trailer with such vehemence that I kept sitting up in bed, feeling for wet patches and turning on the lights to check for leaks in the windows. I tried to think of myself as an adventuresome settler heading West in her covered wagon, but it was hard to reconcile the spirit of pioneering with my fervent desire to have real plumbing.

I was almost into my third trimester, but still I vomited at least twice a day. It was more random and less explicable. I could eat six clementines in a row, burp, and feel completely content. But I could take a sip of water out of a bottle that had been sitting in the car for a couple of days and the next thing I knew, be throwing up all over myself. I'd given up all sense of discretion. At least it's raining, I thought as I glumly wiped my mouth after throwing up next to the pump at the gas station. One night I was headed down to the trailer after dinner with Sam and Kir, the dogs at my heels, when the urge to puke hit me halfway across their basketball court. In between convulsions I realized that the dogs were devouring the vomit as fast as I produced it.

"Oh Jesus," I said. "Where's the fucking hose?" I dragged it over and began spraying down the basketball court, stopping every few seconds to shove the dogs away as I added to the mess.

I'd been in the trailer for almost a month. It was time to get an apartment, if only to have a toilet of my very own.

I went looking for it on an island. Just off the "coast" of Oakland, Alameda was isolated enough to feel somewhat undiscovered, a rarity in the Bay Area. There were wide, tree-lined avenues and a lot of craftsman bungalows mixed in with the Mediterranean and Victorian homes. Canals ran through the Bay side of the island, and people actually had docks and slips and boats in their backyards. The place had a time capsule feel to it; the two main drags were both filled with restaurants, but you wouldn't want to eat at any of them. There were clothing stores too, but they seemed geared more to Edith Bunker than me. Signs of gentrification were creeping in, but slowly. Starbucks had just arrived, and people were actually excited by it. People said Alameda reminded them of the Midwest, but it reminded me of small-town Maine, the big difference being it was only twenty minutes from downtown San Francisco.

Rents were low, relatively speaking, and—I couldn't believe I was thinking this way—the public schools on the island were supposed to be good. Going to look at apartments, I'd wear baggy clothes or hold a file in front of my belly, hoping prospective landlords wouldn't notice. I assumed that tenants with babies were about as appealing as tenants with pet pythons. And I found myself sounding apologetic whenever I explained that it would be just me and the baby. I assumed that even in the famously liberal Bay Area, they'd think there must be something wrong with me. But none of them seemed perturbed in the least by me or the prospect of my bastard child.

Bastard child. I used that word a lot in those early days. Not with landlords, of course, but with my friends and family. If I was up front about the situation, then people wouldn't feel they had to tiptoe around me.

I said it one day on the phone with my father, flippantly as usual. I'd just reminded him that I wasn't coming home for Christmas. Cash was tight, and I thought I'd just be settling into whatever new place I found.

"But I'll come home next summer for sure," I said. "I'll bring my bastard son home to meet the family. I wonder, is that like the prodigal son? Not quite I guess. Well, for one thing, we're not returning."

I was babbling nonsensically, but my father wasn't saying anything.

"Dad?" I said. "Did I lose you?"

"I'm here," he said. Then he cleared his throat. "You must stop referring to him that way."

This sounded to me like a defense of his grandson, and I wasn't about to argue with that.

"Okay," I said meekly.

The thirty-seventh place I looked at was just right. It had two bedrooms, with washer and dryer hookups—my friends with children assured me that having laundry on premises was second only to the epidural on the list of motherhood "must haves"—and it was plunk in the middle of the better of the two good school districts. As I cruised through the neighborhood, my belly pressing closer and closer to the steering wheel, I saw a little boy on a bike, rattling along the sidewalk with his training wheels on, his dad running behind him. *Pleasantville*, I thought. *It's exactly what I need.*

On the day of the move, the crew I'd corralled, Hugh and John, were scheduled to pick up Matt at his place. But he called me in the morning, panicked, saying he had stayed over at a friend's house and was running late. I could hear female voices in the background. In an instant, I convinced myself that he had slept with someone else. We'd been together a few times since Thanksgiving, but it wasn't as though he'd given me a promise ring. And his tone was apologetic, which was unusual.

When he arrived, sheepish and hung over, I could barely look at him. He stank of hard liquor. At the storage place, I sat down on an empty cart and put my hands on my belly. I felt completely forlorn.

We'd been doing so well lately. But here he was staying out all night. With girls. John sat next to me.

"I have this gut feeling that he slept with someone else last night," I told him. "He looks guilty, don't you think?"

"He's definitely incredibly hung over," John replied. "He barely spoke on the way here. Actually, he still seems kind of drunk."

I shot John a look of disbelief.

He shrugged. "We were asking him about what he does at work and he didn't seem to know."

Matt was still temping at the bond trading company. From what I knew, the job was purely clerical. I alternated between optimism that it would become permanent and curiosity about what had kept Matt unemployed for so long.

"That's my baby daddy," I said glumly.

John gave me a pat on the shoulder and then got up and went back to the U-Haul, where Hugh and Matt were wrestling with my antique sea chest. It had been mine as a child, and I planned to use it for Dolan's toys. I sighed and got to my feet. I could still carry lamps and light boxes.

I drove the U-Haul to my new apartment with Matt beside me. Hugh and John followed in Hugh's car.

"So what did you do last night?" I said. "You still reek of alcohol."

"Oh, I was with Terry at the bar and she had some friend with her. Then we went back to her place." Terry was a regular from Finnegan's, but I assumed, since she was engaged, that she was harmless. He rubbed his head. "Stayed up too late. I fell asleep on the couch."

"Did you sleep with one of them?" I asked.

"No," he said, sounding a little indignant. But where men are concerned, indignation is hardly a harbinger of honesty.

"You have to tell me if you did," I said. We were at a stoplight. He looked me full in the eyes. "I didn't," he said.

"Okay," I said. I decided to believe him.

"I feel like crap," he said. "I could use a Mountain Dew."

• • •

MY JEALOUSY MAY HAVE SEEMED ILL-PLACED, given how much I complained about Matt's shortcomings. But the fact was I was new-ly obsessed with sleeping with him. The joys of pregnancy sex had been well advertised to me over the years. "Mythic orgasms," one friend said. "There's so much blood there already. It's just insane. I've never had anything like it."

She was right. What no one had told me was that I would want it constantly, that in the last months of my pregnancy few thoughts would enter my head that weren't about either the baby's room or fucking. I thought about Matt's penis once every ten seconds for every waking hour and for many of my sleeping hours as well. His penis became like a religious totem to me. The rest of him wasn't bad either.

On some level I knew it was a delusion, some biological urge to keep the father of my lion cubs around. But that didn't stop my passion. Matt began sleeping over a lot, generally at my behest, and generally because I had some "task" I needed help with. Usually that task was getting his pants off.

We'd lie on the couch together, watching television or a movie, me hideously aware of his proximity and dying for him to touch me and then finally, sick of waiting, turning to him and making the first move. He always responded, happily, but the next night, I'd be back on the couch with him, like a teenager wondering if the guy I liked was ever going to kiss me. My desire tortured me, and any release was welcome, no matter how lousy it might make me feel that I had to ask for it every time.

I couldn't figure out how to label our relationship. Hardly boy-friend and girlfriend, but still, when he needed a ride to the airport at Christmas, I considered it my role to take him. I was staying in California, saving all my vacation time for maternity leave, but Matt's mom had bought him a ticket home to Baltimore. When I picked him up he handed me a shopping bag, festooned with ribbons. "This is for you," he said. It hadn't occurred to me that he might buy me a present. It had certainly never occurred to me that I'd open the bag and find a scarf in there that I knew I'd want to wear every day.

"This looks like Casco," I said. Casco was my tortoiseshell cat, brown and black and shaggy.

"That's what I thought," he said.

The scarf wasn't some obligatory token; it was a present with heart. When we said good-bye at the curb, I felt shy. "Merry Christmas, Mary," he said as he shouldered his bag and walked away, and just his use of my given name—a rarity—made me feel, at least just a little, cherished.

We spent New Year's Eve together; I'd invited him to join the annual party my friends and I held and he seemed pleased to be included. On his thirtieth birthday a couple of weeks later, I baked him a triple-layer chocolate cake and brought it to the party his friends were throwing for him in the city. I was nervous about meeting them all, nervous that they'd be painfully young or drunken barflies and that the gulf between Matt and me would widen again.

They surprised me. Some were at least my age, and they were a sincere, sweet crowd, most of them far more professionally oriented than he seemed to be. They clearly cared about him, having brought in tons of sushi and filled a table full of presents. The party wound down with a plan to troop off to Finnegan's, the bar where Matt and I had met, and I expected he'd go too. Instead he took me back to his apartment and we lay together on the bed. "You were really great tonight," he told me. We'd touched a lot at the party. "I think you being there made that party." He was grateful and drunk and I was, as usual, on fire for him and excited about the notion of being back in the bed where we had made this baby in the first place. It was actually romantic.

I wouldn't call myself old-fashioned, but some part of me—the dominant part at that point, I confess—felt that it was just *right* that Matt and I were together during the pregnancy. I remember a friend asking me, when I was about six months' pregnant, whether I was "dating." I was offended. How could I expend energy toward anyone but the baby and his father? Every time we had sex I was flush with the knowledge that I was with the father of my child, the source of my baby. It was a rush I couldn't possibly have understood beforehand and one I'm not sure I entirely grasp in retrospect. The emotion was unique to the time.

"You know what my favorite thing about being pregnant is?" I asked Matt, flopping back down on the bed after another amazing session of penis worship. We looked at each other from our respective pillows. He shook his head. His eyes looked very green in his flushed face.

"The fucking," I said. "Having sex with you."

He smiled, a wide, pleased smile, the kind I didn't often see on his face.

"Me too," he said. "It's better than the heartburn, huh?"

While the origins of my attraction to Matt were clearly primal, it wasn't always easy to dismiss it as mere biology. I could tell my friends that's what it was, but there I was in the supermarket, wanting to hold hands with him. Or contentedly cooking him dinner and fondly kissing him on the top of the head as I served it. We'd lie together in bed, watching the baby romp across my belly like something out of *Alien*. In late January, we went to a full-day Lamaze class together, and as he sat behind me to massage my back, he put his arms around me and kissed my head. It felt as though we were a couple.

He had seemed so completely insensitive in those early months, but I was starting to see a more thoughtful side of him. One Sunday we went out for brunch at Rick and Ann's in Berkeley, a place that always has a long line, but for good reason. We were sitting outside on a bench waiting for our table when a family walked by. The mom had a scarf on her head, and her two boys, maybe around six and eight, were being tugged along by a new puppy.

"She must have cancer," Matt said. "They must have got the boys the puppy to make them feel better."

I turned and looked at him. He had on a big sweatshirt and was resting his forearms on his thighs, like a basketball player observing the game.

"The scarf," he explained, gesturing to his own head. "She looked like she must have lost her hair. And she was so thin."

"I bet you're right," I said. "I didn't notice."

I've waited outside many cafes with many boys in my day, making up stories about the people waiting with me as I anticipated my eggs Benedict. But I'd never thought of Matt as someone who played that game. He didn't seem observant. He was the person who had to ask what an avocado looked like when I sent him to the store, even when I'd made guacamole in front of him the week before. His sensitivity reminded me that he had been a little boy who had ridden airplanes by himself to go visit his dad, sometimes returning with a check for his mother. There were sad things he'd lived through that I knew nothing about.

But there was still such an innocence to him. One day, as we were driving across the Bay Bridge together, I asked him when was the last time he'd been in love. Because we'd never technically dated, we'd skipped over all that getting-to-know-you chitchat.

"I never have been," he said.

I turned to look at him and then had to correct the wheel as I started to veer into the next lane.

"Never in your thirty years?"

"I said it, with one girl," he said. "But I realized later that I didn't mean it."

It was starting to dawn on me that maybe he'd had only one real girlfriend, someone from college that he'd been with for a year or so. He called her "she" whenever he brought her up. "I did some yoga in college," he'd say. "*She* wanted to, so I went along." If I said, "Your hair is so soft," he'd respond with something like "*She* thought so too."

I felt terrible for him. To have never been in love, and now to be having a baby. It seemed so wrong for him to be in our complicated, adult situation without ever having had a love story of his own.

"I'd like to fall in love someday," he said. "That would be nice, I think."

Our conversations often had this kind of tenor, a remove, as if we weren't sleeping together, as if we were merely in limbo together, a limbo that involved sex and a baby.

Along with the pregnancy sex came pregnancy dreams, intense and completely neurotic ones that were appallingly easy to interpret. In one, Matt left me for J. Lo, who was desperate to have his baby and had stolen him out from under my nose. I couldn't blame him for hooking up with J. Lo; even in the dream I acknowledged that he'd made no declaration of love to me and was unlikely ever to do so. But I was afraid for our son, afraid he'd be cast aside in favor of J. Lo's beautiful honey-colored child. I told Matt about that one. He was silent.

"I don't know why I'm having these dreams," I said to him. "It's not like we're even dating." I had just picked him up at the BART station and was driving us back to my place. "Not dating exactly." I looked over at him, at his placid profile. Conversation opener. No response.

"I never remember my dreams," he said. He was maddening.

I tried to broach the subject again a few days later.

"I hope we keep doing this," I said. I'd had one of those orgasms that make you think, *Now what's my name again?* I was lying on my side, the lump of baby between us, with my hand in Matt's hair.

He'd smiled, but didn't respond.

I liked the thought of us continuing to sleep together after the baby was born. For one thing, I was eager to have sex on my back again, to look in the eyes of the person inside my body. All that great sex with Matt, yet he was so mysterious, back there behind me. What was written on his face as he made me come, as he came? Once, I twisted around and saw him yawning. I didn't know whether to cry or slap him.

At thirty-nine, I had had plenty of Big Talks with men. I was good at it, having long ago stopped throwing objects or insults. I specialized instead in astute interpretations of our situation, rendered so rationally that sometimes I wondered at my own remove, wondered how, if I was *in* this relationship, I could see it so clearly from an outsider's point of view. The men rarely argued with anything I said, but what I still hadn't learned was to "hear" what their nonresponsiveness meant. I could go wild trying to decipher it, coming up with a dozen interpretations: he was afraid, he was intimidated, he had a secret he wasn't ready to share, his mother didn't love him enough, his father wasn't around enough, he was trying to get his head around the idea of commitment, he knew I was right but wasn't quite ready to admit it. That was all just hopeful bullshit on my part. What the nonresponsive male meant was no. But as I barreled through the last few weeks before my son's birth, I ignored Matt's telling silences.

I WAS ON MY WAY to an afternoon movie, driving across the Bay Bridge. The sky was full of high clouds, and in the distance, the Golden Gate Bridge stood out against all that oyster gray, a rich rusty red. I felt good. I picked up the cell phone. Kir and my friend Sara had just thrown me a baby shower, and I wanted to tell my dad about it.

"Sara made the most amazing chocolate bread pudding," I told him. "With cherries in it and some sort of creamy sauce drizzled over the top. You would have wolfed it down." Then I went on about the diaper bag Liza gave me, the beautiful bedding Dolan would have in his crib, his miniature toiletry kit. He listened quietly as I recounted the generosity of my friends. My pregnancy had been so different from what I'd ever imagined, but the joyousness of the shower had made me feel almost normal.

"This is a wonderful thing you're doing," he said.

I blinked as the tears hit my eyes.

"Really?" I said. "You think so?"

"I was just talking to your Aunt Elizabeth," he said. "Or rather, listening."

Aunt Elizabeth was a talker. She had three children, all older than I. None of them had biological children, although her son had recently adopted a little boy from Guatemala.

"She was telling me that your cousins would have been happy to have such a thing happen to them," he said. "She reminded me that if you were married, we would all be celebrating this, or certainly hoping for this."

I was grinning now, trying not to breathe too hard, wishing the car were quieter. I wanted to hear every word of my father's blessing.

"There's nothing better I've done with my own life then to have you children," he said. "I'm so happy you're going to have this experience."

Thank you, Aunt Elizabeth, I thought. *Thank you for being such a talker.*

ABOUT A WEEK LATER, a package arrived from Kesiah, Aunt Elizabeth's older daughter. I opened it and found a letter on top. Kesiah was the firstborn in our generation, and so the first grandchild. My grandmother was also named Elizabeth, and it was she whose maiden name I was using for my son. In the letter, Kesiah explained that she had always told our grandmother that if she had a child someday, she'd name it Dolan, whether it was a boy or a girl. Grandmother had liked the idea, and she'd made a patchwork quilt for Kesiah. In a demonstration of classic 1960s fashion sense, she had elasticized the top of it. "You can wear this as a skirt now," she had told her, "and when you have your baby, you can use this for a coverlet." Thirty-five years later, the elastic was gone and the quilt was finally ready to be used by a child named Dolan. I unfolded it and spread it across my lap. "This came from your great-grandmother," I told my belly. "Made with her hands."

I always thought of heirlooms as antiques, things that increased in value the farther they got away from their own era, becoming the kind of treasures that made the experts on *Antiques Roadshow* rock in delight. To say you had your great-great-grandmother's hope chest was to say you had something that dated back to before the Civil War. But as I looked forward to the thought of my child and my grandchildren, I realized that an heirloom gains all its true, lasting value from its *physical* connection to our past. My grandmother would never touch Dolan, never even know he existed. But she had created something of cloth and thread that had now come to him. And her past, her name before marriage, her father's name, would be carried forward by a little boy made accidentally one night in San Francisco in the first years of a new century.

CHAPTER 9

Arrivals

"I'D SAY HE'S ABOUT EIGHT POUNDS," my doctor said. Dolan was due in three days. She was feeling around the outside of my stomach like someone trying to shape dough into a loaf. "He's a good size. But not too big. I think you're going to do just fine. Do you have your birthing plan ready?"

A birthing plan is a strategy you come up with during Lamaze classes. I had typed mine up and had multiple copies, including two in my packed suitcase. I was contemplating pinning it to the only jacket that still fit me and wearing it all week, like Paddington Bear, so there would be no doubt about what to do with me.

"No inducement," I said. "Yes to the epidural. I'm totally fine with the drugs. But a firm no to a C-section."

I was vehement on this point. The literature I'd been reading, including a very politically correct book that had come in the Amazon package from Sara—the cover featured a woman cradling her baby in what looked like a hemp sling—espoused natural childbirth all the way. I wasn't looking for the full pain experience, but I didn't want to be sliced open either. The current statistics on C-sections seemed to reflect an eagerness on the parts of doctors to cut to the chase, so to speak. True, a whole host of risk factors were eliminated by taking the cervix and vaginal canal out of the equation. But you also robbed a woman's body of the thing it instinctively knew how to do and created a wound that sliced through the abdominal muscles.

Recovery time for women who had C-sections was usually about two weeks longer. If you had another child, most doctors were loath to let you try it naturally the second time; they preferred to open up the old incision again.

There was also something, I thought, to be gained from pushing that baby out the natural way. Maybe it was just curiosity. But it was something I'd been wondering about ever since I'd been disabused of the notion that babies emerged from their mothers' belly buttons. Even when you knew how it was supposed to work, part of the mystique remained; how could *that* get out of *that*?

I remembered a guy, one of Benet's friends, who had written in his high school yearbook entry that his ambition was to "experience death." Presumably he was just being provocative. But I was fifteen and I thought he was so deep. When it came time to write my own yearbook entry three years later, I recalled that bleak pair of words and realized what I really wanted to experience was *life*, giving birth, feeling a baby emerge from my body. But I wasn't about to write that in my yearbook; I'd just sound like a cheese ball. I went with a Pink Floyd quote instead.

"No one particularly wants a C-section," my doctor said. "But it happens. Birthing plans are not set in stone. Don't be too wedded to yours. Do you have someone to take care of you when you first get home?"

"My sister," I said. "She's coming from Massachusetts tomorrow. Two days before the due date, to get her situated, and then she'll stay for two weeks. Does that seem like a good strategy?"

"Sure," she said. "But don't count on having him on the due date. That would be unusual."

Early on, I'd started asking people to be in the delivery room. Anticipating that Matt might not be enough of a support system, I wanted to be surrounded by friends. But it had gotten out of hand, like one of my dinner parties where I'd invite too many people and then start to worry about their compatibility. I could picture the disapproving look on the other faces if Liza stepped outside to smoke a cigarette halfway through my labor. So the guest list had been pared down to Matt, Wib, and Sara, one of my oldest friends and the giver of the politically correct birthing books. Sara lived in Los Angeles, but it just so happened she'd be in the Bay Area that spring. She was going to function as my doula, which is kind of like a labor coach. She had just had her second child, a boy who was ten pounds, thirteen ounces, and earned the respect of every nurse at Cedars Sinai by delivering him vaginally. She would stick up for me if any of my doctors started talking C-section.

Wib felt like the life preserver I'd been waiting for. When I pulled up to the Oakland airport and there she was, all five feet of her, so cute, with her suitcase at her feet, her hair wild in the wind, beaming at me, I finally felt ready to have this baby. We clutched at each other. No one in the family had seen me since that summer, when I just looked like a woman with a gut. Now, two days before my due date, I had a veritable prow, looming out in front of me.

In Maine, my mother was probably asleep in the nursing home, having dutifully eaten her dinner, watched a musical on the big-screen television, and then allowed herself to be lifted out of her wheelchair and into her bed. She had no awareness of what was about to happen to me, but maybe some younger version of me was in her dreams, playing in the backyard, wondering what was for dessert, asking if I could brush her hair. I had been longing for her, pointlessly, against all logic, but now here was Wib, ready to do for me what our mother had done for her sixteen years before, on the day Matthew was born: hold her hand, be steady, and help usher her baby boy into the world.

I tried to be patient, but the days ticked by without any sign of impending birth. We ate spicy food, which was supposed to induce labor but just increased my heartburn, took slow walks downtown for ice cream, planted flowers in my front yard, and looked at family pictures. Wib went into a cooking frenzy. There was Chicken Marbella in my freezer, along with enough soup to last me a month. We took practice runs to the hospital. We went to the movies and I sat sideways in my chair, trying to get comfortable, wondering if I'd go into labor during *The Eternal Sunshine of the Spotless Mind*. Everything seemed like a portent, but nothing happened. Every night I cried myself to sleep, wanting desperately to no longer be pregnant, wanting to meet my baby.

One by one, the items on the birthing plan fell by the wayside.

"Yes, by all means, strip my membranes," I told the doctor four days after the due date. I was barely dilated at all, and this painless trick she was going to do, separating the amniotic membranes from the lower part of the uterine wall, was supposed to make my body start producing prostaglandins. In theory, that can start labor. (Sperm contains prostaglandins too, which is why people recommend sex to get labor going. But I had finally lost interest in sex.)

Three days later, my feet were back in the stirrups. Still nothing happening. "Let's induce," I said. "My sister has got to leave on the twelfth."

"Okay," she said. "We'll check you into the hospital tomorrow night, get you on some Pitocin, and by morning, you'll be in labor."

A SMART WOMAN would have gone home and sat on the couch watching old movies. But Matt and I had some unfinished business to discuss. Not content to let sleeping dogs lie, I wanted to know if we would keep on behaving as a couple after the baby was born. He was at my apartment all the time in those last weeks, sharing my bed, but what happened next? With poor Wib reading in the baby's room, I summoned Matt into my room and asked him point-blank about our relationship. He stared at the ground and took his time answering.

"I feel the same as I always have," he said. "I told you from the beginning that I wanted us to be friends who co-parent. I want us to get along. That's important for him."

"So nothing that has happened in the last few months has changed that?" I asked him.

He looked into my eyes and shook his head.

"Nothing?" I said, incredulous. "Not sleeping with me every

night, not spending all this time together, none of this has any impact on you at all?"

"It's been nice," he said. "Really nice. It's important that we be friends. But I don't want there to be confusion for him later on."

"So you're okay with us never sleeping together again?" I asked. My tone was getting bitter. "You can do that?"

He didn't say anything.

"Was this mercy fucking?" I asked. "Taking care of the pregnant woman's needs? You felt nothing at all?"

"Of course I felt something," he said. "I just don't want things to be weird with us. If we keep sleeping together, they will be."

I couldn't fathom how he could give it up. All my cravings; did he feel none of that in return? No desperate desire? I suppose I'd seen no evidence of it, beyond a cock that sprang to life whenever I approached it. I was crying now.

"Well, I *have* started to have feelings for you," I told him. "I didn't think I would, but we've been getting along so well and I love having you here and being with you, and I can't believe you don't want that to continue. My feelings have evolved for you, but here you are, saying that you haven't changed your opinion of us since the day I told you I was pregnant? How can you know this for sure?"

"I just do," he said, spreading his hands out, as if to show me how empty they were for me.

"You know that you will never be in love with me?" I said. Tears were streaming down my face now.

"Yes," he said.

"You *know* that?"

"Yes," he said, wearily now. "I can't give you what you need, Mary. I'm sorry."

I ought to be able to recognize an emotionally unavailable man at twenty paces by now. I badgered this one for a little longer, accused him of having no heart, a cold heart, a dead heart, and eventually told him to go home for the night. He'd spoken the most important words of our entire relationship, but instead of hearing "I can't give

you what you need," what I heard was "I don't want you and therefore I won't give you what you need." One sentence is an admission,
the other, a rejection. I chose to be rejected, to believe that there
must be something wrong with me, something that Matt could see
but I could not. I was back on the Bowdoin campus, listening to Peter tell my twenty-seven-year-old self that he didn't want to end up
with me. I was back in a Los Angeles apartment, clutching a phone,
hearing Michel saying much the same thing. No future. I got into my
bed, a beached whale on a deserted shore. I was too embarrassed to
share my rage and sorrow with Wib; my life seemed so messy and
dramatic and *stupid* compared with her nearly thirty years of marriage. What had I been doing with Matt? Why had I given myself
so easily, yet again, to someone who didn't really want me? All this
was so familiar. I felt as if my love life was like some long-running
Broadway play. The lead actress stayed the same; she was typecast
and couldn't break out of the role. Only the actors playing the male
lead kept changing. Some would quit; the actress would fire others.
But damned if they weren't all good at saying the same lines.

I'd have fired the new actor, if I could have. But there were scenes
ahead of me that I couldn't play without him.

"I'M GOING TO RECOMMEND A C-SECTION," said Doctor #1. It
was 11 A.M. Despite the Pitocin, my cervix had crept open only one
more centimeter in the night.

"No," I said.

So everything I'd read about the eagerness of doctors to slash
women open was true. I'd barely begun trying, for God's sake. Go
away, I thought. I embraced my so-called birthing ball (it's really just
one of those giant exercise balls you see in yoga studios) and rolled
around on it.

He sighed. "I'll break your water if you'd like."

Two hours later, he was back in the room, looking disappointed
by my unbudging cervix.

"I'm going to recommend a C-section," he said again, tapping his pen on his clipboard.

"No," I said.

"Let's get going with the epidural," he said. "That might relax you, and then these contractions can do their work. Because they're strong right now, but unproductive."

I'd wanted to hold off on the epidural until I was more dilated, because I'd read it can slow down your progress. Here was the doctor saying it could help, just another example of how contrary information about labor and delivery is. The pain of the contractions was more widespread than I'd imagined, but also duller. I could have lived with it, but use the word "unproductive" around an overachiever and she'll toss another item on the birthing plan out the window. I was grateful to have Matt's arms to hold while they put the needle in my spine. My mood improved considerably once the drugs started flowing.

At dinnertime, a new doctor showed up. She was petite and so young I thought she was a candy striper with the wrong outfit on. She poked around my pelvis and then took a look at her clipboard.

"I'm going to recommend a C-section," she said.

"I'm at eight centimeters," I protested. "I'm almost there. Leave me alone."

She was back a few hours later, trying to put a monitor on the baby's head. Her tiny hands fumbling inside me like a football player with sweaty palms hurt more than anything else had all day. I was up to nine centimeters.

"I'm going to recommend . . ."

"No," I said. I turned to Wib and muttered. "I wish she'd just beat it." When she left, I turned to Sara. "She's awful, isn't she?"

"I don't think she's awful," Sara said gently. "I think she's just trying to do her job. You've been at this awhile and I think they are getting worried that you're going to be too tired to push."

"I'm going to get to ten," I said. "I've just got to get to ten." I felt like Nigel in *Spinal Tap*. *I'll get to eleven, you bitch*, I thought, channeling all my rage toward the tiny doctor.

I looked over and saw Matt snoring on the couch, sleeping sitting up.

"Matt," I snapped. "Wake up!" He jumped. "Jesus!" Yawning during sex, now sleeping during contractions.

The Lamaze instructors tell you to bring a focus point, some object or photo that might help you concentrate during contractions. I had an old photograph of my mother with the four older kids, taken in 1957. They are sitting on a bridge in Venice, in front of the Bridge of Sighs. Skinny Adrian, not yet a teenager, looks into the camera from the far left, Cynthia cocks her head next to him, her hair a dark puff around a small, pale face. Alison is clutched to my mother's breast, looking round and contented. You see only Wib's forehead and eyes peeking out of the far right corner of the photo, squinting in the family manner. *Mum did this six times*, I kept telling myself, looking at the photo. No C-sections for her.

Just before dawn, I hit the magic number, ten, and started to push. It was peculiar. I wanted to squat, but because of the epidural, I was told I had to stay on my back. Sara and Matt and Wib took turns holding my legs up. It all felt so ungainly. I thanked God I'd decided not to have five people in there with me. I almost wanted to be alone. But the pushing was good; it felt as if I was finally getting somewhere. I had them bring a mirror, and in there, inside all that strange mess, I saw the top of his head. He was coming. "Hi, baby boy," I said, certain I'd have him in my arms in minutes.

Two hours later that head didn't seem to be moving at all. I felt as if I were trying to plunge a toilet; I kept thinking that the next push would be the one that would clear everything out, but there was the fear in the back of my mind that whatever was in there was insurmountably large.

"We're going to have to do an emergency C-section," said the annoying doctor.

"How old are you?" I asked. "Are you even thirty? I want to see your supervisor."

If a vet can reach up into a horse and yank out her foal, I saw no reason why they couldn't do that for me.

"What about that vacuum thing?" I wanted to know.

"That can cause stress on the baby," said the attending ob-gyn, who was slightly older.

Two of them now, with their clipboards.

"I'm so close," I said. "I can do it."

"We're going to let you go one more hour," the attending said. "But that's all. After that, we have to do a C-section."

"I won't need it." I glared at her. "I'll get him out."

As she left the room, I sat up and tore off my hospital gown. Sorry Matt. And Wib. And Sara. I decided that I was going to do this like an animal, without silly bits of clothing covering me. I asked for the squat bar. I made myself beet red pushing. I have never been so determined.

Why did I want so much to push that baby out? Maybe on some level I wanted to prove I was tough, just as I had when I'd gone to the trailer. That last hour of pushing passed like five minutes. Then there they were again, handing me releases to sign. The instant my pen lifted off the clipboard, every light in the room came on and people started flooding in. Someone was washing me, someone was shaving me, someone was putting a cap over my hair. I was furiously sobbing. I was not going to be allowed to experience birth, the real birth. I was going to get some man-made version of it, pushed on me by the great conglomerate of lawsuit-fearing HMO assholes.

Thus it was that I was indignant when I first laid eyes on Dolan, and disconcerted by the sense I had that I could feel them pulling my insides apart. It was 8:16 A.M. He was indignant and disconcerted too, by the sudden absence of his warm cave. For just a few seconds, they held him over the curtain that separated my top half from my bottom, sawed-off half, and I saw Gollum, a fuming Gollum, long and lean. My baby. I clutched Matt's hand hard and continued to cry, tears of rage and relief. And then he was whisked off.

I woke up in recovery about an hour later. Matt was sitting in the corner, holding the baby. He was holding Dolan. Before I did, I thought. How strange. Matt looked at ease, far more so than I expected. The baby was fair and pink. The nurse put him in my arms and started wrestling my breast into his mouth. I'd read, in all the natural birth books I'd been browsing, that he'd be less likely to latch on easily after the drugs from the epidural. But he took the breast right away. There was a huge bruise on his head, and a scab from where he'd been repeatedly knocking against my bone while he tried to get out. "I'm sorry," I murmured to him. "You were stuck, and I couldn't help."

Wib and Sara came in, bearing big bouquets and smiles.

"He's beautiful," Sara said.

"Did you see?" Wib said. "He has a dimple in his chin."

I checked. There it was. "Just like Mumma's," I said. The tears flowed so fast, they went into my ears.

I COULD HAVE PAID $200 a night for a single room, but I figured that was a waste of money I didn't have. I was entitled to four nights in the hospital to recover from the C-section, and I thought maybe I'd bond with some of the other moms. My book club friends told me this happened, that this was a way to get a moms' group going.

My first roommate snored like an ancient Labrador and refused to have her baby in the room with her. No one visited until her husband came to collect her, with another child who also seemed to be hers and not particularly cherished. My second roommate arrived in the middle of the night. She was a strident woman with a needy husband. They fought in stage whispers over the issue of the room—he had fucked up, she was supposed to be in a single, could he *fix* it now?—and over the child. You've been holding him for an hour, give him to me. "Well, I feel left out," he whined. They argued over how to change a diaper and who would sleep and when. If that's a husband, I thought, I don't want one. The third woman seemed like someone I could hang out with, but she was too nervous to bond. She kept hitting the call button. "My baby just threw up," she wailed. "That's spit-up," the nurse explained. "Perfectly natural." "Something seems wrong," she cried. "He keeps pooping." Jesus, I thought, cool it.

Meanwhile, Dolan was under the ultraviolet lights in an incubator with a bad case of jaundice. My blood type is Rh-negative, which is uncommon (about 15 percent of the population is Rh-negative). Unless the person who impregnates you is also Rh-negative, your baby's blood will be Rh-positive. Your blood will detect the foreign blood type and develop antibodies to it. In the old days, Rh-negative women were discouraged from having more than two children because the antibodies would have built up in their body to the point where the mother would send those antibodies across the placenta and into her fetus's bloodstream. Having antibodies to Rh-positive blood in your Rh-positive blood is never a good thing. It causes something called the bilirubin levels to skyrocket. Jaundice is one of the early symptoms of that. From there it goes to liver and brain damage and, possibly, death.

There was a drug to counter this, and I'd been getting shots of it throughout the pregnancy. Nonetheless, there had been some crossover, and now Dolan was jaundiced and had a high bilirubin count. If it didn't drop on its own in the next few days, with help from the ultraviolet lights, he'd have to have a blood transfusion.

I was eager to have him beside me, but all I could do was walk to the nursery every couple of hours to try to breast-feed him. They had me supplement with formula, run through a syringe and a tube that I put next to my nipple, so he'd get both breast and bottle at the same time.

Dolan seemed perfectly content in his incubator. Naked except for his diaper, he lay mostly on his stomach with his rump in the air. To protect his eyes from the ultraviolet lights, the nurses had made him a pair of "sunglasses" out of foam, even drawing eyelashes on them. I'd put a finger through the opening in the side of the incubator and stroke his cheek while he slept, but he'd barely stir. Wib went back to Massachusetts; my being so late to start labor and taking so long to get through it meant she had only about thirty-six hours with her new nephew before she had to fly home. Matt had gone back to work and came to visit at night, bringing takeout. I was enormously swollen and the incision hurt. I called my father on the second day after Dolan was born. Wib had already filled him in on the story of the birth.

"It's quite astounding that of all of you girls only Wib, the smallest of you all, managed to avoid a C-section," he said. "Alison and then Sondra [Adrian's ex-wife] and Beth. And now you."

"Uh-huh," I said. "They say external measurements have nothing to do with the internal ones. So you can have huge wide hips and still need a C-section."

"Yes, of course," he said. "She's quite tough, of course, our Wib."

What about me? I thought. *I'm not tough?* I picked at the sheet. They didn't seem to have fitted sheets at the hospital. Why was that? What was the point of hospital corners anyway?

"Not much going on here," he said. "I've been staying away from your mother for the last couple of days because I have a slight cold I don't want to pass on to her. And I have a blasted canker sore."

I made sympathetic noises. My father had canker sores all too often. I got them, too.

"Are you using your medication?" I asked. A few years before, I'd gotten a magic potion from my dentist that made cankers disappear in half the usual time. I'd given the name of the stuff to my father, and he'd gotten a prescription from his doctor. But mostly he declined to take it. "I'm troubled by the idea of a topical steroid," he'd say. He was, for all intents and purposes, a nondeclared Christian Scientist, who believed that aspirin should be avoided, antibiotics were to be used only in the kind of emergency that would otherwise require hospitalization, and, clearly, C-sections were for wimps.

"No, I am not," he said. "I can't seem to find it. Perhaps when you get home you can send me the name of it again and I'll have my doctor give me a new tube of it."

I sighed.

"Dad," I said. "I'm sitting here with a big gash across my stomach praying I don't have to poop anytime soon, just in case I accidentally blow my stitches open. So please, stop complaining about your canker sore."

There was an awkward pause. I felt guilty almost instantly, but still annoyed.

"All right, dearie," he said, sounding more distant. "You get some rest, and I'll talk to you when you get home from the hospital."

I wanted to cry again. "When you go see Mum, will you tell her about the baby for me?" I asked.

"I'm not sure it will mean anything," he said. "But I will tell her."

"Tell her that he has her dimple," I said. "And I think his eyes are going to be blue like hers."

"All newborns have blue eyes," he said.

"Yes, but these seem like her shade of blue," I said. "That soft blue."

MY FIRST NIGHT HOME from the hospital, I was sitting on the couch watching television with Dolan in my arms and Matt next to me when something terrible happened inside me. A wave of pain, a pain much worse than a contraction, swept around my back and into my torso, as if someone were grabbing me from behind and trying to rip me open with his bare hands. It pulsated. I thrust the baby into Matt's arms and began to gasp. It was getting worse. I must be hemorrhaging. Maybe the stitches were ripping open.

"Call 911," I gasped.

Matt vacillated. He was standing now, holding the baby, who had woken up and started to cry. "Are you sure?" he said.

"Yes," I said. "Something awful is happening to me."

I thought that I was going to die, that I would not get to know my son at all. I panicked at the thought of him alone, without me. *But I just met you.* The fire truck and paramedics were there within two minutes. By the time they arrived I'd gotten myself down to the floor, then back up on the couch again, lying full-length on my back. The pain had subsided, but the ghost of it hung around my waist, as if it might come back at any moment.

I realized what it had to be. A back spasm. The paramedics walked me through a series of questions, but it was clear that's what they thought it was too. While they were examining me, Dolan pooped violently and loudly. They all laughed, including Matt. There's nothing like a fart joke to make men chummy. They offered to take me to the hospital, but the thought of going back to that place was too gruesome to contemplate. As long as the spasm didn't come back, I'd be okay. I had my Vicodin and my Motrin. It was time for a dose.

After they left, I wondered, *What would happen if I died? Would Dolan be raised by Matt and his mother? Would he know little to nothing of my family? Miss his mother for his whole life?* I felt foolish for making Matt call 911. But I had just experienced the process of giving life, so death no longer seemed theoretical. I wasn't about to tempt fate.

MY SISTER ALISON flies only if her final destination is Venice. That is her unspoken rule. For about twenty years, she did not fly at all. In the early eighties, she'd gone to Italy with my mother, not long after they both finished college. On the flight back to the States, there was some turbulence. Alison had been seated next to a priest.

"She was asking him about last rites," my mother said, rolling her eyes. "And shaking. I don't think we'll be getting her back on a plane anytime soon."

Mum was right. Alison crisscrossed America by train and by automobile for decades, never setting foot on a plane. Then in 2002, Wib and Sean had enticed her to come to Venice. I flew to New York to meet her, and we took a direct flight to Marco Polo together. Some medication was required, and it was obvious she didn't like it, but if the payoff included being able to lift her face to the sun in Piazza San Marco while drinking a $9 cappuccino, it was worth it.

Over the years I'd tried to convince her to come to San Francisco. "Our most European city," I'd say. "The food. The markets, the cappuccino. The hills, the Bay, the architecture. You would love it here." While I was pregnant, I tried again. Having Alison come after Wib would be the perfect solution to new mother angst. She'd get to see

California and she'd charge through my house, restoring order without ever breaking a sweat.

"I'm sending Katy," she said. "Katy is my proxy."

"Can she *cook*?" I asked. My niece was a junior at Bowdoin. When I was in Maine, we either went out for Thai together or hit one of the seafood shacks that specialized in big oily baskets of fried shrimp or clams. Every Christmas Eve, Katy participated in Alison's giant cook-off of spring rolls. But beyond that, I hadn't seen much evidence of culinary talent.

"Of course she can cook," Alison said. Her tone said, *Don't beg, I am not coming. You are not Piazza San Marco.* "She can do whatever you tell her to do. She takes instruction very well."

"Can she drive?" Katy knew how to drive, of course—our father had taught her—but whether she possessed a legal license was a perpetual question.

"Not in Maine," Alison said. "Not until she takes that alcohol awareness class. But she can drive in other states. Definitely in California."

"Okay," I said. I still couldn't picture Katy sweeping through my house in a tornado of efficiency.

Benet chortled when I told him that Alison was sending Katy.

"What if she and Matt hit it off?" he said. "After all, they are closer in age than you and Matt are, right?"

"Thanks a lot," I said. "I think Matt has a little bit more class than that."

"I hope so," Benet replied.

KATY ARRIVED having just had a fight with her on-again, off-again boyfriend, involving some past violation on her part of the code of proper girlfriend conduct. I was too dazed from the pain of attempting to breast-feed to absorb all the details, but I gathered there was some slight overlapping of her affections. Both young men were angry with her. Both of them wanted to discuss her treachery at length. I heard her muttering on the phone at 3 A.M. She woke up anywhere between 11 A.M. and noon, emerged sleepily, still looking to me like the towheaded, sweet-faced toddler she was not so long ago, sat down to share a cup of tea with me, and, almost immediately, the phone would ring. She'd smile apologetically and retreat outside with the phone and her smokes to engage in yet another round of What Katy Did. I propped myself up on the couch with the not particularly helpful horseshoe-shaped breast-feeding pillow and tentatively offered Dolan the breast again.

Everyone tells you how awful labor is. Everyone tells you how much it sucks not to get sleep when you bring home a newborn. Everyone tells you that breast-feeding is extremely important and that your child will be ten times smarter, stronger, and better-looking if you do it. No one ever mentions that in the early days, breast-feeding hurts like hell. It doesn't feel natural; it feels like torture. No matter how much potion and lotion you slather onto your poor nipples, they still feel as though someone has been chewing on them for days. That's because *someone has been chewing on them for days*. And not lovingly, not tantalizingly, not playfully. Chewing on them as if they were a tough but tasty clam's neck. While Katy was getting verbally spanked by her ex-boyfriends, Dolan suckled and I cried.

I knew I loved him, but he seemed much more like a small animal than a small human. I had imagined him burrowing into my breast sweetly. Instead he fought it, then reluctantly took it, then slobbered over it. He was like a thirsty piglet, and often a piglet without enough sense to find the trough. The best part was when he fell asleep on it. Then he looked sweet. Then he seemed like a real baby. But while the various lactation consultants I'd had at the hospital gave contradictory advice on most aspects of breast-feeding, they were in agreement over one thing: Never let the baby fall asleep on the nipple.

These lactation gurus speak of "the latch" as if the nipple were a key and the baby's mouth a keyhole and there is only one way to get the damn door open. It's simply not that precise. "Oh," one nurse had said knowingly in the hospital, inspecting my tender nipple. "Bad latch." Her tone made me feel like a failure. Then she proceeded to shove my breast into the baby's mouth in a way that seemed not that different from the way I'd been doing it. In my first few days home, a number of friends who had breast-feeding experience came over. "Let me see your latch," they'd say. (It is the baby who is doing the physical latching on to the nipple, but it is the mother's job to make sure he or she is doing it right. Thus it is not his or her latch, but yours. This is a fantastic summation of the responsibilities of motherhood in general.) I'd oblige, and half would say, sunnily, "That looks good." The other half would wince and make some adjustments and instruct me to do it that way and *only* that way from now on or suffer terrible consequences. It was like having someone try to tell you how to have an orgasm. The truth is, I don't think there was any conceivable way to avoid misery. Two things happen in those first few weeks: First, your nipples do get tougher—tougher to the point where you can't imagine how they ever responded to a hand brushing across them. Second, the baby grows and his or her mouth gets bigger and thus is able to get a better grasp on more of the breast.

My incision hurt and I was afraid to even look at it. It wasn't the outside I feared so much as the internal stuff. What if it ruptured or got infected? Every time I sat up, it felt as though there were a chef's knife resting on my belly, with an *Oxford English Dictionary* sitting on top of it. I slithered out of bed sideways trying to avoid using any of my abdominal muscles. Or rather, what was left of them. I had imagined how nice it would be to sleep on my stomach again after the baby was born, but there was no way I'd be doing that anytime soon. I didn't give a damn about having a scar—but I was still pissed about the C-section. It was definitely going to take longer to recover. The only bonus was that because of state law, I'd get an extra two weeks at home now. Between California's disability payments and my accrued vacation time, I'd have eleven weeks with my baby before going back to work.

"Phew," Katy said, coming back into the room, shaking her head.

"Which one was that?" I asked.

"Franco," she said, picking up her mug of tea.

"Is he still mad?" I didn't really care, but felt I should ask.

"Oh yeah," Katy said. She looked around the living room. "Hey, do you mind if I smoke some pot?"

I would have liked to smoke some pot myself. I would have liked to smoke myself into oblivion. But I was pretty sure it would not help with my current state of paranoia about whether I'd achieved a good latch or not. Dolan was sleeping. I put him down on the couch, blocking his route to the floor with a pillow. Social Services would love this tableau. I took Katy into the kitchen and showed her my stash. Dregs in three different plastic baggies, well over a year old now. Some more weed ground down into a fine dust at the bottom of a wooden dugout. "It's not exactly fresh," I told her. "But you're welcome to it."

Her eyes lit up. "Great," she said. "I'll just do it in the bedroom."

Off my caretaker went to get high.

When my best friend from college had her first child, her mother came to stay. The mother had announced on the phone, before her arrival, that all she was going to do was "sit in a rocking chair and hold the baby." In other words, no cleaning, no cooking, just baby holding. "Which is what *I* wanted to do," my friend said to me. She, and others, had warned me about the unhelpful houseguest who comes to "help take care of the baby." Katy wasn't unhelpful; she did everything I told her to. But I had to tell her what to do. I didn't want a servant; I wanted someone to take care of me.

Liza had come that first day when I was all alone with Dolan for the first time and given me a foot rub. She brought magazines, she made me lunch without asking questions, she cleaned my apartment. In between tasks, she sat on the back step and smoked. "I'm the maid," she said. "The maid needs her smoking breaks." But she wasn't the maid; she was someone who could anticipate my needs before I did. She'd even brought me a heating pad for my back, without my asking. Sally, from book the club, was the same way. She arrived on my second full day home with lunch in Tupperware containers and a full dinner, including salad, all ready for me. Sally and Liza were both mothers. Katy was not. Neither was Matt. I wanted my mother, who would not be coming.

Dolan did make it easier on me by being a very good sleeper. He'd go several hours at a stretch during the night, and even though breast-feeding was miserable, I wasn't finding it all that hard to wake up for him. Still I was thrilled on his tenth night home when he truly slept through the night. Refreshed after my seven hours of sleep, I sang his praises all day. Then in the afternoon, I realized I felt feverish. One of my breasts was hard. An angry red flush was spreading across it. I took out my books and frantically looked for possible causes, even though I knew instinctively what it had to be: mastitis. I called the doctor, who couldn't see me until the morning. In the meantime, ice packs. Chicken broth. Pumping. Tylenol. Fluids. And sleeping.

I went out to the living room and barked orders to Matt and Katy, who were watching television. In an hour, I wanted dinner. Wib had left some minestrone in the freezer. They should start thawing it. In a half hour, I wanted a fresh ice pack. I should be brought ginger ale regularly. I was sick and I wanted to see some effective caretaking, starting right now. They both looked at me and nodded.

I went back into my room. Dolan was asleep in his bassinet, his arms above his head. He had resisted being swaddled from the very beginning, which seemed odd for a child who was content to stay in the womb for an extra eleven days. I still wasn't sure who he looked like, beyond my mother's chin dimple and blue eyes, but when he wasn't red-faced and crying, he was a lovely baby. I gingerly got back into bed, turned out the light, and tried to nest. I could hear the TV in the other room. I can't stand the sound of someone else's TV shows. I slid sideways off the bed and went out to glare at them and tell them to turn it down. A half hour passed. No ginger ale. Another half hour passed. No soup. No ice pack. I gave them ten more minutes and then stormed out into the living room, smacking the palm of my left hand with the back of my right hand.

"I said I needed soup," I said. "I said I needed an ice pack." They both looked blank, dopey, and then a little afraid. "I am sick. I have a breast infection. I have a temperature of 103."

There are few things more pathetic than feeling as though you have to remind people to feel sorry for you. But I felt validated the next day when the nurse practitioner opened up my paper gown and grimaced.

"This is bad," she said. "Normally I'd try to push out the blockage or get you to pump it out, but this is all over one breast and in half the other. You need antibiotics."

God, was breast-feeding worth all this trouble? Now I had to worry about the poor baby getting antibiotics in his milk. Sure, the doctors said it wouldn't hurt him, but what else are they going to say? Alison had quit breast-feeding when she got mastitis, and look at Katy—she was fine. Except for being an insomniac stoner.

When we picked Matt up at the BART station that afternoon, I told him that I was planning to quit breast-feeding. He still didn't have a car, or the money or inclination to get one anytime soon. It was a 1.3-mile walk from my place to the station, half of it pleasant, half of it ugly, industrial, and not very safe. From there he could be at work in twenty minutes or at his place in the Upper Haight in another twenty. I was contemplating making him walk back and forth to the station, but I hadn't quite gotten there yet.

"Well, if that's what you want, then go ahead and quit," he said. "I know you wanted to do it for the whole first year, but I can see how hard it is."

He was so reasonable.

"I'll wait and see how I feel tomorrow," I said. "Maybe after the antibiotics kick in I won't want to quit."

Two days later, I felt sufficiently better to take Katy on a driving tour of the Bay Area. She was leaving the next day, and I wanted her to see something of California before she left. This was her spring break, after all.

"I wonder," she said as we neared the end of our loop of the Bay Area's prime tourist spots, "whether there's anywhere in Berkeley where we could just buy a little pot? Just a really small amount."

I turned to look at her. I had a newborn sleeping in the back, a gash in my gut, and I was fighting a bacterial infection of the breast. Technically I was still supposed to be avoiding driving. Did my niece seriously want me to take her someplace to buy drugs *on the street*? She met my gaze, her green-gray eyes guileless. She looked fourteen. Like a fair version of Christina Ricci, pale and petite and curvy, with a sweet moon face.

I turned back to the crowded freeway. "No, Kate," I said.

"Okay," she said.

Someone said to me later that Katy and Matt seemed to be the perfect storm of incompetence. I had to laugh, because it was true. I wasn't resentful, though. If she was the nor'easter and he was the hurricane blowing up from the Bahamas, I suppose I was realizing I had to be the lighthouse—the stability on the rocks. I had always been able to nurture in spurts; I could bring friends soup if they were sick and I could hold their crying babies. I'd be good in a mastitis crisis. But I'd always been able to go home after my fit of nursemaiding to lie around on my own couch and, like Katy and Matt, drink wine and watch television and forget about responsibility. It was fitting then, as I moved into this permanent role of nurturer, to have to fend for myself to a certain extent. That, as almost any mother would tell you, is part of the job. Those two weeks were a rite of passage, an introduction to what lay ahead.

CHAPTER 10

A Gift Horse

DOLAN HAD BEEN the beneficiary of great generosity even before he was born. Liza and Hugh had practically emptied their garage into the trunk of my car: a bassinet, two kinds of strollers, and a white wicker crib. Kir had come by with two enormous boxes full of hand-me-downs in great condition—clothes, toys, even extra diapers. Then there were the gifts, which seemed to arrive every day in the last month of my pregnancy and came from people I barely knew or had never even met. Women at work kept turning up at my desk with offerings: outfits, stuffed animals, soft blankets. Adrian, my gruff big brother, sent me a check for $1,000. Matt's cousins sent a Baltimore Orioles uniform for the baby. His grandmother, about to become a great-grandmother, sent one of those portable cribs, better known in twenty-first-century parental parlance as a pack-and-play.

It was overwhelmingly kind of everyone and I loved it. Until the second pack-and-play arrived.

Matt had mentioned a couple of weeks before Dolan was born that some "girl" (I had been trying to get Matt to say "woman" but hadn't made much headway) who hung around Finnegan's Wake and regularly came to the bar team's softball games had expressed a desire to get Dolan a gift. She'd asked if I was registered anywhere.

"It's weird," he said. "I don't know why she wants to get him something."

"People are incredibly nice," I said. I was holding paint chips up to the wall in the baby's bedroom. "The receptionist at the paper gave me a blanket the other day. What do you think, is Bahamian Blue just too freaking bright?"

"It's pretty bright," he said. "It just seems strange."

"How about this one? Cool Blue?" I said. "I think I like it more. Just say we're not registered anywhere and there's no need to get anything, but an outfit is always welcome."

At the time, I was too busy nesting to dwell on the conversation. The girl probably had a crush on Matt, which seemed misplaced, given that he was about to have a baby, but whatever. Then one night, right after Katy had gone home, Matt called from San Francisco. I was sitting on the couch, Dolan asleep at my breast. He sounded excited.

"So she, this girl, just dropped off all of this stuff," he said. "You wouldn't believe this crap. Another pack-and-play—and it looks like a nice one—and this huge box of diapers, and all of these little clothes hangers and things to separate out his clothes by age. It's like $200 worth of stuff."

He was laughing. I was suddenly very alert. I was still puffy from the C-section, although my ankles were almost back to their normal size.

"Why is this girl buying you all of this expensive equipment?" I asked.

"I don't know. I think she just has a lot of money."

"Have you been flirting with her or something, Matt?"

"No," he said vehemently. "I don't even talk to her. She's always asking if I want to go get a drink or something, but I barely know her."

I've been with some liars, including two of epic proportions. From them I learned women may be irrational creatures, but they simply do not have irrational interests in men. If they are hanging around, if they are crank-calling your house, if they frequent the same places as the man you're with, then something—or rather someone—has led them to believe that the pursuit is worth it. I was a solid decade past being deluded by any man, and Matt, a relative innocent in matters of the heart, was no match for me. I let my suspicions curdle for a few days. Then one night he came over to help with Dolan's first bath, an event we were both dreading. All the books said babies don't like to be naked. Naked and wet wasn't going to be an improvement. But Dolan's umbilical cord had fallen off and his circumcision was sufficiently healed, so it was time.

"Okay, hand him to me," I said. I was kneeling next to a big plastic baby tub, molded so that you could prop the baby up in it. Matt had Dolan in his arms, diaper-free, a pretty pink boy lying rather languidly on a blanket. He was blinking up at his father.

"I don't think he's going to like it," Matt said. "That tub looks so hard."

"I know," I said. "But we've got to wash him. I'm supposed to take him in for a checkup tomorrow and I can't bring him in dirty. My friend Susan told me that she was afraid to wash her son for the first month and her pediatrician scolded her for it. They showed her all the dirt on his neck."

"Okay," Matt said. "Here goes."

He held Dolan out to me gingerly and I took him, just as gingerly. As soon as I lowered the baby into the tub, he started crying. I scooped lukewarm water around him, and that just made him cry harder. He kicked his legs violently, and I remembered the strength of all those kicks I'd felt before he was born. It was sometimes hard to believe that this beautiful boy was the same one who had been living inside me, just a couple of weeks ago. Now that I knew this face, it was almost unfathomable to imagine it, fully formed, hidden from me in the dark.

"Ouch," Matt said.

"This is awful," I said.

"We've got to do it, though," he said. "Maybe faster, though."

"I'm going as fast as I can," I said.

"I know, I know," he said.

"Okay," I said, giving a final splash to Dolan's nether regions. "Get that towel ready."

Dolan was still mad when we took him out. He stayed mad until he was in his sleep sack, wrapped in a blanket and lying in my arms, nursing. Matt sat next to us.

"Whew," he said. "That was rough. I hate seeing him so miserable."

"I know," I said. "Horrible."

We sat for a few more minutes. I could have let it go, but it was hard to pretend we were a happy team when I was harboring these suspicions.

"Did something happen with that girl?" I said.

"No," he said. "I told you."

I turned my eyes on him. I knew they were narrow slits by now. Menacing. I kept them on him until he had to meet my gaze. I was like Medusa. I was going to turn him to stone. But first I was going to yank the truth out of him.

"I don't believe you," I said. "No girl hangs around like this unless she thinks she's getting something for her troubles."

"Okay," he said, running his hands through his close-cropped hair frantically. "We hooked up."

Dolan seemed so small in my arms. I felt a deadly calm, the one that comes before a massive meltdown.

"When?"

"I don't know," he said. "A few weeks ago, or a month or something."

"Right before I had the baby?"

"I don't remember," he said miserably. "It was just one night."

I drilled away at him until I had enough facts to nauseate me. She'd called him late one night after seeing him at the bar. It was the middle of the night. He'd told her she could come over. He'd resisted anything with her since. Yes, it had been while he and I were sleeping together. No, he couldn't remember if it was before or after the baby shower my work colleagues had thrown for me, when his mother had flown in from Baltimore for the weekend and we had been so content together. *No, he hadn't used a condom.*

"I was so intimate with you," I said. "I let you see me at my most vulnerable. I *gave* myself to you. The whole time I was pregnant, and even now, I couldn't imagine sleeping with anyone but you. And this is what you do to me?"

The baby was still asleep in my arms. I felt insulted on his behalf too. We were as one when this happened. Now he was only two weeks old and I hated his stupid, inconsiderate dunderhead of a father. I would have to be tested for STDs. I would have to deal with this girl who was threatening to turn into a stalker. I knew Matt didn't love me, but this meant these last few months of being together, of lying on the couch with his arms around me, of making dinner for him, of screwing him every chance I got, were an absolute lie. That yawn I'd seen, *that* was the truth.

"Do you hate me that much?" I whispered. "You must hate me to have done this to me."

"I don't hate you at all," he said. He seemed anguished. "I just wanted to do something for myself, something that was just for me."

I stood up and walked away from the couch. He was still sitting in exactly the same position, as if he were frozen there.

"You wanted me to trust you?" I said.

He didn't even look up.

"You are going to have to go," I told him. "I can't stand to have you here. You are such an idiot; you have completely blown it. The time when you should be bonding with your son, you make it so that I am not going to be able to stand the sight of you. The time when I need you, when I need your help, you do something so awful that I have no choice but to throw you out."

I went into my room and closed the door. I put the baby down on the bed, curled myself around him, and cried myself to sleep.

In the morning, Matt had packed all his possessions and was ready to go. Except that he needed a ride to the BART station. He was standing nervously next to his blue duffle bag.

"I fed the cats," he said.

Wordless, I buckled Dolan into the car seat and took him out to the car, Matt following sheepishly behind me. I felt overrun with humiliation. The superficial humiliation was driving him to the train, as if I were the mother of the most rotten sort of teenager. But the deeper humiliation was something I don't think I'll ever get over. I had felt beautiful in those last weeks, gloriously with child, fervently sexual. I thought I was someone filled with the unique power of reproduction and therefore invincible, safe from the petty crises of my pre-pregnancy romantic life. In my mind, Matt ought not to have been able to look away from me. But apparently it had been all too easy for him to cheat on me. If that was even the right word for it because how, after all, could you cheat on a woman you said you didn't love and weren't even dating?

AS SOON AS I GOT HOME, I called Kir to recount Matt's sins. I had to bitch about them. I was hurt, but there was something in me that wanted to be told I was right and he was wrong. But she seemed unimpressed, as if this were such a predictable drama that she'd long ago pegged the outcome.

"He just wants you to know that this is not a relationship," she said.

"Just telling me would have sufficed," I said.

"Yeah, but this is easier in a way," she said. "It's so definitive. It makes everything so clear, doesn't it? And you know what? Pretty soon you're not going to care at all. What he does isn't going to matter."

"Really?"

"That baby is going to take over everything." She laughed. "It's kind of bad when you've got a husband because husbands end up feeling neglected, but the more you fall in love with that baby, the less you'll care about what Matt is up to."

I'd walked into the bedroom and was looking down at Dolan. I'd just put him down, and he was already sleeping peacefully.

"How is Dolan?"

"He seems pretty good," I said. "He had his first tubby last night. Which he hated. I felt so cruel, getting him wet."

"Oh, give him a few weeks and he'll love it," she said. "The first couple of times are hard, though. Don't feel like you've got to do it a lot either; you can just sponge him down instead of putting him into the tub. And really, try not to think about this whole thing with Matt and the girl. You've got the baby; that is what matters."

"I know," I said. "I just feel so stupid. This is so not what I expected from my first few weeks of motherhood. I keep thinking it's wrong. Unnatural somehow."

"HONESTLY, IT HAPPENS ALL THE TIME," my doctor said. She was taking a vaginal swab. "The studies on how many men sleep around when the woman they are with is pregnant would blow your mind."

"Really?" I said, propping myself up on my elbows. "Why is that?"

She shrugged. "Fear, I suppose. A lot of them might be afraid that they'll no longer be the center of attention. Resentment of the baby."

I was flummoxed. At least I wasn't alone. I'd been mortified, making the appointment, having to confess to the presence of such sleaziness in my life. Even if I wasn't the one who had slept around, I felt sullied by all that it implied. But now at least I could imagine sharing the pain with women everywhere. Sisterhood. It counted for something.

"Actually, you're lucky," she continued. "Some men really turn on their wives or girlfriends. I had a patient who was just beaten to death by her boyfriend. She was five months' pregnant."

Oh my Lord, I thought, looking at the ceiling.

"You'll get a call from us if there's anything funky in these results," she continued, stripping off her gloves. "Otherwise, you're all good. But you should get tested again in another six months." On the way out of the room, she paused to look at Dolan. He was sitting in the car seat, next to the examining table, and he was watching her. "Wow, he's so alert," she said. "You got a good one there."

In the elevator, I felt less angry than I had going in. Matt was an asshole, but this wasn't the end of the world. A lot of women were worse off than I. For Dolan's sake, we were going to have to find a way to get through this and move beyond. Couples' counseling, I thought grimly. He won't like it, but as we used to say in Maine, growing up, he can just *suffah*.

OUR COUPLES' COUNSELING SESSION was in the same building where I'd gone to discuss the thumb-sucker. I would have liked to see the sniffling therapist again, but she had moved on, so we'd been assigned to someone new. Matilda was in her fifties or early sixties, and she had the look of a cheerful, youthful grandmother. She cooed over the baby, once again being hauled into a doctor's office in his car seat. I made Matt carry him. We hadn't talked much, beyond my telling him he had to come to therapy and his agreeing, in his usual passive manner.

"So," Matilda said. "I am just going to take down some facts about you if you don't mind. Your full name?" She pointed to me, and then to Matt.

"You are not married?" she said.

"No," I explained. "We're not actually together."

If she'd been a dog, her ears would have pricked up. "But you are here for couples' counseling?"

I tried to sum it up for her, as best I could, and swiftly. Her eyes fell on Dolan. He was kicking in the car seat. I stooped over to extract him and started nursing.

"He's a beautiful baby," she said.

"Thank you," I said. "We're here because although we're not a couple, we are going to share some parental duties, and I want us to learn how to work together as a couple. And right now I am very, very angry at Matt, because he slept with someone else, right before I gave birth."

Her eyes swiveled to Matt, sitting there in his work clothes, which were, as always, neat, tidy, and professional. He looked as mild-mannered and sweet as a man could look. Butter wouldn't melt in his mouth, I thought bitterly, then started to parse the phrase. What did that mean, anyway? Didn't that imply you must have some sort of internal refrigeration? I was angry enough to think maybe that was apt for Matt—passionless, inert.

"You *were* a couple then?" Matilda was asking.

"Not declared as such," I said. "But we were sleeping together, and I assumed it was monogamous. Because who would be indecent enough to go screw someone else in between nights at my house?"

Then I went off. Waving my hands, occasionally wrestling the baby onto the other breast, trying to explain why I was so outraged and why she ought to be as well. What I wanted was for Matt to be sent to the gallows. By a professional.

"You look very nice together," she said, when I was done. "A very handsome family."

I stared at her.

"I would not call us a family," I said. "Not now that he's done this to me."

"Matthew," she said, turning to him. "Tell me how you feel about this."

"I fucked up," he said, shrugging his shoulders. "I did something very stupid. I guess I thought we weren't really together so it was okay, but I regretted it right away and I'm really sorry."

"Oh, come on," I said. "Weren't there a few clues in there to tell you it wasn't okay to fuck someone else?" Matilda waved an admonishing hand in my direction. But I wasn't done.

"Especially some stalker," I said. "She's calling him all the time and giving us baby gifts, and coming to his stupid lame-ass barfly softball team games on the weekends, as if they were worth seeing. It's not even baseball!"

Matilda was not coming over to the side of the raving lunatic.

"Tell me about when you and Mary met, Matthew," she said.

He cleared his throat. "Well, there was a physical attraction, of course," he said.

She smiled.

"But we barely knew each other, and when Mary told me she was pregnant, I thought we should just try to be friends. I thought that would be easiest."

"What about these last few months?" she asked.

"They've been nice," he said. "We've gotten to know each other better, which I think is important. But I still think we should just be friends. Otherwise, it's too confusing."

I couldn't get my head around Matt's emotional obstinacy. Or stoicism. Or whatever it was. Did nothing ever sneak up on him? Or, if and when he ever fell in love, would it be because something flashed in the calendar of life he carried in his head, giving him the green light to go ahead and let go?

"So were your actions with this other woman—" she began.

"Hosebag," I muttered.

Matilda waved me off again. Her focus was on Matt. "Were you acting something out with this girl?"

"I guess I was." He sighed. "Trying to say, I'm not in a relation-ship."

"This must be very stressful for you," she said, looking at him.

"Pretty stressful," he said.

Matt had recently revealed that in the first few months of my pregnancy, he'd had dreams in which snakes were biting his penis. "I thought you never remembered your dreams," I'd said. "These you'd remember," he'd said.

"I think we should schedule another session," Matilda said. "Mary, you are going to have to work on forgiving Matthew; other-wise you are not going to be able to move on."

"I don't want to forgive him," I said. "This was unforgivable."

"Eventually," she said, "you will have to, for your son's sake."

I gave Matt a dirty look. "It would be nice if, for his son's sake, he hadn't felt compelled to screw someone else."

She ignored me. Looking back and forth between us, she seemed to like what she saw.

"You know," she said, "in a few years, while raising your son together, you may find that you end up loving each other. You may decide that for"—she checked her notes—"Dolan's sake, you want to be together."

Matt remained neutral, but I gaped at her. Was this couples' counseling or the dating game?

"You do make a very handsome couple," she said again. "You look very nice together."

Then she turned to her calendar. "I could see you next month. I don't have anything open before that, I'm afraid."

We made the appropriate noises of agreement and took the date she offered us. In the car on the way home, we passed my old apartment. Life was so much simpler when I lived there. If I'd never met this jerk, I'd still be up there, I thought, maybe making myself a nice cup of tea or getting ready to go out for the evening. Then I looked in the rearview mirror. Dolan's car seat was facing the rear, but I'd hung a mirror back there so I could see his face. He was sleeping again, his pink lips pressed together in a tiny pout. "He's got your pout," Sara had said on the day he was born.

"I don't think we're going to get much out of Matilda," I said to Matt.

"Yeah, I don't think so either," he said. "She didn't seem to get our situation. What was all that stuff about how we could fall in love someday?"

Matilda's focus on a happy ending had also struck me as absurd, given the way we'd spelled out our problems to her. She seemed like a clueless amateur. But he didn't have to be so dismissive.

"It's not such a crazy proposition," I said, glaring at him. "People do fall in love unexpectedly, you know."

"I know they do," he said. "I just don't think it's in the cards for us."

"Neither do I," I said grimly, getting on the freeway to go home. I wondered whether I was capable of forgiving Matt. I already knew him well enough to know it wasn't cruelty that made him sleep with someone else. It was certainly an effective way of establishing that we weren't in a relationship. But probably all he wanted, just for a few hours, was to feel free of the strange burden that another one-night stand had left him with.

CHAPTER 11

Reality Doesn't Bite

A WEEK OR SO AFTER our trip to the couples' counselor, I picked up Matt at BART on a rainy afternoon. I was still wearing my pajamas, with a sweatshirt over them, and I was cursing Matt for calling to ask for a ride. In general I was cursing his presence in my life. I'd gained enough confidence with mothering to feel certain I could manage the day-to-day caretaking on my own. Moreover, I felt entitled, as the woman burned, to give him the cold shoulder. But if I pushed him away from me right now, I'd also be pushing him away from the baby. I feared doing so would damage his relationship with Dolan. If he felt unneeded and useless, he might want to stay away. Then Dolan might ultimately think fathers were the people who showed up when it was time to start playing baseball in the backyard. I wanted my son to have the best possible experience with his father that he could, no matter what his parents' circumstances were.

Matt walked across the parking lot, and I realized his eyes were glued to the backseat, even from a distance. He was trying to see the baby's face, which at that moment was red with rage; Dolan had been crying ever since we left the house. I popped the locks and Matt tossed his bag into the front seat, then swung his lean frame into the back, next to his son.

"Hey, buddy," he said. "I missed you." Dolan kept on fussing and I watched as Matt tried to entertain him with a stuffed red monkey. It wasn't working.

"Do you think he's hungry?" Matt asked.

"I just fed him," I said. "I think he probably was ready for a nap and wasn't psyched to go on a car ride."

My tone must have said, *Neither was I. Take the freaking bus.*

"Sorry, little guy," Matt said. The squalling continued, unabated. "I am so in love with you, little one," Matt murmured. His voice was as tender as I've ever heard a man's voice. "But you have got to stop crying."

I kept on driving and said nothing. But my heart, bruised as it was for myself, sang for Dolan. His father was in love with him. I didn't forgive Matt on that day, nor did I forget what he'd done. But something in me knew then that I'd survive and that this love, the love Matt had for Dolan, was what mattered.

BIRTHDAYS ARE WORSE than New Year's Eve, when at least you have a world of company in feeling disappointed. That balance of wanting attention and knowing how to handle it had always eluded me. My mother wasn't one for giving her children birthday parties. Other than when I was five and the neighbors' kids came over, I can't remember a party that wasn't exclusively family until I demanded one in fourth grade. I remembered that event only for what went wrong. My mother made spaghetti and left too much water in the pasta, and as I was presenting it with what I thought was an elegant flourish—emulating Rose, my favorite character on *Upstairs, Downstairs*—the noodles slid across the plate and into one unfortunate girl's lap. I can't conjure up their faces, but I can still hear the sound of everyone's giggles.

Before my life took this crazy turn, I had been actively dreading my fortieth birthday. Every day that passed after that would be one less day of fertility. If I were still treading water, all by myself, at forty, I figured I'd be doomed to miss out on marriage with children; there just wouldn't be enough time. I'd even begun planning to compensate for whatever misery I'd be experiencing on that big day by looking at houses to rent out at the beach, someplace with a hot tub, where I could gather all my friends for a weekend party. Essentially I'd started battening down the hatches for what I was sure would be a storm of self-pity.

But here was Dolan. Five weeks and three days old on my fortieth birthday. I felt as though I'd slid under a closing gate in the last few seconds, like Indiana Jones escaping the tomb. I'd beaten the biological clock, the thing that had been tormenting me, but I didn't feel like gloating. I'd imagined besting that clock might be like finishing a marathon, high on adrenaline and ready to mount the podium and pump your fists in the air. Instead I felt something so much softer, something I couldn't quite define.

My dad had sent me a check and I'd spent it on lobsters, inviting some friends over to share them. John came through the door with bottles and bottles of prosecco, April with a stack of gourmet chocolate bars, Karen with flowers. The women all made an immediate beeline for Dolan.

"God, he might not be a girl, but he's as pretty as one," Karen said, running her fingers across his downy head. Then she leaned in, closer to my ear. "You let Matt come?"

"Yeah," I said. "I kept imagining looking at pictures from this night, years from now, and Dolan noticing that his dad isn't in them, and then I'd remember why, and that almost seemed worse."

"That's good," Karen said. "Forgive and forget. So, how's being home? Do you miss work?

"No," I said. "Not one bit. I'm sure I will at some point, but days are so full right now. We don't do anything, but even that seems to take a lot of time."

"And how's he sleeping?" she asked, fussing with Dolan's blanket. He was sideways in my arms, eyes open, looking around curiously.

"He's up to about four hours at a time at night," I said. "I thought it would be so much worse." I leaned closer, afraid to say it too loudly in case I put a hex on it. "I think he might be an easy baby."

"Oh, you have no idea," she said, opening up her arms. "Not until you've lived with a colicky baby. Now go get yourself a glass of prosecco while I get some Dolan time."

The doorbell rang. It was Liza and Hugh. They were officially back together after more than a year apart. No one understood exactly why, except that Hugh had started dating and Liza hadn't liked it. John and I were laying bets that the reunion was temporary. They'd just returned from spending Easter week in the Bahamas with the boys. Hugh was glowing with love. Liza was glowing as well, although it could have just been her fresh tan.

She handed me a yellow silk bag. "It's a piece," she said. "From the Bahamas. I think when you turn forty, you need a piece."

I opened it up. It was an aqua necklace, made of chunky, uneven stones. It was the kind of jewelry I don't even look at in stores because I know I can't afford it. I put it on, and it was heavy, lustrous, and cold against my neck. Liza's taste is exquisite. I've never been anywhere with her when she wasn't the most stylish woman in the room.

"This is what the water is like in the Bahamas," Liza said.

"Oh my," I said, touching it. "It's spectacular. I feel like such a grown-up. It's too much, though, Liza."

"Well, this is a big deal," she said. "Your first birthday as a mother. You deserve it. And little mister is going to love looking at this. And playing with it."

I could picture that, so easily. And I could also picture the decades ahead, wearing my "piece" when I turned fifty, or sixty. Or seventy. It would look good with silver hair. The necklace was warming on my neck.

"Now where is that baby?" she demanded.

Dolan went from one friend to another, all evening. Every time Matt or I tried to put him into his bassinet, he cried. He seemed to want to be a part of the party. Eventually he fell asleep in Hugh's arms, head back, mouth open, arms flopped at his sides, and I went looking for Liza. She and Matt were out on the back steps, smoking. He tended to gravitate toward her in social gatherings. It made sense; she was so gracious, she always made an effort to make him feel comfortable. Some of my other friends were still stiff with him, maybe because they weren't sure what to make of him. Was he going to be a regular part of our social scene, or would he fade into the background?

Liza, it turned out, had some privileged information in this regard. She had mentioned Matt's and my situation to her psychic. Little Deer—who lived in Montana and could, for a fee, interpret Liza's cosmic state of being by telephone—had told her Matt and I "would be in and out of each other's lives for a long time." Liza had passed this information on to me very gravely, as if it were a state secret I might find helpful. "Well *yeah*," I'd said. "We're having a baby together. I think it's a safe bet we're stuck with each other on some level." But even as I scoffed, I appreciated that she was always kind to Matt.

She stubbed out her cigarette and headed back into the house when she saw me coming out. Matt and I hadn't talked at all that night, except about baby logistics. "Keep it light," she whispered in my ear as she went by.

I hugged myself against the chill of the April night. Matt was using his foot to prop himself up against the wall. He was drawing hard on his cigarette.

"Shouldn't be doing this," he said, holding the butt out to squint at it. I couldn't tell whether Matt actively tried to do a Marlboro Man thing when he smoked or whether it came naturally. Either way I knew it was fucked up to find it at all attractive.

"That Liza," I said. "She could talk Laura Bush into having a cigarette with her."

We stood there together, me upwind of his exhales. In my dress-up clothes and high heels, I felt for a minute as though I'd followed the cute guy at a party outside. I had to remind myself of the fact that the two of us had a baby inside, passed out in Hugh's arms. Our levels of intimacy didn't track like any normal relationship. He'd watched me being cut open five weeks before, but still, he often felt like a complete stranger. For instance, who was this guy who could have had sex with someone else a few weeks before? What did they talk about? What did they *do*? I couldn't imagine. Well, that wasn't true. I'd been tormenting myself with images of it. But I couldn't fathom it.

"Thanks for inviting me," he said. "It was a really nice party."

"I am still mad at you," I said.

"I know," he said.

"But I'm glad you came," I continued. "It would have been weird not to have you here."

"I would have felt weird not being here," he said. "I just want us to get along."

I think when you've been cheated on—although this wasn't technically cheating, what Matt had done—a lot of us believe makeup sex is, while not a cure, a fine Band-Aid for hurt feelings. At least that was the wicked thought chasing around in the back of my wine-fogged mind until Matt trotted out the Rodney King-ism. That's right: friends. We were going to be friends.

"Let's go for a hike tomorrow," I said. "I would really like to breathe some fresh air into my forty-year-old lungs."

John poked his head out the door. "Birthday girl, some of your guests are getting restless," he said. "Let's cut into that cake."

As I got ready to blow out the candles, I looked across at Dolan, awake again and now in Liza's arms, looking entranced by the flickering lights. That soft feeling I hadn't quite identified earlier was, I realized, a kind of contentment I had never felt before. The worries I'd had about turning forty had evaporated, and that astonished me. I'd gotten so used to worrying, I thought it was as permanent as a scar. I owed it all to Dolan. I smiled at him and then blew hard. Extinguishing forty candles takes a lot of work, even if all the angst I'd associated with the age was gone.

MATT AND I HAD WALKED only about one hundred yards beyond the Mt. Tam ranger station before Dolan started crying. It was overcast and chilly along the Marin coastline, and he was wearing a fleece hat that was about as tall as he was long. He looked like a really pissed-off court jester. Matt turned back to look at us. "Should we stop?"

I shook him off. "I'll nurse while we walk," I said, unsnapping the baby Bjorn and starting to reach up under my sweater. "We'll see if I can get him to sleep that way. If not, *you* can carry him until he falls asleep."

"I've got the pacifier," he said, holding it up. One of the dads we knew had told Matt that his primary function as a parent in the first six months would be to keep track of the pacifier. Matt had been very dutiful about that so far, but every time we put it in the baby's mouth, Dolan let it drop out again. I was fine with that. After my thumb-sucker experience, it would suit me if my child just skipped the oral stage entirely.

We entered the woods. The mist was so heavy it dripped off the leaves. Matt turned up his collar. I watched appreciatively as his long legs covered the ground. Some people can drive you crazy on a hike. I have one friend who has a peculiar habit of walking at a slight angle across my forward path. She's like a trucker butting into your lane on the freeway. My nephew picks up a stick and whacks every tree or bush that hangs close to the path. Adrian starts speed-walking at the thought of the beer waiting for him in the trunk of his car. Coming off a long hike with him on Mt. Whitney once, I ended up at least two miles behind him. I was so mad I barely spoke to him on the four-hour drive home.

With Matt, even though there were always at least five things about him that irked me at any given time, I found not a single fault with him as a hiking companion. We never disputed how far to go or how fast to get there. He was eager to explore, but he wasn't a dare-devil or a show-off. When he was at my house he frequently whined about being tired, to the point where I sometimes wondered if he suffered from depression, but on the trail he never complained.

As we left the woods and headed out on a grassy path that curved around the steep hillside, I wrestled Dolan back into the baby Bjorn. He was asleep now and barely stirred as I snapped him into it. "Do you have that blanket?" I asked. "I want to wrap it around him."

"How far do you want to go?" he asked as he handed it over.

"I feel pretty good," I said. This was my first attempt at exercise since the C-section. "I'd love to make it down into the enchanted broccoli forest part of the trail."

"Enchanted broccoli forest?" he said, looking at me blankly.

Of course Matt, with his limited exposure to all things green and leafy, didn't get the reference. I didn't even like vegetarian cooking, but Mollie Katzen's *The Enchanted Broccoli Forest* was ubiquitous in every shared household I'd lived in or visited in the nineties.

"The trees," I said. "They look like broccoli. Kind of short and then really bushy at the top. Forget about it. Haven't you ever been out on this trail?"

"Nope," he said. "Aside from those other hikes we did in Marin when you were pregnant, I haven't been out anywhere up here."

"Three years you've lived in San Francisco and you've never been out on Mt. Tam?" I asked.

"Not having a car, it's hard," Matt said. "None of my friends are into this kind of thing. I used to ask, but they never wanted to go."

When I was thirty, I had a car and my friends and I were out exploring California every weekend. I'd cross-country skied at Tahoe, camped in Yosemite, and done mushrooms on a full-moon hike through Joshua Tree. I had exactly the kind of youth I had wanted, short of sharing it with a soul mate (whatever that was). I was torn between feeling sorry for Matt for all that he hadn't had and frustrated by his own lack of initiative. He simply waited for things to happen to him, and I wondered: if I hadn't come along on that June night, would he still be unemployed, living off his parents, and killing time at Finnegan's Wake?

We stopped at a rocky vista point to take a few foggy pictures of each other against the mountainside. Then I handed Dolan over to Matt to carry, helping him adjust the straps of the Bjorn. "Not bad," he said. "I always thought guys looked so stupid in these. But it's kind of nice having him up against my chest."

"He's pretty snuggly," I said. "Especially when he's not howling."

I remembered Matt telling me, after his trip east at Christmas-time, how his friends with a newborn had handed the baby to him and how uncomfortable he'd felt. "It was weird," he'd said, sounding disgruntled to have been tested so. "I didn't know what to do with him. And he cried."

I'd said at the time, "I'm sure it's different when the baby is your own," but inside I'd felt a stab of panic. What if he wasn't capable? Now such doubts seemed absurd; he could be clueless about most practical matters, but his natural parenting instincts were solid. One night very soon after Dolan was born, when I was desperate for sleep, I had told Matt to take him out for a walk. Cool night air was supposed to help babies sleep. "Just fifteen minutes," I said. "If I even slept for fifteen minutes, I'd be more sane." I buried my head in the pillows and listened to Dolan's cry recede into the night, thinking, *I should have told Matt to dress him for an outing.* Then I went to sleep. I woke up to the sound of the cry coming back up the block. I stumbled out of my room and found Matt in the living room. He'd wheeled the stroller right into the apartment and was bent over the baby, unstrapping him. Dolan was wearing a hat and a coat and was swaddled in blankets. "You remembered," I'd said stupidly, thick and slow with my exhaustion. "Of course," he'd said.

I made Matt pose under the trees with the Bjorn on and took a bunch of shots to send to his mother and father. They'd have to like those. And Dolan would like them someday too. His very first hike, during which he'd gone a good six miles with only minimal complaining.

"We'll have to bring him back when he's older," Matt said as we strode down the path toward the car.

When the future came up, at peaceful moments like these, I felt jarred, the way you do after a minor earthquake in California, one so small it doesn't even shake a dish off a shelf, but it reminds you that fault lines are everywhere, under your feet. Our future was so ambiguous. I had no idea if we'd be taking family hikes together in a few years. We could both be married to other people by then. Or one of us might be married and the other might be resentful. There were so many possibilities, all of which made me nervous.

"Listen," I said from behind him. "I've been thinking we need a rule for dating."

"What kind of rule?" he said, with evident trepidation.

"I'm not planning on dating anyone anytime soon," I said. "But when it happens, I think we need to agree to tell each other about it once it becomes serious enough to mean we'd want to introduce that person to Dolan."

"Okaaaay," he said, still uncertain.

"Then, if you're still seeing that person six months *after* the notification, then an introduction is permitted." He kept walking. "Wait, would you stop?"

He obliged, but didn't look at me, choosing instead to adjust Dolan's hat.

"Does that seem reasonable to you?"

"Sure," he said.

"I just don't want a lot of random people traipsing through Dolan's life," I said.

Now he looked up at me, his green eyes serious. "I wouldn't do that."

"Neither would I," I said.

We continued on down the path, with me feeling vaguely unsatisfied with the conversation, but glad at least I'd got it on the record books. Later, though, when I loaded all the digital photos from Mt. Tam onto the computer, what struck me was how similar Matt's and my expressions were in the shots where we were holding Dolan. We looked like the people in that other emotional landscape, the one that Sam had made me think I wouldn't be privy to. Blissful. We both looked as though we were in love. Except not with each other, but with the baby. I knew I was going to keep being neurotic about the future—I couldn't help that—but we did have common ground. And values. That was a good start.

That's not to say I didn't still feel inappropriately, freakishly jealous. The next weekend, when he went to play softball, I went with him. I made him point out that girl to me. I shot daggers at her until she skulked to the far end of the stands. Then when Dolan let loose with an enormous poop, I put him down in front of the whole team, called Matt over, handed him the wipes, and made sure she saw us changing the vile diaper together. We might be a fucked-up version of a nuclear family, but nonetheless, that's what we were: family.

BENET SENT AN E-MAIL in the first week of May with the subject heading "Sperminator." When I opened it up, all it said was "I am." No *way*, I thought. Not another one already. His daughter Julia wasn't even two yet; Isabella was about to turn four. Was he going to have a third kid? I called him. "Yep," he said. "Wow," I said.

My father went into action immediately. He wanted to sell our family house to Benet and Beth. They'd need more space than they had in their cramped old brick house in the next town over. He was ready to move into a retirement community, only a few blocks away. Conveniently, he'd just managed to get my mother into the dementia wing there, so he no longer had to drive eight miles to visit her every day.

But he wanted our approval first.

"Just in case you yourself had some interest in ending up in the family homestead," he said on the phone.

"It's not that I wouldn't love living there," I said. I had sometimes had that fantasy. But that dream had nothing to do with the new reality. "But I certainly can't see it now. Careerwise. And I don't know that I could take Dolan so far away from his father."

"Well, I hope you're not going to be too beholden to that young man's choices of where to live," my father said. "You aren't married, after all."

"No," I said, not wanting to get into my complicated feelings. I *wanted* to be free to do whatever the hell I wanted. But my priority was Dolan, who deserved to be near his father. "I love the thought of Benet raising his family in the house," I continued. "But Dad, are you ready to move into some apartment? Aren't you going to go crazy in a retirement community? You can't stand socializing."

"I didn't say I was going to socialize," he said. "I'm just going to live there. And it's quite a civilized place. I won't take all my meals there, but the dining room is very good."

"Well, if you're really okay with it," I said.

"I am," he said. "I'm weary of all the upkeep."

"So when I bring Dolan home to visit you all this summer, will I still be able to stay at the house?" I asked.

"You'll have to ask Benet, but I don't imagine he'd turn you away," he said. "But to be clear, it will be *his* house. I know that may be strange for some of you."

"Better than it being some stranger's house someday," I said grimly. "You're not getting any younger."

"I'm getting quite ancient," he said. "But I'm in good health. Except for this aggravating hernia. I did tell you about that, didn't I?"

"Yes," I said. "I thought you were going to have it fixed soon."

"My doctor wants to do some blood work first," he said. "To make sure I'll be okay with the general anesthesia. I was a bit gripey last week so we put it off for week."

My father was the only person I knew in the world who used the term "gripey" in place of diarrhea. He was like the fussy old Victorian bachelor in Trollope novels. Except with six kids.

"I hope you're taking care of yourself," I said. "You were such a bag of bones last summer. Are you still so skinny?"

"I'm fine," he said. "I do miss you, though, my dear. And I'm eager to meet my namesake."

I promised to bring Dolan in August and signed off. The idea of home not being home anymore was unsettling. It was the only house I'd ever lived in as a child, other than the sabbatical years we had had in Europe. I always thought of wherever I lived in California as "my place." My true home had always been the white house on Columbia Avenue, with the black shutters and row of hemlocks out front. Would Benet want us to stay there at Christmas, or would that be too much for him and Beth to take on?

But at forty, wasn't it silly to be anxious about such things? Your childhood home was what you hung on to until your own life began in earnest, until you created your own home. I looked around at the

Alameda apartment. It did seem like a temporary stop. But I couldn't deny that my life *had* begun. Finally.

EVERYONE WHO CAME to see us told me that I was lucky, that Dolan was a breeze compared with a lot of babies. At first I had been dubious. One day I'd taken him up to Kir's house, and he'd literally cried for forty-three straight minutes on the drive, practically the whole way from Alameda to northern Marin. I'd wondered whether I should get off the freeway and nurse him, but I'd fed him right before I'd left the house. I eyed him nervously in the rearview mirror. The reflection was not pretty. His face was red, his eyes looked mad, and he was exhaling a steady stream of irate howls. They slowed only when he had to catch his breath.

A few days later, Sara stopped by for a visit.

"Sometimes he seems so angry," I said to her. "Really furious. I worry that he's an angry baby."

Dolan was lying on the changing table, blinking up at us angelically. He was doing what your car does when you bring it into the mechanic: refusing to misbehave in front of someone who might actually know how to fix it. I felt as though I was asking Sara to listen for some rattle that wasn't going to start up again until I was on the freeway home.

She laughed. "He's perfect, Mary." She was changing his diaper—gently, carefully, and so much more efficiently than I did. She cooed at him, and he answered her with a soft, cheerful noise. "Look how sweet he is,"

"But he cried about nothing on the way to Kir's," I said. "He was fed and changed and cozy and still he cried."

"He's just freaked out by being in the world," she said. "Think how nice it was for him in there, all warm and content. He didn't have to work for his food or do anything. Being out here is a major adjustment."

As for me, I hadn't been out in the world by myself since he'd been born. I'd had this expectation that motherhood would be something I'd need to escape from on a regular basis—like the friend who went out into the garage to do bong hits—but that wasn't the case. When I did finally go out by myself, around the time Dolan was eight weeks old, I felt strangely naked without him, as if I'd forgotten my purse. And my bra. And my shoes.

The occasion was the wedding of an old friend from Maine. The last time I'd seen him, we'd been commiserating over the perils of online dating. While I'd gotten pregnant, he'd soldiered on and made a match with a divorced mom with a young son. I made a mental note of that. It was good to be reminded that single moms still got laid and found love.

I didn't expect to see Nancy at the wedding. I'd practically forgotten she existed; she felt like a person from an entirely different life I'd led. A skinny Canadian with a thing for horses, she was one of those six-degrees-of-separation people. Not only had she been Benet's roommate in Washington, D.C., for a brief time, she'd also been mine. Our original common link was the bridegroom, but Nancy was also the person who had set me up with Peter. They had gone to college together.

At dinner, we were seated next to each other. I was wearing a loose-fitting top and had wedged myself into a pre-pregnancy skirt. After having been so eager to shed my capacious maternity clothes two months before, now I missed them.

"So, Mary," she said. "What have you been up to for the last fifteen years?"

Her Canadian accent always sounded slightly British, and her tone naturally veered toward the condescending.

"Mostly journalism," I said. "A lot of journalism. And I just had a baby."

"Oh!" Nancy said. "I had rather wondered. You always used to keep yourself so slim. I thought you must either be pregnant or have recently had a child."

Nice. I agreed that I was fat, although this was an overstatement. Of the thirty-five pounds I'd gained during the pregnancy, twenty had vanished right away. The other fifteen had not melted off during breast-feeding, the way so many relentlessly cheery veteran moms had promised me. That hadn't bothered me until now, but suddenly, out in the world again and facing down a part of my past, I felt fragile. All it took was a reminder of how I had once been a woman in control—a woman who kept herself so slim—to make me feel as though my life was now totally out of control. Because, as soon as I put it out there that I'd just had a baby, all the other old friends at the table wanted to know all about my husband, and I had to come clean about my lack of one, trying to joke my way through it. None of my jokes seemed funny, though. I thought I'd come to terms with the situation, but with Nancy next to me, I wished I had a slightly happier ending to crow about. I hated to think of her telling Peter: "I saw your old girlfriend Mary in San Francisco—looking *quite* plump—and she still seems to be having trouble finding someone who wants to be with her."

I wanted to be cool enough not to ask about him. I made it until near the end of the salad course before I brought him up. I had to. I hadn't heard a word about him in a good ten years.

"Oh, he's doing wonderfully well," she said, forking up a tomato wedge and a big leaf of radicchio. "He went to business school, you know."

I never would have pictured him at business school. It didn't quite fit with the holier-than-thou, save-the-world intellectual I'd been tortured by.

"He's quite successful," she continued. "He lives outside of Boston with his wife. I was just at his wedding last summer."

Well, I thought, at least it had taken him this long to find someone. Nancy could have stopped there, but she didn't.

"His wife is just lovely," she said. "He met her at our fifteenth college reunion. She's pregnant already. And they're having twins. She's due this fall."

I grabbed a roll and began buttering it lavishly. *Don't cry, you silly cow*, I told myself. *Who gives a shit if he's happy?* Nancy was still talking.

"You were quite devastated when he ended it with you, weren't you?"

Did I ever like this woman? I picked my way through dinner and then, as soon as the cake was cut, slipped out the door. I'd brought the breast pump so that I could stay late, but all I wanted to do was go home and see Dolan. There were fireworks in downtown San Francisco for an outdoor music festival, and traffic was backed up. For an hour, I sat in the car, creeping along, feeling forlorn. It wasn't as though I'd expected Peter to still be single. But the confirmation of his traditional married life was something else altogether. I couldn't stop myself from juxtaposing it with my own situation. I'm sure he'd had hardship. But his life sounded so much closer to that Christmas card vision I'd wanted. Probably there were no trailers in his recent past. My life seemed infinitely less photogenic.

At home, I shed my tight skirt, stripped off my nursing bra, which felt—and looked—like a torture chamber for breasts, and got into my biggest pajamas. Then I peeked in at Dolan, stretched out in the crib with his arms above his head. The night-light bathed him in a soft, lemony glow. He was so gorgeous and so vividly *there*. I felt better just looking at him. I reached down and gathered him up, putting his head against my collarbone. He stirred, sighed, and relaxed against me. I loved the weight of him, his undeniable substance. I carried him into my room and put him on my bed.

I loved to watch him sleep, although in truth, I fell asleep much more quickly when he was in the crib. My love felt so overwhelming, I couldn't get myself to quiet down about it; it was as if my heart were up on the roof of my soul, crowing about my beautiful boy, and the rest of me couldn't relax with all the noise. I just wanted to look at him. If I'd ended up with Peter, maybe I would have had his children, maybe his twins. But I'd never have had *this* baby. I stroked those wisps of blond hair, remembering my mother stroking my hair under the grape arbor and all the pain I'd felt. Then the bad night and the bad times it had evoked receded. I was back in the present with the boy I was meant to have.

CHAPTER 12

Careers

IN THE MOVIE REVIEWING BUSINESS, you can fall behind in a week. Some of the critics I knew never missed a screening. I wondered when they saw friends, when they cooked themselves a nice dinner, when they read books. We didn't say hi to one another as much as we checked one another's agendas and probed for opinions. "Have you seen *Super Size Me*?" someone might ask. "God, have you seen the new Lars von Trier film?" Or "Are you going to the press conference for the San Francisco International Film Festival?" If you answer no three times in a row, it's like saying, "I'm a part-timer, a mere dilettante."

I'd been determined to keep the dilemmas of my personal life separate from my professional life. I feared the perception that I'd become a slacker at work once I became a mother. Or that I'd lose my analytical edge and turn into a gush machine, weeping over any movie that tugged at the heartstrings. The assumption always seemed to be that lactating made you lax. Full-time jobs as movie critics are few and far between, and not only did I not want to lose mine, I wanted to be considered for better jobs at better papers. Dolan and I were going to need the money. As a single mother, I figured I'd look less desirable as a potential employee, with the assumption being that I'd always be running off to pick up the kid from day care, calling in sick when he was sick, and saying no to working late, weekend screenings, and traveling for assignments. Pregnancy had already cost me one Sundance Film Festival, and breast-feeding would likely cost me a second.

New releases were usually screened for critics in San Francisco at one of a handful of theaters, including my favorite, a private screening room on Market Street. But getting there was a half-hour schlep on the train. If I drove I might spend an hour sitting on the Bay Bridge. I'd often go to a movie at night and have to write my review by noon the next day. Matt was willing to babysit when I had evening screenings, but Dolan was such an easy baby that I fantasized about taking him to some movies during the day, at least for the first few months. That could cut back on day care costs. I decided to do a test run while I was still on maternity leave.

Off we went to a press screening of *De-Lovely*, the Cole Porter story with Kevin Kline and Ashley Judd. For my first trip back to my former and future stomping grounds, I'd worn white jeans, a pair of hand-me-downs from Sara that fit fairly well. I knew most of the critics in the room. Some of them came to ooh and aah over Dolan before the movie began. He was about nine weeks old and doing a lot of smiling. I sat down next to an older woman I'd seen a lot, but didn't know by name. She walked with a cane, which she had a habit of thrusting out with no regard for who might be standing in front of her. She was also a heavy breather. I figured anyone as physically irritating as she was couldn't complain about having a baby next to her.

Twenty minutes into the movie, Dolan stirred and the big woman harrumphed in disapproval. I put him on the breast and he started to suckle, noisily, more noisily than he had ever done before. I put a blanket up around his head, trying to muffle the sound. He pushed it away. Then, three minutes into the feeding, his bowels emptied. Loudly. The big woman shifted in her seat. I decided to ignore the full diaper, but then I felt a telltale wetness on my jeans. I picked the baby up and scooted out into the lobby. I was slathered in poop.

I cleaned him up as best I could, going through most of my package of travel wipes. I was hopeless myself, the white jeans now marred with a yellowish brown on both legs. "Fuck," I said. "Fuck

fuck fuck." I put him back on the breast and headed back into the theater. The big woman rumbled as we sat down again, but I wasn't about to give up so easily. Yes, Matt had said he'd stay with Dolan while I was at night screenings. But what if he backed out? I didn't have a choice between a career and motherhood; they had to work together. And selfishly? I just really wanted to see a movie.

Dolan kept eating. Then he paused, nipple in his mouth, and gave me a conspiratorial grin so wide I could see it in the dark, a *Hey, whatcha doing?* It was hard to be annoyed with him. I smiled back and stroked his cheek. Then he pooped again.

I whisked him back out to the lobby. As I changed his diaper, he started to cry. I knew how poorly the theater doors blocked out sound. I'd stalked out into the lobby myself on many an occasion to tell chitchatters to keep it down. I didn't want to piss off the entire jury of my peers. I tried to silence Dolan with my pinkie. He twisted his head away, wise to that old trick. I looked around frantically. I had to go back for my coat. I hadn't brought the stroller or car seat in with me from the parking garage, hoping to have less baggage to drag around for once. I could either carry him back in with me to the screening room or leave him wailing on the lobby floor. Then I remembered David's office. David was the projectionist. I saw him three times a week and I knew he usually left his door open. It was ajar. I gave a soft knock. It was empty. Perfect. I put Dolan down on the floor and pulled the door shut and ran back into the theater for my stuff.

When I came back, I put my hand on the knob. It didn't budge. I had locked my baby in an office I'd never even *seen* a key for. My crying baby. I ran back into the theater and leaped up the steps into the projectionist's booth. The reel was flickering away in front of the light, making its old-fashioned racket. I loved that noise. It usually made my brain launch into a silent chorus of "Hooray for Hollywood." This time I just scanned the room in a panic. No sign of David. He might be out front smoking a cigarette. I ran out of the building. Not there. What if he was at lunch? What if the baby had rolled over and put his face in some electric socket? I raced back into the theater and up the steps of the projectionist's booth. I opened the door again, letting out the *click-clack, click-clack* sound for all the other critics to hear. Behind me, there was a chorus of squeaks as people turned in their chairs to see what the fuss was.

Inside the booth, I saw a movement: David, the stealth projectionist, sitting in a corner.

"David," I hissed. "I've locked my baby in your office. Can you please come open the door?"

He looked bemused when he walked out into the light of the lobby.

"How did your baby end up in my office?" he asked, reaching in his pocket for the key.

"He was crying," I said lamely. "I was trying not to disturb everybody. I didn't know the door would lock when I closed it."

"Yeah," he said, looking at me, deadpan. "It locks."

When he opened the door, Dolan was lying just where I left him, on his blanket. He looked up, idly pumping his arms and legs. He had stopped crying. He was none the worse for wear.

"That's your last press screening, Bunny," I said, scooping him up.

SO I WOULD NOT be toting my child to screenings once I went back to work. Day care remained the most daunting part of this whole single-mother adventure. How would I pay for it? How would I find it? Given the horror stories I'd heard about waiting lists and all the terrible places your child could end up if you weren't a discriminating day care shopper, I thought I was doomed to months of searching. Instead, I went on a popular East Bay parents' network, posted a request to share a nanny, and had half a dozen responses by the next day.

This isn't bad, I thought, reading through an e-mail from a woman named Cindy whose Laotian nanny had been taking care of her little girl Stella for six months, with no ill effects. They already did "share care" with another family, but they had room for a third parent to pick up twenty to twenty-four hours a week. Splitting the nanny's fees came out to $8 an hour. Even with Matt chipping in (and I practically did a jig when he offered), I could barely cover the twenty to twenty-four hours a week that "share care" arrangement called for. But it was my best alternative. My boss at the paper had agreed to let me work Sunday through Thursday, so that on Sundays, Matt would be with the baby and I would write. I'd miss some Friday screenings, but that would be okay. That left me with ten work hours when I'd have to improvise, either by hoping the baby was napping so I could write, or working at night, after I came home from screenings. I thanked God I didn't have an office job that required me to be there every day looking smart and professional in pantyhose and heels. I worked at home in yoga pants and old sweaters most of the time. After maternity leave, I would be going into the office only once a week.

Cindy and her husband, Tim, lived on the other side of the island, a little more than a mile away. They had a spacious old house, and the minute I walked through the door I thought, if my baby spends the day hanging out in digs like this, he's never going to want to come home with me.

My other instantaneous reaction was that slim, pretty Cindy, an obvious type-A personality, would vet any prospective nanny within an inch of her life. I could coast on the coattails of her considerable research. I was learning one of the first rules of motherhood: make it easier on yourself whenever possible.

"I must have interviewed fifteen nannies," she said with a cheerful grin. "And we had one that I fired because I wasn't happy with her. So Ken has been great. She's got four kids of her own, right, Tim? Or is it five?"

"Her English is pretty good," Tim chimed in. "It's not perfect, but we can definitely understand each other."

"Yeah," Cindy said. "I do get frustrated with her sometimes, but in general, I think she understands. She gets nervous about money, though. So if you meet her and like her, I think you'll need to give her like a month's pay in advance."

Wow. Down payments on nannies. Who knew? I had heard the drill about holidays and vacation pay; just because you were paying in cash and there was no social security involved didn't mean you could treat your nanny like crap. Ken wanted a week's paid vacation and six holidays a year, including the Mien New Year.

"When's that?" I asked.

"Sometime in February, I think," Cindy said. "I'm not sure I want to agree to that, though. We didn't do it this year, and since it's not a holiday I get off from work, I'm not sure I want to give her that day off. Presidents' Day makes sense."

I nodded, overwhelmed. So much to negotiate. I was going to have my first employee, a complicated dynamic I did not particularly want to venture into. But if I was going to work, I was going to have to have someone working for me.

WHEN I WASN'T THINKING about my own career, I was fretting about Matt's. He'd held on to that temp job for nine months now, but he hadn't sought out anything more permanent, either at the bond trader or elsewhere. Every few weeks he'd mention that he needed to work on his résumé, and I'd offer to edit or proofread it, but nothing would come of it. I couldn't understand why he was dragging his feet. Even slackers had fantasy jobs, didn't they? It was almost as though he refused to believe that there was something else out there for him besides temping. Or maybe it was paralysis brought on by fear of failure.

When his mother came to meet her grandson, I decided to do some emotional reconnaissance.

"More tea, Katherine?" I asked.

She was staying with me. Matt had nowhere to put her up, and though we weren't technically in-laws, I wanted to pay her at least that much respect. Even if we barely knew each other, conversationally we could always fall back on the two subjects we'd quickly established we agreed upon: the awfulness of the Bush administration and how amazing Dolan was. But first there were things I wanted to know about her mystifying son.

"How about some more toast?"

"Oh thank you no, I'm fine," she said. She was holding Dolan and she was glowing.

"So," I began. "I was wondering if Matt had talked to you about his job search?"

"No," she said. "I've been waiting to see if he'd bring it up."

As Liza was fond of saying, that'll be the Eleventh of Never. I sipped my own tea. Dolan stirred. "Should I take him?" I said.

She smoothed his blanket. "There he goes," she said with wonder. "Back to sleep. He's so sweet."

"Does he remind you of Matt?" I asked.

"Not really," she said. "I don't see much resemblance."

She'd given me a photo album filled with pictures of Matt from babyhood through the Little League years. Even in the squalling infant, the adult Matt's strong jawline and expression were visible. I saw none of that in Dolan, who was as round-faced as I was. But their bodies? Long and lean and proportionally identical.

"I can't figure out what to think about Matt's career path," I continued. "Or lack thereof. It seems, since he's been at this company for nine months, as if he could probably ask for something permanent. I just want him to have health insurance, something that will lead him somewhere."

"Me too," she said, reaching out for a piece of toast.

"I'm worried about how long he's spent not working in the last few years," I pushed on. "Why is that, do you suppose?"

"I don't know," she said. "He keeps saying it's a bad market, that he moved out to San Francisco at the wrong time, just when the dot-com business was falling apart."

Nice excuse, Matt. Except that he hadn't come out to San Francisco seeking the dot-com dream, or any specific dream that I'd heard about. And there were always bartending and waitering jobs to be had while you planned your breakthrough. Finally I asked the question that had been eating away at me for months, the one that I feared was true.

"Do you think he's . . . lazy?" I asked.

Katherine answered right away. "No," she said, pushing her plate away from her. "I don't. When he was living at home and working at Home Depot, he worked long hours and he didn't complain, and everyone there was very happy with him."

She started to cry.

"I know people think I wasn't tough enough with him," she said. "But I tried. If I got mad at him about his schoolwork, that didn't help. And when he was living at home, after college, I told him he was going to have to pay rent. Three hundred dollars or something like that. Just a contribution. Charlie and I agreed. I don't think we ever actually asked for it, though. He was so insulted, so mad at us for asking."

I felt guilty for upsetting her. But I also felt some grim despair on my own behalf. He'd been a problem kid, and now he was my problem. Also, there were times when I felt as though he were my kid now, like when he'd show up at BART with a sack of dirty laundry he planned on doing at my place. Or at the grocery store, where I always paid and where he had a habit of disappearing down the wine aisle and then returning with some $28 bottle of wine marked down to $20, a bargain he didn't think we should pass up. He'd stand there with it, hovering over the basket, looking hopeful, and I'd remember myself at age eight, trying to persuade my mother that this was the day for the biannual purchasing of Frosted Flakes.

Maybe I could live with paying the tab at Safeway if when we got home he'd pop open that wine and then whip those groceries up into a sumptuous meal for me. But I had never met anyone who knew less about food and its preparation than Matt. He refused, entirely, to eat vegetables, although I was fairly certain he'd never tried any. This was the man I'd seen painstakingly pick a lettuce leaf off a cheese-burger, as if even a shred of it would cause him to spontaneously combust. Fruit he claimed to tolerate, but I'd seen evidence to the contrary just the day before when we'd taken Katherine on a picnic to celebrate Mother's Day. We had deviled eggs, chicken breasts, and potato salad. I'd also dipped strawberries in melted chocolate and let them harden. I had handed one to Matt.

"I don't like strawberries," he'd said, waving me off.

"It has chocolate on it," I said, not retracting the berry one inch.

He finally took it and cautiously bit into it. I watched him. Then he nodded.

"It's good," he'd said. "It doesn't taste like strawberry candy."

Could it be? Had I just given the father of my child, a thirty-year-old man, his first *strawberry*? I'd stolen a look at Katherine, wondering what they ate in that house.

Now, with his tearful mother at my breakfast table, I wondered, should I cut Matt free to sink or swim on his own? Everyone I knew was urging me not to engage in his problems. But I kept seeing such good qualities in Matt, glimpses that made me believe that with time and experience he could, if not outright blossom, at least be rooted in the ground. Not to offer a hand to my son's father would ultimately be bad for Dolan. To be so harsh that I drove his father away would be worse. But I couldn't turn into his enabler. I had to find a balance, and balances were not my specialty.

KATHERINE LEFT, and Miles and Frances arrived two hours later. Cleaning up the house for another set of visitors, I wept with exhaustion. I might be single, but somehow I still had four quasi-in-laws to impress. And I did want to impress them all, to make them think their grandson, though he'd arrived unorthodoxly, was going to be fine. No, better than fine. Someday, he'd be eating the likes of cream of asparagus soup with an asparagus flan floating in the middle. When he had teeth, he could follow that up with crab cakes drizzled with a yellow pepper aioli. Because that is what I, insanely, decided to make for Miles and Frances for their first meal in the presence of their new grandson.

If Matt had been happy to have his mother visit, he was beside himself over the prospect of introducing his father to his son. "This is your granddad," he said tenderly to Dolan as he deposited the infant in Miles's arms. Dolan lay there, sleeping, oblivious, while Miles chuckled over how little he was.

"What are we going to have him call you?" he said to Frances.

"How about Semi-Grammy?" she answered.

I smiled to myself as I headed back into the kitchen to attempt to make mayonnaise. I liked the way Frances's mind worked. It went a long way to diffusing the awkwardness in the air.

I did have a selfish interest in their visit. I assumed that Miles, having just met his grandson for the first time, would be inspired to take Matt off for a heart-to-heart about manhood and responsibility. This was how it happened in the movies, right? The father led his now-grown son off for a walk, and the boy came back a man. At the very least, Miles could convince Matt to ask to be made full-time at the temp job. Then I wouldn't have to.

One day we all met for lunch at the Ferry Building in San Francisco, where Matt worked. He was wearing a blue shirt and he looked very handsome, cradling Dolan in his arms. Pictures were taken, lunch was enjoyed, pleasantries were exchanged. Then I walked Matt back to the elevator. He and his dad had been out alone together the night before.

"So did you have a nice time with your dad last night?" I asked.

"Yeah," he said. "Hold on, I've got to go to the mail drop and pick up the afternoon mail."

"Did you guys have a heart-to-heart?" I asked, hopefully.

"What do you mean?"

"Well, like a career talk or anything," I said. "Did he give you any advice? Encourage you to try to go full-time at this job?"

Matt looked distracted, and somewhat annoyed by my line of questioning. "No," he said. He went off to get the office mail and I stood there, waiting for him. I was going to have to give him the father-son talk. Dolan started to fuss. I leaned against the wall and opened my shirt for him.

"Matt," I said when he reappeared with a heavy postal bag. "Let's talk."

"I've got to go," he said.

"Just give me a minute," I said, putting my hand on his chest. "Now listen. If this company is willing to keep giving you work and paying that temp agency a fee to keep you around, they are going to be willing to give you a full-time job. But it's not going to happen unless you ask. Nothing in this world comes to you if you don't ask."

He'd backed away from me, the mailbag slumped at his feet. His head was tilted back at an awkward angle, and I realized he looked like a boxer waiting for the next punch. His eyes were almost deliberately vacant, as if he'd pulled down the shutters so I couldn't see in.

"You have got to be your own advocate," I said, thumping his chest. Dolan was wedged between us now. "You have got to ask, do you understand? There is no reason in the world why they shouldn't hire you."

Then I thought I saw moisture in his eyes. He was *afraid*. My own eyes filled with tears.

"I believe in you, Matt," I said. "I do. You just have to ask. And soon. I'm going to pester you about it once a week until you do it."

"Mary," he said, helplessly. "Okay. Not this week. The boss is out. But okay."

I watched him get on the elevator, headed upstairs with the mailbag over his shoulder.

THE NANNY TOOK DOLAN out of my arms with utter ease on that first day I went back to work. He went to her without protest, too little to offer any reproach to his mother. I expected to cry. Everyone had told me that was unavoidable. As I drove away, I did shed a tear or two, but they were over the sadness of saying good-bye to this person I'd just spent eleven weeks with. I didn't feel guilty. There wasn't an option not to work. And the truth was I still needed my job for reasons beyond the paycheck and the health insurance. I was looking forward to writing again. With the exception of one short freelance piece I'd written while Dolan wailed from his bassinet, I had touched the computer only to e-mail photos of the baby to his grandparents and my siblings.

Motherhood is so often described as a transformative experience that when you're on the outside, looking in, you wonder if you'd even recognize yourself after it. I didn't expect I'd suddenly decide it would be better to stay at home with my child. But when so many moms are exchanging knowing looks in your presence and remarking on how they'd never thought this or that, but *now* it was all different, you start to question how you'll react in the face of this all-powerful motherness. What if the sea of mommyhood swept over me and writing about movies just became the obstacle between me and my true love? I was relieved to discover, as I got back into my job, that my transformation into a mother didn't subtract from the pleasure I had always taken from work. I think I'd assumed that something good had to go away from the old life, to be replaced by the everlasting glory of the baby, because life was supposed to be about balancing. You didn't just suddenly get *more*, I reasoned. But actually, you did.

In the end, the adjustments in my working life were all logistic. I used to breeze out of the house with only a notebook. Now the breast pump went with me everywhere. I was supposed to send Dolan off to day care with at least two full bottles, and it took a long time to fill them. So I learned to use the pump while driving, plugging it into the car just like the phone charger, and then sticking the suction cup up under my shirt. On the freeway, this was easy, although in traffic, I'd find myself anxiously edging up to avoid being right next to any other drivers who might notice that woman cradling her breast in the black Jetta. The noise the pump made was mournful and dreary, like the sound life-support machines always make on TV shows, but with attitude: *Whha, whha, you're, whha, whha, such a, whha, whha, cow!*

I'd always had a highly scheduled workweek, but now, with the structure of day care pickups and drop-offs, and only two full days a week when Dolan was with the nanny, there was no room for error. On the upside, with less time to write, there was also less time to procrastinate, and I got sharper and faster out of necessity. All in all, I thought that first month back at work went fairly well—tiring but not unbearable.

Then Marlon Brando died. It was late on a Thursday night, but the news didn't start to break until Friday morning. Technically this was my day off, and I didn't have day care. When my editor, Karen, called, I was still in my bathrobe, worn out from successfully making it to all my screenings that week and hitting all my deadlines.

"No choice, sweetie," Karen said when I reminded her of my Sunday-to-Thursday workweek. "Not when the executive editor wants it. And after Katharine Hepburn, there's no way he's going to take no for an answer."

I always liked Katharine Hepburn. My mother and I had watched *Bringing Up Baby* together every time it showed up on television. But now I'd forever associate her passing with the day I peed on a stick and said no to an assignment.

"Can't I do it Sunday?" I asked. "We could run it Tuesday. It would be more thoughtful then. He was one of the greatest actors that ever lived. I want to take some time with it."

Karen wasn't just my boss, she was one of my best friends, and I knew she hated telling me it had to be done that day. And by 4 P.M. It was going on the front page. I couldn't call Matt; the bond trader didn't give its temporary employees days off or sick leave.

I started to cry. "I'm a single mother. I'm breast-feeding. I have no day care."

"Look, you've just got to rally," she said. "It doesn't have to be a masterpiece. Just get it done."

This felt like a test. I checked the clock: 10:15. I had five hours and forty-five minutes.

I put the baby down on a blanket and dug furiously through my DVD collection. Somewhere I had a copy of *On the Waterfront*, the movie that first showed me what Brando was all about. He has a scene walking through a park with Eva Marie Saint. She drops her glove and he picks it up, but instead of handing it back, he begins to play with it. He's so manly that the white glove looks ridiculous in his hand, almost as if he's mocking her. But it's also flirtatious, as if in touching her glove, he's touching her. She reaches for it, sort of ineffectually. He ignores her and eventually wedges the dainty thing onto his own meaty hand. Her character is flustered and so is the actress; Brando was improvising. That bit of business with the glove made all the difference in the scene. I played it twice, my bathrobe open, Dolan on my breast.

"Go to sleep," I told him. "Just fall asleep on the nipple. Chew it if you want. Just sleep, I implore you."

Instead he grinned at me, his hand patting my breast. His face was so eager. His eyebrows would go up and he'd pump his legs as if he had something very important to say. He reminded me of the baby pictures I'd seen of Benet.

"Let's try this bouncy seat thing, Bunny," I told him. The bouncy contraption seemed very high-tech. This was my first attempt to get it up and running. It had headphones, which I didn't understand. Could it play music? I wasted seventeen minutes turning it upside down and inside out and looking for a screwdriver to pry open the tiny door on its underside, which turned out to merely house the batteries.

Four hours and fifty-two minutes. Dolan started crying.

I brought out the blanket with the pop-up toys on it and moved him to that. Then the phone rang.

"Hey," Karen said. "Listen, deadlines are going to be really tight today. There's a homicide out in East County, and Metro is going nuts about it. So we're talking more like 3:30 instead of 4 for moving your story over. Can you do that?"

"Oh, sure," I said. Four hours and nineteen minutes. Newspapers are not just the first draft of history, they are the rough first draft of history.

"One more thing," she said. "Don't forget *The Godfather*." She lowered her voice. "You know they all get hard for *The Godfather*."

"They" were all the male higher-ups, who liked to debate the greatness of Robert De Niro versus the greatness of Al Pacino over lunch in the cafeteria.

"Check," I said.

I needed to spend some time looking at Brando. I had *The Godfather* and *A Streetcar Named Desire*. But something was missing. I threw on my yoga pants, my nursing bra, and a T-shirt, and then wasted four minutes looking for my clogs. Dolan had resumed crying in the living room. He stopped briefly while I was driving to the closest video store on the island—eleven minutes!—then resumed just as I walked up to the counter, the handle of the car seat resting in the crook of my arm.

"I need *Last Tango in Paris*," I said to the clerk. "Can you tell me if it's in?"

He looked me up and down and then turned to his keyboard. "Did you say *Save the Last Waltz*?" he said.

"*Last Tango in Paris*," I said. "You know, the one with the butter."

"I don't know that one," he said. I hated big chain video stores. He went tap tap tap on the keyboard. "Oh," he said, looking from me to Dolan with some concern. "We don't stock that here," he said. "It's considered pornographic."

By the time I got back from my trek to the independent video store, where Bernardo Bertolucci is not considered a pervert, I was down to three hours and twenty-nine minutes. On the upside, Dolan was yawning. All that yelling had worn him out.

As I watched chunks of the movies, I pored over the indexes of books from my film library. Whom could I quote? What did Pauline Kael say about Brando? Manny Farber? Agee? Wait, was Agee already dead by the time Brando came around? Or just thoroughly pickled? God, pickled and done with film criticism before Brando became "Brando." And then dead at forty-five. Now there's a cautionary tale. What about Ebert? No one cranks out more copy than that man.

As Karen said, the story didn't have to be a masterpiece, but it was so hard for me to let go of that aspiration. I wanted to make people pause in their morning ritual and stay with my story from beginning to end. I wanted to offer them some insights that they wouldn't get otherwise. This wasn't just some movie star; this was the greatest natural talent of the twentieth century, the man who inspired a veritable acting revolution. I wished I'd read that fat Brando biography sitting on my desk in the office, eighteen miles to the east.

The story ended up getting great play on the front page, with a huge photo of young Brando smoldering in black and white. I'd spent plenty of time on the front page in my hard news days, but for a critic, there isn't much cause to get on page one, so this was a nice reward. You have to be pretty jaded to feel nothing when you see your name on the lead story of the day. I was pleased. But at what price? In order to get it done, I had actually wheeled my child into the living room and closed the door, leaving no one but my two alarmed cats to supervise him. In the course of the day I'd been a puppet, at the whim of my employers, feeling barely adequate as a journalist and less than attentive as a mother. I took out a blue marker and wrote on my desk, just below my keyboard:

JULY 2, 2004: ONE YEAR FROM NOW, IT WILL BE DIFFERENT

I had no idea how it would be different, or how I would make that happen, but somehow, I had to. I felt somewhat embarrassed by my own gesture; it seemed so desperate for self-empowerment, so unlike anything I would normally do. But what was normal anymore? In my frantic search through the movie books, I'd come across one that quoted Pauline Kael, a single mother herself, saying that there was nothing like the need to support a child to jump-start one's ambitions. *I hear you, sister,* I thought as I picked up the DVD boxes that were littered across my floor.

PART II

One Year from Then

CHAPTER 13

The Red Cable-Knit Sweater

DOLAN RAN AHEAD OF ME toward baggage claim, his long pale legs churning in his little denim shorts. At seventeen months he was so fast and so eager to run that in public spaces—shopping malls, department stores, sidewalks—he made me nervous. But the airport in Portland, Maine, is so small that I knew he couldn't get very far. Plus I felt sorry for him; cooped up in a plane coming across country once again. He'd made five round trips between San Francisco and Portland in the last year, and at this point, he probably knew exactly where he was going. He certainly would recognize our big red suitcase if and when it rolled out onto the baggage carousel. When I caught up with him he was standing transfixed, watching as a lone bag trundled round and round.

"Ours is coming soon, Boosty," I said. The harder I fell in love with him, the more ridiculous the nicknames got. Then again, Benet survived a childhood of being called Bendy-boodledy-do. I laced my fingers through his tufts of blond hair, longer now and getting wavy. "But where's Aunt Wibby?"

He grinned up at me. "I'm going to see Wibby," he said in the reverential tones he usually reserved for discussing ice cream and cookies. The adoration of Wib had not skipped a generation. Benet had three kids now, and with the exception of his newest, baby Sid, who was only six months old, Wib's nieces and nephew would happily deck one another just for a chance to sit next to her at the dinner table.

It was almost midnight before she pulled the Subaru up to the sidewalk. I'd had time to change Dolan's diaper, reclaim our bag, wheel it out front, and compulsively check my cell phone at least four times to see if she'd called. It was like her to be late, but not when it came to picking up a toddler coming in on an evening flight.

"Look how much Dols Pols has grown," she said, stooping down to admire him. He played bashful, hiding his head against my thigh, and my hand went automatically to the top of his head. This was my mother's gesture, one that I could feel her doing with me and picture her doing to Benet, another beautiful blond boy. "Are you going to say hi to Aunt Wibby?" I asked him.

"I so happy to see you," Dolan said.

She stepped back, hands over her heart. "I'm so happy to see you too," she said, then looked at me. "Slay me."

"I know," I said. "That's his latest thing. I can't get over it."

After I'd convinced Dolan to climb into his car seat and we'd belted ourselves in, she nosed the car forward. "Now which way should I go?" she asked. Wib has been to the Portland airport plenty of times, but she still approaches a trip there with a blend of urgency and fear, as though she's been wrested out of her art studio, dropped into a Cambodian minefield, and told to leave with a piece of bamboo, three blades of grass, and a rare breed of toad.

"Just forward," I said. "Follow the exit sign."

"But if I want to go to the highway?" she said. "Is this going to take me there?"

"Yes," I said. "So how's Dad doing today?"

"Not so good. This way?" I nodded. Dolan was grumbling from the backseat. He was both bored and tired, which I was learning was a deadly combination in a toddler. "That's why I'm late actually. Bodwell called and said he's having some serious respiratory distress."

She took a deep breath. "They think he might not make it through the night."

. . .

WHEN I WROTE THAT MESSAGE to myself on my desk, I had been thinking, of course, of the ways I would make my own life different. By this I meant better, more sane, more directed. I hadn't factored in all the events or circumstances that might happen and would make my life different but would not be of my own doing.

A mere twelve days after I'd taken Magic Marker to unfinished pine in that desperate bid toward self-improvement, *different* had begun. That was the day an e-mail arrived from my father mentioning that some tests he'd had in advance of a minor hernia surgery showed an unusually high white blood cell count. This was the crack that by the end of the next week had become a chasm: a diagnosis of chronic leukemia. Since then he'd developed a mysterious throat condition and his weight had dropped to ninety-eight pounds. Then he'd had a heart attack. I couldn't keep track anymore of all the times he'd had pneumonia. Wib could, though; she'd become the unofficial keeper of all information related to the tenuous medical condition of Edward Pols.

How astonishingly naïve it was for me to feel I'd beaten the biological clock. A much bigger clock had taken over my life.

I STOOD BEFORE a low-slung, fifties-style brick building, with long wings that poked into the woods. It looked like the junior high I'd attended, which was just a few blocks away. Dolan was safely asleep back at our house. I corrected myself. Benet's house.

Everything felt terribly familiar. There was the hum the street lamps let off and that dim, yellowish light they cast over the almost empty parking lot. Half the cars in the lot belonged to members of my family. As I stood looking at the bright fluorescence inside, even the smell of the thick, warm August air seemed the same. I looked at the keypad that after-hours visitors had to use to get into the building and reached my finger up to punch out the code. I needed no reminding of what it was.

I walked past the paintings and photographs of boats and Maine seascapes. "Not unpleasant," Mum might have said. I invoked that thought every time I walked by them last August, trying, I suppose, to hear her voice in my head, trying to make it seem like not such a bad place for her to be living. *Dying, you mean.* Down the hall was a print of Casco Bay, the waters of which had been rendered an unfortunate yellow. Liza and Hugh own the same print, and every time I see it in Hugh's kitchen, I want to ask him to put it away, down in the garage, anywhere, just somewhere I won't see it and remember her hands grasping fruitlessly at nurses, blankets, life.

I walked past the reception area, the bathroom where I cried so much the summer before, past the lock-down hallway where my mother took her last breath, eleven months ago and, what, five days? I turned left down another hallway, and there I was, in the place where I knew my father would soon die.

Where would I want him to die? Nowhere. Never. But failing that, in some beautiful place, I suppose, looking out over the ocean maybe. Not one of these sterile, dingy institutions with their bad lighting, plastic food, and depressing noises. Not even his still new apartment, which was just on the other side of this retirement community. This place had everything, the soup to nuts of the end of life, from independent living to the last circle of hell—the nursing home. It was all connected by covered walkways. When he first moved in, we'd joked about how he'd be walking over in his pajamas to visit my mother in the dementia wing. Now here he was himself, in the rehab wing, with me hoping for small compromises. May my father, if he must die here, at least have a single room. He dislikes roommates more than he dislikes the Yankees.

He smiled a ghastly smile when I came into the room. Age and illness can distort even a sincere smile into something frightening. He was a skeleton, gray, sweaty with fever, sitting up and struggling to breathe. They'd given him antibiotics to fight the pneumonia, but there wasn't much else to be done. Benet had just gone home, but Wib, Alison, and Katy were all there. It was getting close to 2 A.M., and the late hour showed on their faces. Alison got up to give me a hug. She smelled like sweet soap.

"His fever is down a little," she said.

"He definitely sounds better than he did an hour ago," Katy said as she hugged me. After all we had been through in the last year, the little college girl who had smoked me out of house and home had grown into someone calm and competent.

I was wired from the trip and the realization that I might have come just in time, so I offered to stay with him through the night. Dolan would be fine at Benet and Beth's house without me; in fact, he'd be thrilled to wake up to the happy clamor of his cousins.

Dad told me he was tired.

"I bet," I said, smoothing his forehead. "It's a lot of work, being so sick." Such a nice brow, above that beaky nose and those bushy eyebrows. As a teenager I used to tease him about how long the hairs would get, until he handed me a scissors one day and asked me to trim them. I remember being taken aback, to realize he would actually listen and want to change something that, in fact, I didn't want him to change at all. He was just as he was meant to be.

I bent to kiss him. "You can just rest, Dad. You've been fighting for so long. You've been a phoenix already."

"That's what my doctor calls me," he said, hoarsely.

"I know," I said. "You surprised us all."

He had. On the day of my mother's memorial service the previous fall, he'd been rushed to the hospital, and I'd stood, watching him being unloaded from the ambulance in the chill of an autumn night, thinking, *He's going, right now, he's going.* That was the night of the heart attack. He'd barely recovered from that when his doctor had said his throat condition was so poor he'd never eat normally again, and suddenly the man who could tell you, in vivid detail, about the meal we had at that corner bistro in Arles in 1973, how the lamb melted on his tongue, how the roast potatoes crunched under his teeth, how soft and sweet the accompanying garlic cloves were, was subsisting on some horrible concoction of liquid nutrition poured into a feeding tube in his stomach. Then, miraculously, he'd rallied. His throat seemed better. He'd tried eating again. Not long after his eighty-sixth birthday, they'd been able to take out the feeding tube. Alison had gone back to roasting chickens and mashing Yukon Gold potatoes for him. That's when his doctor made her famous pronouncement about how he'd risen from the ashes.

He'd even put on his cap and gown and marched at Katy's Bowdoin graduation that spring. As I sank into a chair next to his bedside, I remembered pushing Dolan's stroller through the crowds, scanning the gray heads in the faculty section for him, then the elation of finding him in the front row, looking tiny and thin, his hair nearly white, his crimson hood a stark contrast to his black robe. He had squinted against the bright day. I waved but couldn't get his attention, so I took out my camera and got a few shots of him listening to the speaker. Once he noticed me, he took off his mortarboard and tipped it in my direction. Always the courtly gesture. My eyes filled, and as I turned my head to surreptitiously wipe the tears away, I saw Benet only a few feet away from me, with his zoom lens trained on Dad. If he was the phoenix, we were like feverish bird-watchers, recording every glimpse of a creature we knew to be rare, bordering even on extinction. That had been only three months ago.

He wasn't sleeping now, but his breathing seemed easier. He looked toward the ceiling but not actually at it. I'd spent enough time at his bedside in the past year to know he wasn't about to launch into any big speeches.

"You're looking well," he said. His voice was very hoarse.

"Weight Watchers," I said. "I've been trying to get into shape before the fellowship. I want to impress all my fancy new colleagues."

He smiled, then fell silent.

In the year of things becoming different, this was the only thing I could claim responsibility for. The previous winter, I'd applied for a competitive fellowship for mid-career journalists at Stanford—something I'd been fantasizing about for ten years at least. On the spring day I'd learned I'd be spending a whole academic year there, studying film and whatever else I pleased, and getting paid for it, I don't know who was happier, my father or me. I think that having spent his whole working life living fairly comfortably within academia, he saw it as the perfect refuge for a single mother with a baby still in diapers.

In classic father-knows-best fashion, he'd told me he hoped I'd use the year to "get your head out of the movies." All these years of my being a movie critic, and he still regarded my profession as somewhat lamentable. I remember his tone when I called him once between my second and third movies in a single day: "*Another* movie?" he'd said. You'd think I'd just announced I'd escaped Dunkirk but thought I might head off to Paris to see what the Germans were up to there.

"I just got the course catalog," I told him. "I'm thinking about taking Italian. It's about time I actually learned how to speak another language."

Even as I said it, I realized how ridiculous it was to be trying to please him with hints that I'd be getting my head out of the movies. He was way past that. I reached out for his hand on the bedcovers. "Is there anything I can do for you, Babbo?" I said. "Anything you need at all?"

"I should sleep, I suppose," he said, looking at me anxiously, as if sleep were a dangerous thing he might not emerge from.

"That's a good idea," I said. I got up to look for a cloth to wipe his forehead with. There was a black tube of Chap Stick standing on the bedside table. I held it up. "Shall I put a little of this on your lips? You seem parched."

He blinked his assent. I smoothed it on, and as I did so, remembered doing the same to my mother's dry lips the summer before and having the desperate sensation that I was not doing it right, that what I was doing was too little, that there was really nothing I could do except sit there and tell her that I loved her.

THE TIMING HAD BEEN BIZARRE. I'd brought Dolan, an infant almost six months old, home to meet the family. We'd stayed a week, and then we'd gone back to California. Two days later, my mother had had a stroke. Everyone assumed it was another minor setback, but then the doctors realized she couldn't swallow anymore, not food, not water. She had a living will, so there would be no intervention. "The nurses are of the opinion that the end will come in a week or so," my father's e-mail had said. I was on a plane with Dolan the next afternoon.

My mother's room had been in the Alzheimer's/dementia wing adjacent to the rehab center. The layout was essentially identical to my father's, the view into the leafy woods, mostly birch, about the same. I'd watched him sitting next to her bed in the same sort of chair I was sitting in now. During those long days and nights at her side, my siblings and I had either been overwhelmed with emotion or cracking jokes with each other, trying to lighten the weight of a situation we'd never been in before. My father had just been getting ill then, and when he'd come to visit her, he sat silently at her bedside, but very alert, as if he were waiting for her to speak to him. When I looked into my mother's eyes, I saw only dark confusion and beseeching, as if she wondered whether we might show her the way out. He looked as though he understood exactly what she was asking, and it seemed he could answer her without words.

They'd told us it would take five to seven days for an old woman consuming nothing to die. After five, she seemed no closer to death. The seventh was her eighty-fourth birthday. We told ourselves she'd go then; the nurses had all talked about those mysterious tricks of the internal clock, how people hang on until they reach the signpost they've been waiting for, be it a special day or the arrival of a longed-for visitor. But the next morning, her vitals were still strong. We'd basically taken up residence in the room. There were copies of the *New Yorker* everywhere, packages of half-eaten Oreos, reading glasses, bottles of Coke with one tepid flat inch in the bottom, sweaters tossed over the backs of chairs. It was hot and muggy outside, but in my mother's room, the air conditioning droned on perpetually. Dolan slept in his stroller or in my arms. Alison held his head to my mother's face and let her smell his milky baby smell. We took turns in groups of two. We didn't want her to be alone at the end. We didn't want her to be afraid.

Her physical endurance seemed to baffle the hospice workers, who had started to ask if there might be some unfinished business she needed to settle. But I knew she wanted to go, had been ready for years. Three years before, as she was being driven to the hospital after she'd broken her hip, she'd asked Adrian to hit her over the head.

"I can't do that, Mum," he'd said to her.

"Just put me out of my misery," she had pleaded.

When she awoke from that hip replacement surgery, she seemed disappointed to still be alive. The anger I saw in her eyes then was the most cogent emotion I'd seen from her in years. She never walked again. We were almost grateful; at least then we were finally able to persuade my father it was time for a nursing home.

IT WAS DIFFERENT WITH MY FATHER. He never wanted to die. Alison had told us that his doctor had given him two choices the week before. Either he could work harder at his physical therapy, since the rehab center was for people who were supposed to be getting better, or he could be discharged and go home to his apartment, where he could have hospice. Those were his choices. He told the doctor he'd take hospice *and* get better.

He had things he wanted to do. The previous fall he'd finished a poetry manuscript, elegant, formal poems that knitted across the breadth of his life, from his days as a young man in World War II to his years as a caregiver to my mother. He'd enlisted Wib as his literary agent, and he'd been pestering her to track down editors at the few publishing houses that still bothered with poetry. She'd walk into his room and he'd ask if any mail had come from the editor of the *Sewanee Review*, or from an obscure contest out in Michigan that sounded promising. He'd also finished a new philosophy manuscript, and he wanted her to do something with that too. He was a man who was not yet done with life, even if, it seemed, life was done with him.

My fierce father. He'd finally fallen asleep. By dawn I could tell the antibiotics had staved off death, at least for another day. I kissed him as he lay sleeping and then drove home to Benet's and climbed the steps to the Barn Chamber. When we were young, this had been our playroom, a big old barn with walls blackened from some long-ago fire. My father had had it redone in unstained pine planks and turned it into his lair, the room we were supposed to stay out of, where he did his thinking and writing. He'd built himself a platform bed out there. Now this was where Dolan and I slept when we were visiting.

Dolan was sprawled in the portable crib. Last August he'd looked so small in it; now he had to lie diagonally across it to be comfortable. I took him into the bed with me and tried not to look up. There was a series of knots in the pine on the vaulted ceiling that had caught my eye last summer. A nose, two eyes, a mouth open in anguish, a face that looked like my dying mother's, some silently howling Irish banshee. I knew I was supposed to be brave, but it was too much that it was August again and someone else was dying.

TWO DAYS LATER, when I brought Dolan by to see him, my father was in the hallway. The fever had broken and his physical therapist reported that he'd been up and down the corridor twice. She seemed pleased. Worn out from the exertion, he sat there in his gown, scrawny legs stretched out in front of him, and smiled at Dolan. As his grandson played at his feet, he reached out his hand, slowly, carefully, to touch that flaxen head. Dolan stole a glance up at him and smiled back. He was young enough to not be afraid of an old, sick man.

My father was Elizabeth Dolan Pols's firstborn. When he was about Dolan's age, she had dressed him in velvet and ruffles, like Little Lord Fauntleroy, and taken him to get his portrait made. He posed for the camera with chin in hand, looking languid and pretty. I used to pore over that photo when I was little, amazed at how girlish my father had been. His hair was as golden as Dolan's. I wondered if my father thought of that when he touched Dolan's hair.

At least they knew each other a little, these two. Admittedly most of their time together had been at bedsides, but I felt grateful for even that. My mother and Dolan had barely passed each other in the world, meeting each other just a week before her stroke. Wib and I had gone over to the nursing home together. We'd found my mother hunched over in her wheelchair in the television room. She wasn't watching the screen; such things didn't seem to interest her anymore. Nothing really seemed to interest her. I held Dolan in my arms, like a present I was proud of, the best present I would ever give my mother. We'd pulled up chairs and sat down in front of her.

"Hi, Mum," I'd said, feeling weepy already. "How are you?"

She'd looked at me consideringly. No matter how long it had been since we'd seen each other, she usually reacted as though I'd just been there a few minutes before and what was I making such a fuss about? She was often confused about how old I was, but she always seemed to know me. The same was true for my siblings. My father was the only one she really brightened up for, and she'd hold his hand while he visited. In my whole life I never remembered seeing them hold hands. "I don't believe she said 'I love you' as much in our whole marriage as she has in the last couple of years," he had told me once.

"Fine," she said. The blue of her eyes had faded. There was a curious mix of vagueness and intensity to them; she'd study our faces, not as if she was trying to figure out who we were, but, rather, as if she was determining the content of our souls. Under her questioning gaze, I often felt as though I'd done something wrong. There always seemed to be disappointment in those eyes. I didn't know if it was real or my own projection that the woman who loved to travel, who was always plotting her next trip, hated being trapped in this place.

I'd held Dolan up to her. Her long finger came out, gnarled by her arthritis, and touched his perfectly rounded cheek. His eyes were open, wide and blue.

"Here's your newest grandson, Mum," I had said, feeling my voice start to tremble. "My baby. This is Dolan Edward Pols."

Her eyes were only on him. She stroked his cheek again. "He's beautiful," she said, her tone serious and somber. There were tears in her eyes. I had put him into her arms for just a few seconds and she held him, but for the first time ever with a grandchild, she seemed too timid to relax and enjoy the weight of a baby in her arms.

We had sat awhile longer. Visits to dementia and Alzheimer's wards were like entering black holes. The time there seems endless, yet you never felt as though you've been there long enough. I remember feeling that way as we left.

I was right. It never is enough.

THE SIGHT OF MY FATHER actually out of bed and walking should have been encouraging, but he'd had so many ups and downs in the past year that I'd learned not to be optimistic. I'd also learned that the only thing that really made me feel better was to be with Dolan, who was so vibrantly, definitively alive. Later that afternoon, I was sitting out in the yard at Benet's house, watching Dolan chase the cat, when Beth's red minivan pulled in. While she extricated Sid from his car seat, Isabella and Julia came tumbling out and began making their way to us. Isabella was wearing a very ladylike floral dress and a stern look that was pure Benet.

"Don't chase Tishy," she admonished Dolan. "She doesn't like that."

Julia chimed in with her high, breathy voice. "Leave Tishy alone."

Dolan stood stock-still. He glared back, a look I recognized from the mirror. But he didn't say anything. He was smitten with Isabella and more than a little scared of Julia, who policed his every movement in the house, lest he touch anything of hers. Together they were confounding, both fascinating and daunting. I thought back to how much I'd wanted a girl and realized that if I'd had one, the three of them would have been like a keg of dynamite.

Isabella softened. She was fond of her smallest cousin. She was five, after all, the mature one in this group. "Do you want to go on the play structure?" she asked, coming over to take his hand. He allowed himself to be led away to it. It was an impressive thing, ladders, swings, a slide, and monkey bars. We never had anything remotely like this as kids.

Benet came walking across the lawn, carrying a couple of glasses with limes in them.

"Stimulating beverage?" he asked.

That was our mother's expression, used just about every afternoon. Usually she meant something caffeinated, though.

"Don't mind if I do," I said, taking one. I sniffed it. Gin. "So, does Dad think this play structure is an abomination?"

"I thought he might grumble but he hasn't said anything," he said. "Could be that he just didn't focus on it. It's not like he's been out in the yard much since we moved in."

We sat and watched the kids playing. Dolan was climbing a ladder.

"He's coordinated," Benet said. "Clearly not from his mother."

"I just wish he'd got Matt's skin instead of mine," I said. "He's doomed to a lifetime of sunburns."

"How is Matt?"

"He's okay," I said. "He doesn't like his job, but at least he's employed."

Matt's temp gig at the bond trading firm had evolved into a full-time job with benefits shortly after my mother died. His work there was mostly clerical, and I knew he found it unspeakably dull. But we both knew he needed to get something solid on his résumé, and I for one was grateful that he'd been steadily employed for this long.

"I think he's looking forward to me being on the fellowship so that things will be less stressful in general for us," I said. "And he's planning a trip to Baltimore with Dolan in October, for his mother's sixtieth birthday."

"Sixty," Benet said. "Jesus. Adrian will be sixty in two years."

"Matt has no idea how lucky he is to have such young parents," I said. "It's good for Dolan too; he ought to have those grandparents around for a long time. Meanwhile, here we are, you and me, in our forties with little kids. Just like Mum and Dad."

"Yep," he said. "We're old."

My parents had planted most of the trees in the yard: the hemlocks behind us, the row of pines in front of us, the lilac bushes that filled in the borders. It felt so comforting to know that a whole new generation was going to grow up there. "It's good you bought the house," I said. "You going to turn into the Wag or the Grinch?"

The Wag was our nickname for our mother. It had become a proper noun, a verb (to wag, as in, to behave like our mother), and an adjective.

"Bit of both, I expect," he said.

THE NEXT DAY, the head nurse said she no longer felt my father could make informed choices about his own health care. We decided that there would be no more antibiotics after this cycle. It was inevitable that the pneumonia would return, and when it did, it would be allowed to do its work. "Pneumonia," my father used to say. "The old man's friend."

When my mother was dying, it hurt tremendously—much more than I thought it would, given how desperately I wanted her to be free of her misery—but we'd still found ways to laugh. We grew punchier with each day that passed. She'd gone nine days without hydration or nutrition, then ten days. Suddenly it was September. The Republican Convention was in full swing in New York. The Red Sox were at the end of a three-game series with Anaheim. My teenaged nephew Matthew sprawled on the empty bed across from my mother's, watching the game on the tiny TV that came out from the wall on a retractable arm, like a piece of dental equipment. Wib had pulled a chair up to the light and was turning the pages of a magazine. Dolan was lying in my arms. He'd finished nursing and was staring up at me, reaching for my face and hair. Benet had come into the room. "Hey," he said. He nodded at Matthew. "Anything happen while I was driving over here, Termite?"

"Nope," Matthew said. "Still winning."

"Could be three for three," Benet said. "So you're not watching the convention?"

"Like we're not already depressed enough," I said.

Benet stepped to Mum's bedside. He stroked her forehead. She didn't stir.

"Hi, Mumma," he said. "You want to watch some Red Sox?"

He turned her TV on. George Bush's face filled the screen. Benet stepped back and listened.

"Why are you turning that douche bag on?" Matthew said. As a teenager, it was his due to be surly, but in this case, his tone of voice was dead-on.

"If this doesn't kill her, nothing will," Benet said.

"We can't have her die with that voice in her ear," I said. "That's just cruel."

"And if there is an afterlife she'll be pissed at us when we all get there," Wib said.

"You're right," Benet had said, turning the channel to the Red Sox.

On the twelfth day, Alison announced she couldn't go back anymore. We'd been summoned to the nursing home the night before for what we thought would be the final good-bye. We'd all wept and stroked her and told her how good she'd been to us. The space between her breaths seemed to be growing.

But my mother had rallied once again. While Benet and Beth were putting their brood to bed, the rest of us gathered gloomily for another dinner of Thai takeout at Alison's.

"I'm done," Alison said. "I've said good-bye. I just can't do it again."

Benet strode into the house with a wineglass in his hand. With his house and Alison's only a block apart, mugs of coffee and glasses of wine went back and forth almost every day. "Okay," he said. "Who is going to go over there and put a pillow over her face?"

"I think it should be Wib," I said. "No one would ever suspect her."

"But Alison is so *efficient*," Wib said. "No fuss, no muss."

"It should be Adrian," Alison said. "He's the oldest. Let's call him and tell him to get up here."

Then we laughed until Wib snorted and Alison said she was

about to wet her pants and even Benet, who smiles sparingly, had to walk out of the room to cover his grin.

But with my father that week, even if we could have thought of anything funny to say to one another, none of us could have laughed.

BENET AND I took Isabella and Dolan on an outing to an island in the New Meadows River. I felt guilty leaving Dad's bedside, but we had been there for four straight days, and it seemed safe to steal away for an afternoon. I was desperate for Dolan to get some fresh air, and especially to give him a chance to be in a boat. He was practically panting by the time we got down to the dock. He sat with his face thrust into the wind, chin buried in his life jacket—which he found aggravating but a price worth enduring for this ride—hair blowing back from his brow, eyes squinting into the sun, a look of pure bliss on his face.

Maine is known for its beautiful, rockbound, dramatic coast, but what I love most about it is the crazy length of it. We were a twenty-minute drive from home, but as the crow flew, it was only a few miles away. If you stretched it all out, they say, took the whole state and unpeeled every inlet and neck of land as if you were yanking the wool out of a sweater, you'd have a coastline as long as the whole East Coast. Hidden in there, in the folds of that sweater, are all the secret inlets, the forgotten islands, the coves that families believe belong only to them, not realizing that the kayaking couple from Freeport who come in the early morning and the teenagers from Bath who come at sunset with a case of beer also imagine that this place is theirs alone.

All I could think, looking at all this beauty, was that my father would never see this coast again, never walk through woods that speak, in their small scale, in their bent shapes, of winters past and future springs. He left New Jersey and came to Bowdoin College on a train in 1949 and thought that the pretty campus and the quiet town and this spacious, uncrowded state would be a good place for his growing family. And it was, not just for us, but for him.

In the summers of my childhood, we'd escape the humid heat in town—"hum-dee-dee" my mother called it—and drive down Harpswell Neck. We'd go past houses that Dad would say they could have bought, back when they were new here and shopping for their future, for $10,000. We'd pass other houses, ramshackle ones, set far back from the road, with overgrown lawns and dirt driveways, and Dad would say, thoughtfully, "You could do something with that house." We'd look hard to see if there was a telltale light coming through the woods behind these houses, the hint that there might be the much longed for ocean frontage back there.

"Why don't you write a book that people would want to read?" I'd say, from the backseat. He'd written three dense philosophical books already. Every time I came upon one of them, I'd leaf through it, looking for something I could comprehend, and each time, be utterly disappointed. "What about a detective story? Something like Lord Peter Wimsey. Then we could have our own beach."

In the meantime, we had Lookout Point. There was a small hotel, and a big dock for the commercial fishermen to use, but there were no restaurants or lobster shacks. It was just a place to go to swim. Other Bowdoin professors used it too, and we'd run into them sometimes. "There's Harv with another pretty young thing," my mother would say darkly. "Probably a coed," my father would mutter.

There were two islands to the left, reachable at low tide if you didn't mind walking across the squelching, sucking mudflats. The beach—no sand, only pebbles and craggy rocks—was on the other side of a small promontory attached to the land by such a slender spit that you could pretend it was an island unto itself. We'd park our big old silver Mercury on the dirt, just above the tide line, marked by piles of blackened, dried out old seaweed, and then we'd head up the promontory.

Prickly blackberry bushes acted as the gatekeepers to the point, but also, as they thinned out up the hill, provided sanctuary in which to change into your suit, with Mum holding up a towel. The path was narrow after that, and the rosebushes and wild grasses grabbed at you as you went by. When you arrived at the clearing, you had reached what we thought of as the true Lookout Point, a grassy clearing at the top, crowned with a clump of gray rocks. Sitting there, you felt as if you had all of Middle Bay spread out in front of you. I thought this was the most beautiful spot on earth. We always paused there before taking the footpath that wound down the hill on the northernmost side of the point and onto our beach.

"Maybe we'll find your sweater today," I'd say to Dad. He'd be wearing shorts, cut from chinos and hemmed by my mother, and one of the sporty white shirts he owned for tennis.

"What sweater?" he'd say, absently looking out at the bay, his hand protecting his eyes and saluting the sea at the same time.

"The red cable one," I'd say. "The one Mum made for you. That you left on the island."

"That was a long time ago, Buglet," he'd say. "That sweater is gone." She'd be nearby, kerchief tied over her head, denim skirt on over her suit, a tote bag filled with our towels in her hand, looking out at the bay from the other side of the point. "Let's not speak of it in front of your mother."

There's a picture of him, looking barely thirty-five, in that red sweater, at the helm of the little sailboat he had, for a brief time, in the early sixties. I think it was the last sweater she ever knitted him; she was so indignant over its loss. Legend was that he'd left it on an island he'd walked to at low tide. I liked to think it was one of the small islands off Lookout Point, because I could look at them and imagine my father, amid the glory of a summer afternoon, maybe watching birds, forgetting the time, and then having to swim for it, too swept away by his surroundings to realize that he was leaving the red sweater behind. My father was always the kind of man who loved days more than things. After my last visit, just two months before, he'd sent me an e-mail with the subject heading "Miss You." "Here I have been slightly compensated for your absence by a totally splendid day," he wrote. "Cloudless, crisp but warm, mild breeze, salubrious air."

He signed off with "It was marvelous to have you and Dolan Edward here."

I had smiled at his obvious enjoyment of seeing his own name reflected in Dolan's. Then I tucked the note away, not realizing it would be the last I'd ever get from him.

WE WERE SUMMONED home early from the island. The end was near, and this was not another false alarm. We gathered at his bedside, tentative about our good-byes, for how did you know precisely when to say them? I remember little about the first few hours, except that they were awful. I remember that at about 10 P.M., Benet brought Dolan to me because he had woken up and cried out for his mummy. He leaned against Benet's shoulder, looking very blond and, at this hour, dazed and discombobulated. But when he saw me, he smiled and held out his arms. "Mommy." It was a plea, a greeting, and a reminder of my future all at once. I was a daughter saying good-bye, and a mother saying hello. I took him from Benet and brought him out into the hallway.

"Let's go run around," I told him.

"Let's do that," he said. He was just shy of a year and a half, and his predominant approach to all offers that didn't involve eating or going to sleep was eager enthusiasm.

There was a big meeting room just down the hall, and we went in there. The chairs were pushed up against the wall, stacked in threes, as if to say, *No party here.* The fluorescent lights were dimmed. I put Dolan down on the ground and he toddled off. I couldn't get over the way he moved, pumping his arms at his sides as if he were running a marathon. I thought of my father, striding purposefully down the town common, swinging his arms.

"Ball," Dolan said, triumphantly, emerging from a dark corner with a huge yoga ball, just like my birthing ball.

"How about that?" I said. "Can you kick it?"

He tried and knocked himself over. He lay there, giggling. I picked him up, lifting up his shirt to kiss his stomach. "How can you be so beautiful?" I said.

"Ball," he commanded, suddenly serious, wanting to be put down.

We rolled the ball back and forth to each other, five times, ten times, twenty times. He was having a good time, but I knew he should be home in bed, and I should be next to my father.

"Sweetness," I said. "Are you tired?"

"No," he said. But his hand went up to rub his eye. The telltale sign, the one that never lies.

"I'm going to take you back to Uncle Benet's and put you to bed," I said. "But first let's go say good-bye to Babbo."

"Babbo," he sang out as I carried him toward the room. "Bye to Babbo."

It was the first time he ever said the name we use for my father. I took him into the room and he said it again, cooing it out in long syllables. Then I took him home and waited for him to fall asleep so I could get back.

The nebulous area between pain and snatches of sleep lasted for hours. Whenever Dad woke up, he tried to get out of bed. He fought death. He looked in our eyes, whispered a few things. There was an agonizing torrent of vomit, an expulsion so violent it seemed to be death itself. I used a suction tube to try to clean out his mouth while the nurse changed his soaked gown. After that, they offered morphine and we responded eagerly, yes, please, as much as you can give him.

We said, "We love you" a hundred times over. Wib, trying so hard, as she always does, to give comfort, walked over to his apartment and brought back his poetry manuscript. One of his newer poems, "The Winter Hexagon," was about death, the way he used to imagine it, under the winter constellations, as a young man, and the way he imagined it as an old man. We ringed the bed, Alison on his left, then Katy, then Wib, then me to his right; I read his words to him, trying not to choke over them as they warred with the tears in my throat, in my heart.

> When I was young and full of careless vigor,
> I often thought the end of life should be embraced
> in some old pagan way one's heard of; go forth
> to meet with dignity what must in any event come.
> The Winter Hexagon then seemed a refuge: walk
> out under it as though it were a canopy:
> Walk till you can walk no more, or perhaps go striding
> along on your battered old skis till you can
> stride no more. Choose some great hard-frozen lake
> somewhere in Maine; or perhaps those blueberry barrens
> on the great ridge out Camden way
> either way you'd pass without knowing that you passed.
>
> How was I to know that such pagan resolve
> requires strength and vigor—the same qualities
> that make life persist? I have seen loved ones wane
> till no purpose was left, even as I now fade:
> no trace of any pagan resolve at all.
> Nonetheless, immortal hexagon, I revere you still,
> For you are there in glory whenever at the proper season
> I look towards heaven—shall be there in glory
> When, weak or strong, my time shall have come.

He closed his eyes and a single tear rolled from each eye. Alison reached out and put her hand over his heart, then grabbed mine and brought it there as well. She collected hands, Katy's and Wib's, until they were all stacked on his heart, beating slower and slower. Then he was gone.

We dressed him in a white shirt and chinos. Alison combed his hair. We picked up his possessions and put them in a box. Reluctantly, we went home. There was nothing else to do.

MY MOTHER HAD DIED without any of us there. She too went in the middle of the night. It was the thirteenth day after her stroke. Wib saw her last, a few hours before the end. She'd worn us down. A nurse had walked by her room and noticed that she had stopped breathing. They called us, to come say good-bye to her body. I woke to Benet's touch on my arm and had risen in the dark, throwing on my clothes quietly so as to not wake Dolan. Wib was waiting downstairs for us and we'd driven over together. I had dug out a pair of old pajamas for Mum to be cremated in, pale blue polar bears on flannel. I'd bought them for her a few years before, at Nordstrom, in the era when gifts had started to seem pointless but I hadn't been able to give up the idea of trying to reach her with some small pleasure. Bowdoin's mascot was a polar bear, and my mother had loved her college. I could still see her in my mind's eye, standing next to my childhood self, passionately chanting, "Go U Bears" at hockey games.

In death, the beauty of her high cheekbones and her elegant nose was more obvious. I stroked a long shin and remembered those slim legs, kicking up through the water at Lookout Point, the tips of those sneakers sticking out of the water. Her swimming costume always included the sneakers, a modest suit, and often a cap. I'd snuck peeks at those legs then. They were covered with varicose veins, the fascinating but horrifying evidence of her motherhood.

"Do you want to help me wash her?" the nurse's aide had asked. She was sweet. They were all sweet.

I'd hesitated for a second. So private, my mumma, would she want this? Then I remembered how she'd talked fondly about the way of Irish wakes, how loved ones prepared the body for viewing. "Yes," I'd said, and taken the warm cloth from the nurse. We moved around her body, tenderly taking off the institutional gown, slipping the pajamas up over her hips and around her arms. I straightened her top, then slid my hand onto her belly. I laid my hand on a surface once soft, now practically concave after weeks without food. Her skin had felt dry and cool already, papery and wrinkled. I put my other hand under my shirt and felt my own belly. I stood for a minute, touching the twin sources of my being and Dolan's.

THE MORNING AFTER my mother died, we had had something to do. We had to go tell my father. We drove over to his apartment and waited for Alison, then all went upstairs together. Benet had a key. He went in first and shook Dad's shoulder gently to wake him. He blinked, looking from face to face, knowing without asking. We waited in the living room for him to get dressed. When he came out, wearing a navy blue blazer, a pressed shirt, and chinos, I had ached for him. He had just been diagnosed with leukemia, he was so sick, so tired, yet he dressed like a gentleman to say good-bye to his wife.

I had walked behind him on the pathway between the apartment complex and the nursing home. He'd lost his strong gait, his purposeful stride we'd always called it, and shuffled now, listing to one side. I thought of him in his fifties, coming into the room while my mother and I were watching *The Carol Burnett Show*, focusing on the screen for a few minutes, then leaving the room in an imitation of Tim Conway's old man shuffle. The space from joke to reality seemed outrageously short.

More than sixty years they'd spent together, had known each other, had loved and tolerated and, I was sure, sometimes hated each other. He stood looking down at her body and began to recite part of the Requiem Mass in Latin, words from their Catholic childhoods, words learned in Newark, words from long before any of us. He clutched a napkin in his hand, spoke softly, in his solemn teacher's voice, and as I watched, again from behind, his thin shoulders shook inside the wool and he began to cry. And we all cried again, with him, in the quiet room that smelled nothing like my mother, or anything alive.

He had touched the hands of the nurses on the way down the hallway afterward, let them hug him, big women embracing a frail old man. We were walking away from my mother, leaving her to be taken away by strangers, a lonely journey to the crematorium. She would soon be gone in every sense. No part of her left, just scattered reproductions. The dimple in Dolan's chin, the set of Katy's eyes, the high curve of Alison's cheekbones, Wib's mouth. I stopped at the nurses' station and asked for a pair of scissors.

Her hair was like fine steel and curled, as it always had, at just the right place. Variations on white and gray, wrapped around my finger. "I hope this is okay, Mumma," I said, as I snipped a curl. *Your corporal self, soon to be gone*, I had thought. *I must have something of you to look at. I must have something beyond photographs and memories. I must hold on to something.*

WITH DAD GONE, there was just a vast emptiness. There were no ceremonial good-byes needed. I took nothing from his body, no lock of hair. My mother had been absent in so many ways for so long that her death had somehow seemed more acceptable. But he had just been there. He had just been talking to us. He had just been our father.

We set out to clean his apartment, to banish all the remnants of his illness. It was Alison's idea. "If I don't do it now," she said, "I am never going to be able to do it." I took my cue from her. My own choice would have been to wallow, but I was grateful to be given direction.

There were so many bottles of medicines that didn't help at all, or helped just a little, or never even got tried. Cases of Ensure. A fridge full of ice cream for smoothies never made. Under the bed, crumpled Vanity Fair napkins, left by a man too fragile to find a waste can. On the desk, the first few lines of a new poem, in black ink, in his chicken scratch, slanting across unlined white paper.

Alison moved with her usual efficiency, sweeping things into plastic bags, piling up food and toiletries that could go to Benet's house or her place. I went slower, looking at things as I went, try-ing not to cry over the family mementos he'd chosen to put on the shelves in his bedroom.

"We might as well do the closets," she said when she finished with the kitchen. "Matthew might like some of his jackets. And his sweaters. Maybe even some pants, although I suppose they'll be too short."

You realize, when you're packing up the life of someone you loved, that much as you'd like to devour it whole, preserving it for-ever as it was, a museum to that person, it just isn't feasible. No one has the room for the museum. Moreover, the meaning dissipates. His selection of narrow-tipped felt pens in a cup means something only in the context of his being alive, because he might return to them, use them to write you a note. With him gone they'd become just a motley collection of pens with and without caps, mixed in with some paper clips that will never be used, and a grimy plastic pencil sharpener that came out of a set you got for school back in 1975.

I got a suitcase out of the closet and opened it up on the bed.

"You should take this," Alison said, coming out of the closet with the Pendleton wool robe we bought for his birthday a few years ago. "You masterminded this purchase."

"I did," I said. My mother had bought him a Pendleton robe long ago, sometime in the seventies, and he'd worn it until it was in shreds. I'd gotten the idea to get him a new one a few years before while I was in the Pendleton store in Park City, Utah, killing time be-tween movies at the Sundance Film Festival. I'd made a quick round of calls to my siblings, assessing interest in a group gift. Now I took the robe from Alison. I'd wear it. I'd write reviews in it, sitting at my kitchen table.

Then I went into the closet myself and stood in there, looking at the neat piles of sweaters on the shelf. There it was.

"IF YOU LOSE THIS ONE," I said, lecturing as I stitched away at the last seam, "I'll have your head." The wool was a deep berry red, the color of the raspberry in the basket that makes every other berry look less ripe, less enticing. "Two of these in one lifetime would be too much."

"I'll guard it with my life," he said, amiably. He nibbled on a cookie and drank watery tea. We were in Venice, in a rented apartment with high ceilings and what seemed to be bearskin blankets on the beds. The balcony looked out over a canal in Cannaregio. It was March of 2000 and Dad had finally been coaxed away from my mother's side. Benet was taking care of her in his absence. We had been trying to persuade him to enjoy life a bit more, to get away from his responsibilities here and there.

"Now this one isn't going to be enormous, is it?" he asked.

I shot a glare his way. The last sweater he watched me finish was for Benet. I had less control over my gauge back then, and as I had laid it out on the kitchen table to piece it together, it did seem to cover the distance from one side of the table to the other. My father had sat next to Wib, both of them silently watching like jurors. His hands were crossed in his lap. Mirth played around his mouth as he watched me realize how huge the thing was. Then finally he couldn't contain himself and he'd said, "I hope Pavarotti likes his sweater." He and Wib had dissolved in laughter.

"If anything, it might be a tad small," I said, making the very last knot at the armpit. I held it up. It was the nicest sweater I'd ever made. I had been knitting frantically, all the way from California, through Paris, racing to finish before I saw him in Venice. Instead I'd had to settle for finishing it halfway through our stay.

The trip to Venice had its complications. For the first few days, Dad was ready to go early in the morning, happy to be visiting old haunts, making delighted noises over the Bellinis at the Frari. But he had not come with a warm enough coat, and he complained of the damp air. He got a canker sore. He wanted to stay in the apartment instead of going sightseeing. On our evening constitutionals, Wib and I walked along the Fondamente, speculating that he felt guilty, coming without Mum. Not that he could have brought her. Not that she would have even known this place that she had loved.

One day as he was gazing out over the canal, looking wistful, I asked him if he was homesick.

"No," he said.

"You seem sad," I persisted.

"I'm sad because I don't want to go home," he said gravely.

Who could blame him? Going back to dirty diapers, my mother's occasional tantrums, and her incessant repetitions? Meals he prepared himself, for the two of them to eat at a table once filled with children, now so empty? His energy sapped at the end of the day, when what he wanted to do was write poetry?

"Okay," I said, holding the sweater out to him. "Let's give this a try."

"Ah," he said. "So warm." He went to look at himself in the giant gilt-rimmed mirror, threw his shoulders back, and struck a pose. "I shall be the grandest tiger in the jungle."

THIS RED SWEATER was not lost on an island's ledges. This red sweater was not forgotten on a day that started out chilly enough to beg for wool and ended in the kind of warmth that made a plunge into the northern waters palatable. This sweater, made with heathered wool from Maine sheep, saw only four winters with its rightful owner. On an overcast August day, it came back to its maker. She shed tears on it, folded it into a suitcase, and thanked whatever twist of fate it was that brought her a son who might someday run across a Maine beach, wearing his grandfather's sweater.

CHAPTER 14

Orphan Girl

IT WAS MY JOB to call Adrian in Virginia to tell him how Dad had left us. He listened to all the details of that last night without interrupting. We both knew there would be no more fresh stories about our father.

"I can't believe I never get to talk to him again," Adrian said. "Not for the rest of my life."

The enormity of it, the end of a conversation that had gone on for forty years for me, almost sixty for Adrian, rose up in front of me like a rogue wave and slapped me down. If I was lucky, I was about halfway through my life now. Half my life without the people who made me.

"We're orphans now," Adrian said.

Orphans were not adults; they were children in books. They were despairing and alone, ragamuffins in the street clinging to a single penny, or Sara Crewe huddled in her unheated attic, trying to be optimistic. But I couldn't shake the label Adrian had given us. I said it to Benet later, in the kitchen as I was putting on the kettle for afternoon tea. I could hear Dolan chattering away with his cousins in the front room.

"Adrian says we're orphans," I told him.

He had been standing over the table, reading something in the *Times Record*. He glanced up at me. He looked weary.

"We're not orphans," he said dismissively, dropping the newspaper and moving to the window. No one scoffs quite as effectively as Benet. "We can't be." He put his elbow on the sill and looked out toward the poplar tree in the neighbor's yard. There had been a beautiful elm next to that poplar tree when we were kids, two tall, elegant trees, growing companionably together, but long ago it had been felled by Dutch elm disease. I'd never be able to look at that poplar without remembering the elm.

The kettle came to a boil. Benet was still looking out the window.

"I suppose he's right," he said quietly.

I WAS FORTY-ONE YEARS OLD, and as far as I was concerned, the three most important events in my life had happened in the past two years. I'd had a child in circumstances I never would have predicted. I'd lost my mother. Then I'd spent a year watching my father die. Geographically, I'd lived in California during that time, but mentally, I'd been in Maine, following every twist and turn in his health saga. I had my siblings, but now there was no one left on earth who remembered my beginning. No one there from those first moments. No one there in the secret time when I was *made*. If the beginning and end of life are the bookends, one was now vanished and the other loomed larger. Any book on such a shelf would be about to fall over.

I'm not sure there is anything new to be said about loss. But when it is new to you, you form the words because you have to. You feel yourself delivering dialogue from a bad movie, saying things that sound as though you must be reading off a Hallmark card, because they *are* just that trite—but feeling as though at least these words might help you start bailing the boatful of your own tears, because no matter how bad it feels, it is worse than you thought. I had always been an imaginer of the darkest sort. In my childhood I would sometimes kill off Benet in my head and then try to picture life without him. When I'd seen enough to believe I did not think my own survival would be possible without him, I'd turn off this stream of thought and return, somewhat guiltily, to real life. Back then, I had never done this with my parents, perhaps because they were such a given. Now I knew their absence. It was a loneliness of the sort that must happen when you've been lost in deep woods for days.

Yet even when I was most mired in sadness, I looked at Dolan and thought, *Yes. But.* Had I been looking backward at my life with my parents and forward at nothing but myself, I would have been crushed. That was the self I felt truly sorry for, that alternate Mary, the one who stayed home that June night and drank more wine with John and Liza and fell asleep on the couch and then went on with the life she'd been living. Not the Mary who had blundered into a productive one-night stand and had, unwittingly, provided a sort of salvation for herself.

Dolan was so *essential*. There had been so many times when I had watched death circling my loved ones and put my face down into his hair and smelled life and had known that time had somehow been on my side just as much as it had been against me. I had spent so long obsessing over the biological clock, aware, yet at the same time ignorant on some level, of the power of the bigger clock, the one ticking away on my parents' lives. That I'd had Dolan when I did now seemed like a miraculous stroke of luck.

When it came to Matt, though, I admit I did not always feel lucky. I swung between gratitude that he'd stuck around, that his participation in Dolan's life had ceased to be a variable and become a certainty, and trouble accepting that there was this person in my life whom I could find no easy description for. Lover? Off limits. Friend? Not quite. Little brother? Disturbing on *so* many levels. Co-parent? "Co" implied an equal share, and in my mind, Matt didn't pull enough weight to qualify. I suppose I thought of him as my quarter-parent. To be more accurate, that was what I had decided he was. From the moment I'd told him I was pregnant, my goal was to make it possible for him to be a vital part of his child's life. But his purpose in *my* life was far from resolved.

• • •

WHEN I GOT BACK to California after my father's death, I had a week to pack up my apartment in Alameda and get it ready for my subletters. I had movies to see and reviews to write because the fellowship money wouldn't start for another month. And I had to get us moved into the apartment I'd rented for the year down at Stanford.

"I just can't believe how much I have to do," I said to Matt. I was sorting through Dolan's toys looking for things to leave behind, trying to pare down, to live a simple life for the year.

"It'll all get done," he said.

"I don't want to be organized and energetic," I said despondently. "I just miss my father."

"I know it's hard," he said. "You'll get it done, though. You always do." He picked up an enormous talking frog I'd just tossed in a cardboard box destined for storage. "Wasn't this from Aunt Rose?" he asked. "Did we ever send her a thank-you note?"

"We?" I said. "We?" I stared at him until I had his attention. "No, we didn't. We got sick of sending thank-you notes to your family because we are not your wife. Have you ever sent a thank-you note to anyone in my family?"

"Okay," he said, dropping the creature back in the box and holding up his hands against me. "Okay, okay, okay."

The lights on the frog's chest began flashing. "Hello," it chirped brightly. "I'm Baby Tad! Do you want to sing a song with me?" I left the room. Matt had missed his cue, the one where he was supposed to come and put his arms around me and let me cry on his shoulder. He was always missing his cue, but then again, he'd never asked for this part. He'd had a front row seat on the spectacle of parental sickness and death I'd endured and he had given me sympathy, although mostly when I was so desperate for it I asked. Because he was the main witness to my grief, it was easy for me to start expecting him to say the right thing. But I was not his wife. He was not my husband. It wasn't his fault that his heart did not break for me. He didn't even know my parents. He had no idea how great they were.

Matt had met my father just once. I'd asked him to come home with me for my mother's memorial service. With my father's poor health, I had worried we were running out of time for introductions. However unusual the situation between Matt and me was, it seemed only right that my father should meet the man who had fathered his grandson. Nonetheless, I had felt chagrined, traipsing into my father's hospital room with a stranger, the man I had sex with two hours after I met him and accidentally made a baby with. This awkward introduction had seemed an affront to my father's dignity, already compromised by all the indignities of serious illness. But he looked at Matt with interest. Matt was holding Dolan against him, and as always, he looked just right holding Dolan. He looked like a man who found something that belongs to him and will never let go.

My father surveyed Matt and then spoke slowly, raspily.

"You're a fine-looking fellow," he said.

Another man might have joked. Another man might have made small talk. Matt acknowledged the statement with a nod and a slight smile. It was, after all, a statement, not a compliment. It said, dryly, *I see now why my foolish daughter took a fancy to you. She always liked pretty things.*

I think it's safe to say my father never hoped for a happy ending for us. Individually, certainly, but not as a couple. "Good," he'd said a few months later when I told him Matt and I would never get married. "Of course, if he marries someone else and has more children," he added, "he may lose interest in Dolan. He's young."

"He could," I acknowledged. "Although I don't think he will." I couldn't make promises for Matt then or now. It is not my place and I'd hate to be wrong about it. But there have been only a few times when Matt has been absolutely emphatic with me. Once was when I had suggested that if someday he had a wife and other kids, a "real" family, Dolan would be less significant to him. He had answered immediately, and with unwavering conviction. "That will never happen. I will never lose interest in him." This he said before he ever looked into those blue eyes and long before Dolan started stroking his hair and saying, "I need my daddy."

There was a soft knock on my door. I hadn't felt up to going back to Matt and the talking frog and had flopped down on my bed instead.

"Yeah," I said, reaching for a tissue. "Come in."

Matt had his über-neutral face on, the one that says, *Hello, stormy sea, I am a placid pool and I'd like to stay that way, so can you keep your waves to a minimum?*

"Are there any boxes I can carry out to the garage?" he said. "Anything I can get out of your way before I go to sleep?"

I'd bought a twin bed for Dolan's room the previous winter. It was intended to be Dolan's whenever he was ready to graduate from the crib, but in the meantime, it was where Matt slept when he stayed over. I'd gotten sick of coming home from night screenings to find him in his makeshift bed on the couch. The sight depressed me, reminding me that he still didn't have a car and that he was still in the same lousy apartment in the city where we'd conceived Dolan. The twin bed was serving as an hourglass for us; I told Matt he had to be in a better situation by the time Dolan was ready for his big-boy bed. "I am not buying the two of you bunk beds," I had told him. "My psyche cannot handle that."

"No, thanks," I said now. "Nothing is ready. Maybe next time you come over."

"Just stack them by the door," he said. "I'll take care of them when I come on Tuesday."

I nodded through a fresh load of tears, and reached for another tissue. Even a small kindness is such an invitation to lose it.

"I just peeked in on him," Matt said. "He's out solid. Down at the bottom of the crib, with his butt up in the air." He laughed. "It looks pretty comfortable. I'd kind of like to sleep that way."

He hesitated in the doorway. "Should I close this?"

"No," I said. "I've got to get back to packing."

"He kept telling me, 'I so happy to see you,' tonight," Matt said.

"We were in Maine for almost two weeks," I said. "He missed you."

"I missed him too," he said. "I missed both of you guys."

Poor Matt. Emotionally, he might not be in tune with me, but it wasn't just Dolan who was important to him. He and I spent more time together than we did with anyone else, except for Dolan. There were so many contradictions in our relationship. I wasn't Matt's wife, but I knew I was the woman of primary significance in his life. "He never uses your name," Benet observed after he met Matt. "He always calls you 'she.'" "I know," I'd responded. "It makes me feel like he thinks I'm the alpha bitch." But in a way, I liked being his "she." Even I wasn't sure what I wanted from him.

THE TRUTH WILL ALWAYS OUT on a spa date with your girlfriends, though. Karen arrived to pick me up that weekend as I was issuing the last directives to Matt about dinner. I'd set him up with a roast chicken and mashed potatoes. All he had to do was keep an eye on the bird, take it out at the right time, and steam the broccoli.

Matt waved the head of broccoli at me. "Do I cook this whole thing?"

"No," I said. "You just cut off a chunk of it. Enough for the two of you."

He looked vaguely unsettled. "Here," I said, taking it from him and whacking off a two-person portion.

"Bye, sweetheart," I said to Dolan. "Be good for Daddy, okay?"

"I don't want you to go," he said, grabbing my leg and starting to whimper. "Stay."

"Can you walk me out to the car?" I coaxed. "Wave good-bye to me outside?"

He nodded. By the time Karen and I had gotten into her minivan and were buckling our seat belts, he was smiling from Matt's arms and waving cheerfully.

"Whew," Karen said. "Good-byes are hard. But what a little trouper. And what about Matt and that broccoli? He's like a vegetable virgin."

"He's gotten much better about eating them," I said. "But cooking is the new frontier."

She pulled away from the curb and turned to look at me. Her tone became conspiratorial. "So did you bring a swimsuit?"

"I did," I said. "A roomy one-piece. I hope you did too. The pool is tiny, but so nice."

"I brought one," she said. "But the idea of being in a bathing suit with Kir and Liza is kind of terrifying."

"It's genetic," I said. "They can't help it. I used to think I didn't look like them because I was lazy and loved chocolate. But when I was living with Kir she ate enormous bowls of ice cream every night. She's like a whippet; just burns it off. As for Liza, I haven't seen her exercise in at least two years."

Liza had found this spa in one of San Francisco's posh hotels during one of her many tiffs with Hugh. Never one to scrimp, she'd spent a few nights there. When she dropped by the spa for a facial she discovered the indoor pool, which was high up in the hotel and faced a wall of windows looking out over the city skyline. It was a perfect way to start a girls' night out.

"Ah," Liza said, turning her head as a white-clad waiter approached. She assumed her faux French accent. "We have some champagne coming. A leettle refresh-monte to toast our new Stanford student."

"Ooh," Karen said. "You know how to celebrate."

"I'm an expert celebrator," Liza said. She handed out the glasses and then raised hers to me. "Here's to us," she said.

"And those like us," I added. We finished the toast together, "Damn few left."

"Is that some sort of Maine thing?" Karen said.

I laughed. "Actually, it is. Here's to new beginnings as well," I said.

Liza had officially begun the divorce process. She and Hugh had tried, but the reunion had not lasted. She'd moved into her own apartment, a two-bedroom in an old brick building high up in the hills, with a rooftop deck that had views of San Francisco Bay. Her boys would be going back and forth between her place and Hugh's. Karen started grilling her about the apartment. Kir listened, but I suspected that her distant smile masked disapproval; she'd been pulling for the marriage to last. This was the struggle Liza faced constantly when she socialized with those of us who knew both of them. Although she was convinced Hugh was not the *right* good man for her, there was no denying that he was a good man. As a result people tended to treat her as if she'd tossed a cashmere coat into the garbage. (Liza was far more likely to press the cashmere coat upon someone she knew couldn't afford it—as her former babysitter now in possession of a black Max Mara overcoat could attest.) I hoped she didn't notice Kir's lack of enthusiasm for her plans to divorce. Fat chance. Liza hated to be judged, but nature had cursed her with an uncanny ability to pick up even the smallest current of judgment, like a weather vane shifting direction when you haven't even felt the wind on your face yet. I just wanted everyone to get along and talk about fascinating things. On these rare occasions when I got a chance to check out of baby mode, I wanted to get right back into life as I once knew it, or rather an idealized version of what I'd had. I wanted to hear stories of adventures I wasn't having. The sooner we got to the anal sex and blow job discussions, the better.

A phone rang. Mine. I'd put my cell in the pocket of my spa robe, just in case. I got out of the hot tub and flipped it open, walking away from the group. When I rejoined them, they looked up at me expectantly.

"Matt," I said. "Asking where the diapers are. I guess the middle of the coffee table wasn't obvious enough."

Karen nodded her head. "Just like a husband."

"It often feels that way," I groused. "Except of course for my conjugal rights."

"Anything going on there?" Karen asked. She poses questions with such a light and pleasant touch that to hold anything back seems unsportsmanlike. Before she became my editor, she'd had my job, and I pictured her in celebrity interviews twinkling at, say, Matt Damon—"So what about these rumors about you and Ben Affleck being gay?"

I hesitated.

"Mare," Liza said. "Not a good idea."

Kir's wide eyes were on me. "I thought that was over," she said, in a voice that implied, *It ought to be.*

"It is," I said. "But before I went to Maine, I did make a pass at him. We haven't slept together in months. And he said no. Which made me feel wonderful."

No one said anything.

"I just needed some comfort," I said. "Just some affection."

Karen patted my shoulder. "It's been a rough time for you."

"There's that," I said. "But also, if you had this hot young guy hanging around your house a few times a week, and he had the perfect ass and sometimes he'd lift his arms up above his head and then you'd see his flat stomach . . ."

"This is like Penthouse Forum," Karen said.

"You just can't go there," Liza said. "Trust me. I know."

"And he's the father of your child and he looks so good holding your baby," I continued. "And your baby loves him. It's sexy. You guys know what I'm talking about, right?"

They all nodded. There really was nothing like witnessing that father-son closeness, seeing Dolan fresh from his tub, nestled against Matt's shoulder. He was as comfortable with his father as he was with me, and that was powerful. It made me feel as though we were a unit of love. I had no idea if Matt ever experienced a similar feeling when I was holding his son, but for me, the image of him as a father was a turn-on.

"But let me tell you, that feeling can fade," Liza said.

In my moments of weakness with Matt I'd think, *Oh come on, I know we've agreed we aren't going to be in a relationship, but couldn't you just scratch my back, so to speak?* I guess I was angling for what they call friends with benefits. Couldn't platonic co-parents have an occasional benefit? But Matt was not interested in allowing such a gray area in our relationship.

"I know, it's pathetic," I said. I waited for them to tell me it wasn't. They didn't. "I don't want to be with him. It's just that I feel as though I've got this *husband* around, that I do so much for, you know, I cook for him and I take him to the doctor and I worry about him and he watches sports in my house and I'd just like some payoff. You know what I mean?"

"I really admire him for resisting," Kir said, evenly. "He's trying to keep it clean and simple. He's being smart."

I felt deflated. Admiration for *Matt*. "So I'm being stupid."

"More like not smart," Karen said.

"You're being Mary," Kir said. "Looking for a connection. And affection. And sex. Which I don't blame you for, but honestly, you'd be better off screwing just about anybody other than Matt."

Some of this attraction I needed to shake was hormonal too. I'd realized that whenever I started eyeing Matt, it was typically when I was ovulating. This put that whole night at Finnegan's Wake into new perspective. My body was on a biological quest, and on that June night, it had led me out of the house. When my father had asked me if the pregnancy had been accidentally on purpose, I'd denied it. But now I was convinced that on a purely subconscious level, there was some truth to that.

"I know that," I said.

"You're absolutely sure you guys couldn't be together?" asked Karen. Ever the romantic optimist.

"She'd get bored after a few years," Liza said. "And then she'd be so nasty to him. Even nastier than she is now."

"I'm *so* nice to him," I said.

"You are," Kir said. "Except when you're mean to him."

"I've been cooking without *gluten* for him," I said, defensively. "Do you know what it means for me to give up gluten?"

"So wait, is it celiac disease?" Karen said. "That's the gluten allergy, right? I thought he had colitis."

"He does," I said. "Ulcerative colitis."

Matt's digestive system was a shambles; there were open sores all over his lower intestines and colon. It's a stress-related condition, one that started soon after Dolan was born (yet another way that things became different that year). Matt told me about it a month or two after my mother died. He'd asked if I could pick him up after a colonoscopy because he'd be too groggy from the anesthesia to get home on his own.

"Why do you need a colonoscopy?" I had asked. "Is this a regular thing?"

"I've had some problems," he'd said. "I've been bleeding."

"Bleeding?" I'd said. "For how long?"

"A few months," he said. "Maybe four."

I was aghast. "Why didn't you tell me? Why didn't you talk to me?"

"I didn't see the point," he'd said. "I didn't have health insurance yet, so I couldn't go to the doctor. But as soon as I got my insurance all set up, I made an appointment."

Once, early on in our relationship I'd been irritated with him for being so nonreactive. "Are you made of stone?" I'd said. "I keep it inside," he'd answered. "My mother and I both do." But this was ridiculous—four months of not knowing what was wrong with his body and he'd never breathed a word to me. I had thought he'd spent an unusual amount of time in the bathroom after every meal we had together, but I'd just assumed he was trying to dodge dish duty.

"Never do that again, Matt," I'd said. "You have to tell me this kind of thing. I could have married you to get you on my health insurance. You can't go around bleeding when you poop and not telling me."

"Okay," he said. "I'm going now. That's what matters."

Now he was taking a lot of different pills, but still seemed sick. Beyond saying it was stress-related, his doctor seemed blasé about the source. I kept thinking food had to be an issue, and I'd recently unloaded my doubts about his condition to my sister Alison. She'd asked if he'd been tested for celiac. Now, as I explained to Karen, we were waiting for the test results and I'd eliminated pasta and flour from our diet just in case.

"Dr. Alison Pols is good with a diagnosis," Liza said.

"She is," I said. "But my gluten-free cooking doesn't seem to be helping, unfortunately. At least not yet. Probably because he eats sandwiches for lunch every day."

"I couldn't think of anything else to get," he'd say, and I'd just want to swat him. In terms of parenting, Matt and I were almost always in agreement—which I found both shocking and a great relief—but when it came to what he ate and drank, we never saw eye to eye. I'd threatened to start pulling out a tape recorder during our debates, because there were so many times when I'd heard him admit that beer seemed to bother his colitis, only to retract it a week later when he really wanted a cold frosty one. "But what about last week?" I'd say. "Oh, I'm sure that was the burrito I had," he'd answer, popping open the beer. I'd glare and he'd say, "I'm having a good day, okay?" But I'd ceased to believe he was telling the truth about the good days; it seemed he was always disappearing into the bathroom. "Are you in denial?" I'd say. Then he'd do the thing that I hate, the sort of man-in-prayer gesture that signifies that I am driving him crazy. His knees bend, his eyes roll heavenward and he casts his hands out, as if begging God for mercy from my nagging self. "Just leave me alone, all right?" he'd say. Whether soft or firm, my attempts to nurture were so often rebuffed.

"He never listens," I said.

Kir got out of the tub and sat on the side. She picked up the champagne bottle and topped off our glasses.

"I think you've got to let him deal with his own health problems," she said. "You should focus on Dolan."

"Definitely," Karen said.

"And I think you need to spend less time with Matt," Liza said.

But that was easier said than done.

EVERY DAY, I rode my bike from the new apartment in Menlo Park onto the Stanford campus. It made me feel like a kid, both to be on the bike and to be on a campus, even though Stanford had to be ten times the size of Bowdoin. I took a side path that went right by the mausoleum Leland and Jane Stanford had built for their son Leland

Jr., who died just before his sixteenth birthday. The heartbreak had spurred his parents to found the university in his honor. A few yards away from where all three are interred is a monument Jane erected in memory of her brother. It's an angel, bent over a stone pediment, grieving. Even her wings sag with sadness. Whenever I went by her, I thought: *She looks the way I feel.*

I suppose when people say, "It hasn't sunk in," what they mean is something is hovering at the front of their consciousness and they haven't been able to push it to the background yet. I felt as if my brain was encircled with a layer of thought devoted purely to Edward Pols, a fog so dense I couldn't think about much else. But I didn't particularly want it to go away, because then there would be less of him in my head. Nor did I want time to pass, because that would put more distance between us. If he had *just* died, I could say, "Oh, well, I saw him just last week." Part of me kept thinking this had to have been a practice run. As if he'd bounce back and announce, "Good job all of you, that was just the way I'd like this handled. When the time comes of course." Then he might say: "Mary, that was a dreadfully maudlin thing you did, reading me my own poetry at the end. And for God's sake, why read to me about death? What about one of the other poems? Something more cheering." I'd be happy to take his criticism. I'd be happy to take anything more of him.

The Knight Fellowship was the best distraction anyone possibly could have devised. There were twenty-one fellows from around the world, ranging from writers to radio and television reporters to editors. There was even a cartoonist. Most came with their spouses and a lot of them had children. Everyone had a study plan that related to the sort of journalism he or she practiced. I was the only critic in the group, and my goal was to take every film and film history class I could. But in a broader sense, creating an actual *fellowship* was our task for the year. From the first days of orientation, the fellowship was like being at the best dinner party in the world, one where you want to get to know everyone at the table. Since we'd have ten months together, we could relax, knowing we'd all have a chance to sit next to everyone eventually.

Dolan had his own fellowship experience. There were two dozen kids in the program, and they had come with their parents from Poland, Nepal, Colombia, Chile, Mexico, Korea, and South Africa. They all went to day care on campus together twice a week, during our group events. At first Dolan cried whenever I walked away, something he never did at his regular day care. Among the sea of self-sufficient eight-year-olds and five-year-olds, he looked so small and vulnerable. But as the year went on, he started to ask hopefully, "Knight kids?" whenever we passed that turnoff. We went everywhere as a pack, and the kids came with us, even to the graduate students' pub, the only place where we could bring the kids *and* get a beer. "We go bar?" Dolan would say. I kept him up too late, rode him to school on my bike, and started taking him on mother-son "dates" to restaurants. I was meeting new people, luxuriating in film history, and spending more time with Dolan. *This* was the way I had wanted things to be different.

THE MOVE DOWN to Stanford made for a longer train ride for Matt, but he still came to see Dolan two or three nights a week. He'd spend the night in Dolan's room, then get up at the crack of dawn to go back to the city. It was by no means ideal for him. Most of the spouses and partners took classes with the rest of us. As someone who wasn't technically my partner, and who needed to work full-time, Matt couldn't participate. In order to give him a taste of the Stanford experience—and thinking of his résumé, of course—I'd paid for him to take a class at the business school at nights. But he didn't seem to find it scintillating.

On the other hand, his enthusiasm for Dolan was impossible to miss. That wide grin of Matt's, the one I'd felt I didn't get to see enough of before, I now saw every time they greeted each other. I'd watch him say good-bye or good night, and hear him murmuring, "I think about you all the time." If they went three days without seeing each other, Dolan would begin to complain. "I miss my daddy," he'd say. "I need my daddy." When he'd hear Matt's key in the lock, he'd go dancing over to the door.

Matt had started talking about taking Dolan on trips to the East Coast back when I was pregnant. "I'll take you fishing, buddy," he'd say to my belly. "We'll go to the lake." I'd cringe. I knew full well his notion of male bonding over fishing was the equivalent of my fantasizing about picking out dresses for a baby girl, but still, it set off all kinds of alarm bells for me.

"No boats," I'd said. "Not unless I'm there."

"I'm not going to let him fall in," Matt said indignantly.

"Your father did," I'd said.

I'd heard the family story, the one about the time Matt was left on a dock, six years old, with a fishing pole in his hand, while Miles and Frances went out in a canoe. I imagined them in the sun, so in love, the way they still seemed to be. As they approached the dock, little Matt leaned out too far and fell in. A stranger fished him out as Miles and Frances raced toward him in the canoe.

"That was my fault," Matt had said. "I was trying to wave to them."

"It was not your fault," I'd said. "You were *six*. No one should have left you alone on a dock. The point is that dads can be kind of oblivious."

That had been the end of that discussion. But it had repeated itself every six months or so. While I'd been breast-feeding, during that first year, it was easy enough to keep Dolan by my side. But once that was over, once he was walking and talking, I had run out of excuses. After all the times I had taken Dolan to Maine over the last year, I could hardly have said no when Matt told me he wanted to take his son to his mother's sixtieth birthday party in Baltimore. He had the right. And I had the obligation, not just to Matt and Dolan, but to Katherine. Not only had she not once uttered a disparaging word about our unusual situation, she'd stepped up to the grandma plate with gusto. I'd find myself at every major holiday, and many of the minor ones, opening the door to find yet another package for

Dolan on the front step. "A Valentine's outfit for a one-year-old?"
I'd say to Matt, holding up a tiny red sweater. He'd shrug. "She likes
to shop." I wasn't Hallmark-oriented myself, having grown up in a
household of mannerless heathens, but I was touched by any and all
manifestations of her devotion. Dolan meanwhile was too young to
appreciate the packages, but he'd voted with his heart on the issue
of Grandma from the very beginning. He'd never been anything but
comfortable in her arms. So even though my heart trembled at the
thought of all the terrible accidents that could befall him between
San Jose and Baltimore, I had to let go.

While they were gone, I felt the luxury of free time for about a
day. Then I felt aimless for the next two days. Driving to the airport
to pick them up, I was like a woman about to meet her long-lost
love. I spotted them in baggage claim and sped up, trying to sneak
around the side of the stroller and surprise Dolan. He was buckled in, but craning his neck around to see the conveyor belt. He
looked absolutely content, as if he hadn't missed his mother at all.
As I squatted down in front of him, he gave me a half smile, the kind
of polite smile you give someone you aren't sure you know. Then he
redirected his gaze to the conveyor belt.

"Oh my God," I said, burying my head in his tiny lap. I was instantly crying, like an idiot. "He doesn't even remember me."

"Of course he does," Matt said. "Don't be ridiculous. He's just a
little tired. He didn't really have a nap today, did you, sweetheart?"

Dolan twisted in the chair to look up at Matt. He smiled big for
his father.

"Dols," I said, taking his hand. "Mummy missed you so. Did you
miss me?"

"Yes he did," Matt said. "We were talking about you on the plane,
weren't we, Dolan? You were saying Mummy's name."

Dolan gave a bashful smile. I kissed him all over his face, inhal-
ing his Dolan smell, his beautiful essence. "Look, Mummy," he said,
pointing at the conveyor belt.

Matt slipped me a worn-looking bag of M&M's. "I told him you'd
have some candy for him when we got here," he whispered.

I was struck by Matt's tone of voice. He sounded so at ease, and so much more confident than I was used to him being. And the M&M's—that was one of my travel tricks, to make sure that Dolan gave his father the time of day whenever we'd been away for two or three weeks. Now Matt was doing it. I might feel sad that Dolan hadn't needed me desperately, but whatever had gone on between him and his father in the course of that long weekend had been important for both of them. They'd become a team, and even if I had to watch from the sidelines, I had to admire how they looked on the field together.

THIS SPORTS METAPHOR could also be extended to my dating life. Or lack thereof. Since Dolan's birth, I'd essentially sidelined myself, and apparently this worried Karen.

"I want to fix you up," she said.

"Oh, Karen," I said.

"Now don't say no before you hear me out," she said. "All that talk in the hot tub got me thinking you need a date. You haven't met anyone on the fellowship, have you?"

"Just a bunch of wonderful married or otherwise taken men," I said.

"No cute professors?" she said.

"Married or gay," I conceded.

I couldn't stand the thought of going back online to look for a man; my time and energy were far too limited already. But I had hoped that a change in environment would introduce me to some new men. When that hadn't happened, I felt some relief that I wouldn't have to worry about negotiating a fourth party into our delicate family arrangement. I was, for the first time in my life, ambivalent about the matter of having a man in my life.

Karen was persuasive, though. "Dave is such a doll," she said. "Totally smart. And he's so sensitive. I would go out with him if I was single and ten years younger."

Dave was another writer, someone I already had a passing acquaintance with, and who I knew to be a nice person. So I agreed to make an effort. We had a very pleasant dinner together; he was easy to talk to. His father had died recently too, and both of us teared up as we compared our tales of loss. *He gets it. So different from Matt.* I thought, maybe, just maybe, I could do this again. But as the night seemed to be drawing to a close, he mentioned he'd brought a movie with him, an imported copy of a new Korean film he thought I should really see. "I love this movie," he said. "It's the best film I've seen all year. By far."

I don't much like having movies pushed upon me—I get enough of that when I'm working—but I said I'd certainly watch it sometime.

"I thought we could watch it together," he said. "If you're not too tired."

I was taken aback. I was not the slightest bit interested in watching a movie that night. Especially not alone with a guy who might try to grope me. Having given my body to Dolan for so long, between gestation and all that breast-feeding, it no longer felt solely mine.

"I've got to get home," I said. "Babysitter." I gave a shrug with the last word, which I hoped would convey, *Babies. What can you do? This is a world you know nothing about, so take my word for it and back off.*

But he persisted. "I was thinking we'd just go back to your place. Let the babysitter go home. Make some popcorn. Drink some wine. Watch some awe-inspiring Korean violence."

Right, I thought. Sounds great. After almost two years out of the dating pool, I no longer felt any obligation to pretend I wanted to spend my evenings watching awe-inspiring Korean violence. On a grainy bootleg tape.

But even if I had wanted to bring this guy home, what kind of scene would that be? My babysitter was Matt. I hadn't spelled it out for him that I was going on a date, but I figured he suspected as much. I hadn't picked up any vibe of jealousy from him. But I still couldn't walk in the door at 11 P.M. with a guy in tow and a movie in

hand and tell him he was relieved of his duties for the night. Logisti-
cally, it would be impossible; he couldn't drive off and leave me cuddling with my date on the couch because he didn't have a car. And
the bus stopped running at that hour. The next time I ventured out
socially with a man, I'd have to find myself a real babysitter first.

But more than just the awkwardness of such an encounter, it
also would have seemed unnecessarily cruel, walking in that door
with a guy, as if I were saying: *Here's the one that might replace you in
the daddy role.* Maybe early on, when Dolan was tiny and I resented
Matt's lack of romantic interest in me, I'd imagined "replacing" Matt
in some manner of speaking. But as their bond developed, those selfish thoughts had faded, and I didn't want him worrying about it any
more than I wanted to be worrying about him introducing another
woman into our lives.

I resolved not to bother dating again for a while. I didn't have to
be a nun, but there was no urgency. The man of my dreams was fast
asleep in his crib.

GRIEF IS UNREASONABLE and has a terrible sense of timing. Walking down the frozen food aisle at the supermarket, I found myself
stopped dead in front of the Sara Lee pound cakes, starting to sob.
My mother used to slice strawberries on top of them, then spoon
fresh whipped cream onto the berries. I'd refuse the strawberries and
the cream and then try to peel the butter crust off the top. At the dinner table, I always sat just to her right, Benet just to her left. She'd
still be wearing her apron, and she'd be twirling her wineglass. I took
a pound cake out of the freezer case. At home I thought how much
loftier the loaf used to look when she'd taken it out of the package.
Then I devoured three slices, hoping to find the taste of my mother's
company.

I held out a piece to Dolan, who looked at it skeptically. It was
not chocolate. Why bother? He was standing in his high chair, be-
havior I kept forgetting to discourage. "It's *cake*," I said. "This is the

kind of cake your grandmum gave me." He turned his back to me, standing with his hands on the top of the chair's back. He began to sing. I ate his slice too.

He might not want pound cake, but whenever I dipped downward into overwhelming gloom, Dolan could pull me back up. He'd always been a merry baby, but as he gained vocabulary, his sense of humor became more evident. One day, when I was changing his diaper, he twisted and squirmed so much that I had to push him back down on the bed and hold him there with the flat of my hand. He looked up at me with my mother's eyes and my round face. He was wearing the crazy love expression, the one that says he can't decide whether to yank my hair or throw his arms around me.

"Be still," I told him. "I have to get this diaper on. Stop squirming."

I caught one of his legs in one hand and used the other to smooth down the diaper underneath him.

"Dolan," I admonished. "Cut that out."

He looked up at me, clasping his hands together. Lately I'd taken to telling him, "I'm serious" when I needed to be the enforcer.

"Are you *serious*?" he shouted, his eyes filled with merriment.

I tried to swallow my smile, but couldn't. I couldn't believe how much this little boy already had my number.

Not long after that, I was driving him to day care on a gray and overcast morning, one that felt almost like winter. I peeked at him in the mirror. He had a book open in his lap and I loved the way he looked, so absorbed, as though he could actually read, even though of course he couldn't.

I picked up my cell phone and thought about calling someone. I wanted to talk to my father. I looked up his number, which I'd left in my cell phone, as if, by doing so, I could make him less gone. An elderly family friend who died recently asked Wib, in the last days before she went, "But how will we keep in touch?" Such a plaintive question. Wib tried to give her an answer that fit within the framework of her beliefs but that was also loving and true. She said she recounted the conversation to the woman's daughter, who said, "Oh yes, she asked me the same thing." "What did you tell her?" asked Wib. "I said we'd talk on the phone," the daughter said.

I hit send. Rationally, I just wanted to hear his voice on the outgoing message. But Benet is too sensible not to have disconnected the phone. I knew this, but still I called. The recording started, "This number has been disconnected or is no—" and I snapped the phone shut and looked out the window. The tears hadn't even left my eyes yet, my nose hadn't started to run, but my shoulders must have shaken a little, because from the backseat, Dolan asked:

"Mummy sad?"

"Yes, honey," I told him. "Just a little."

"Babbo?" he asked. He knew that when I cried, it was usually about Babbo.

"Yes, sweetie. I miss Babbo." I reached back and took hold of his slender knee.

AT LEAST TWO YEARS BEFORE his illness began, my father had sent us all a list of household possessions and asked us to tell him which things we wanted. He would then devise a way to distribute these items—mostly furniture and artwork—equitably. My father was always equitable with all six of his children.

No one had wanted to deal with the list and all that it implied. Then once he got sick we really didn't want to do it; it would have seemed too much like we were anxious to get our "stuff" before he died. Now that he was gone, it was up to us to conduct a lottery and split everything six ways. We gathered at Alison's house the night after his memorial service, got liquored up, and tried to joke our way through the process. As individuals, we clutched at certain items that meant the world to us—*But I love that wooden candlestick most!*—but knew as we did so that they meant just as much to the collective. There were many moments of dismay as we dismantled the household that had once been all of ours. The next day, Benet watched with some disgust as those of us who were departing dug through boxes and opened drawers in the Barn Chamber, collecting our items. It wasn't our finest hour. I no longer regret not getting my mother's carnelian ring, but I do regret feeling a kind of desperate need to have it. The possessions, after all, had lost some of their magic when their owners left them behind.

I shipped a few objects and went back to California with the family's everyday silver in my suitcase. The forks are squared off, heavy, comfortable in the hand. The knives are rounder. Nothing matches; it's a set only in that my parents kept it all in one drawer. Except for holidays, when the much vaunted Danish silver had come out, this was what I had eaten from all my childhood. I put it into the silverware tray in my narrow kitchen in Menlo Park, where it gleamed against my motley collection of flea market flatware. I felt like a criminal, having taken anything out of my parents' house. I felt as though I had just robbed my own home. Except that my home was no longer my home.

A week later, the box with my mother's lamp in it arrived. It was the second item I had asked for in the lottery. It always sat on her bedside table. Made of stainless steel, it was originally a kerosene lamp, long ago converted to electricity. The shade is white porcelain, which gives the light a soft, warm glow. It's a pretty object. But the reason I bid for it in the sibling auction was because of the noise it makes when you turn it off or on. When I pull the metal cord, the rattle of it bumping through its housing sends me hurtling through time and space to my own childhood, when I would lie in bed, listening to my mother prepare for sleep in the next room. Dolan, I thought as I unpacked it, would come to know that rattle and feel its comfort as I did. I wished I had an actual house for him, a place to call home.

But when you are not yet two, home is a simpler concept. That winter, Wib flew out and we took Dolan up to Sea Ranch, a modern, eco-friendly community built on the bluffs looking out over the Sonoma Coast. We rented a house with weathered shingles, a hot tub, and a good kitchen. On the second night, we drove out in the late afternoon to get some groceries and came back just at dusk. As I pulled the car into the driveway, Dolan sang out from the backseat.

"Home. We're home."

I turned to look at him, sitting back there, gripping his favorite airplane, and realized that for him, home is wherever we are together. He gave the word back to me.

SO BEFORE THE AGE OF TWO, Dolan had served as my grief counselor, banished my loneliness, and helped me find a new sense of home. I was ambitious to pay him back in any and all ways I could think of. This is how I came to find myself shivering on a January day by the side of one of Stanford's many swimming pools, trying to jam my hair up under a nasty rubber cap and fighting the urge to run away.

For while I have always been the first one in the cold Maine water, and the last one out, I harbored a terrible secret, known only to my siblings and a few friends who noticed and asked. I couldn't put my face in the water. I swim head up, nose out, like a seal perpetually scanning the beach. When, under great peer pressure, I've jumped, I've pinched my nose shut with the urgency of an old lady guarding her purse on a busy street. I watched people dive with admiration, feeling embarrassed that I would never be able to plunge headfirst into the water. In a shipwreck, I wouldn't stand a chance. More important, if Dolan fell off a dock in front of me, I would be of no use when it came to fishing him out. And when it came time for him to learn how to swim, I wouldn't even be able to teach him how to blow bubbles.

The swim coach who doubled as instructor to Bowdoin professors' children during Friday Night Faculty Swim had done me no favors. His method was to drop us all into the pool like unwanted puppies, a trick intended to tap into our survival skills. Apparently my natural instinct was to drown. It's all Charlie Butt's fault, I'd tell myself. But inwardly I blamed myself. I knew I was my own worst enemy, and privately I thought I was an unconquerable foe. However, past fellows had spoken of the magical teaching skills of Zora, the instructor for "Advanced Beginning Swimming." She was a legend in the Knight Fellow program; this suggested, comfortingly, that a fair portion of otherwise successful middle-aged journalists also had swimming issues. In fact, on that January day, I was huddled with two other Knights, Pam and Jo-Ann, amid a sea of Lycra-clad college students.

The first lesson was fine. Zora talked about breathing and had us do a lot of yoga on the lawn. We practiced bouncing up and down in the water. I sank underneath and blew bubbles out of my nose for the first time. It wasn't so hard. Then in the second class, we added strokes. Zora beckoned me over after one set.

"I don't think I've ever seen anyone make it all the way across the pool without breathing once," she said. "Try to take some breaths, okay?"

I put my face in the water and promptly forgot everything she'd said about breathing. Gasping and spitting, I almost drowned myself. With each passing lap I became more spastic and frenzied. I kept my head under, but that was the only part of the instruction I followed. At the end of class, I clung to the side of the pool, exhausted and miserable. Zora's feet, clad in her sporty Keens, appeared in front of me, and she bent down to look in my eyes. "You know, there is nothing wrong with swimming with your head out of the water," she said gently. "If doing the breaststroke up and down the pool works for you, that's okay. That's what my own mother does. Don't put so much pressure on yourself."

In the showers, I started to cry and didn't stop for an hour. When I finally turned the water off, Pam and Jo-Ann were long gone. I was still weeping. I never placed much faith in the whole concept of repressed childhood trauma, but I truly felt as though I were five years old again. If the lovely and supportive Zora couldn't teach me, I didn't think I could be taught. Wrapping my towel around me, I realized how much I wanted to tell my mother and my father about my failure.

I barely spoke, except to Dolan, for the next few days. Then I called Wib, who also swims in the manner of a curious seal, and told her about the swimming lessons. "You can get yourself out of that cove and around the Bigelows' boat and back into the dock just fine," she said. "That's good enough."

But was it? These swimming classes seemed like yet another example of the confluence I was at, between childhood and being a parent. All this time, as the youngest child of Edward and Eileen Pols, I had been a bad swimmer. Now I was Dolan's mother. For him, I couldn't be a coward.

Mum was afraid of pigeons, my inner voice said. *She couldn't ride a bike. But she would have torn apart anyone who came near her kids. Remember how she was with those scary gypsies in Italy? Practically beating them off with her purse? It's okay to be a coward about little things as long as you don't wimp out on the big stuff.*

I decided to go to the next class, just to thank Zora and tell her I might try again in the spring. Then I'd flee. But in order not to feel like such a quitter, I put on my suit. After I talked to Zora, I thought I'd go by one of the other pools and do some quiet head-out-of-the-water laps. Maybe I'd try the breathing routine on my own, at my own pace.

Zora spotted me as I was locking my bike up outside the pool.

"Oh good," she said with a warm smile. "You're early. You want to hop in and we'll work on this breathing stuff together?"

I stood there for a long minute, struggling with my desire to give up. Did I want to change this? Was I capable of fixing a weakness I've lived with for so long? Part of me *had* already given up, and was busily reminding myself that I was hopeless. But was that the same part of me that had been so terrified of having Dolan, only to be proved completely wrong? The part of me that had refused to see the possibility that having a child on my own could be the single most empowering act I could undertake?

If I'd listened to that naysayer, I wouldn't have the best thing in my life. I kicked off my shoes, pulled my sweatshirt over my head, and got in the pool.

By the end of the fellowship, I could dive.

• • •

IN THE MOVIES, change is often illustrated with a montage, a passage into a new life, love, or state of mind covered in the course of a couple of minutes or the length of a song. In the space of time it takes Van Morrison to sing "Brown-Eyed Girl" in the 1991 thriller about an abusive husband, *Sleeping with the Enemy*, Julia Roberts goes from being a woman paralyzed by years of being terrorized to a woman who is ready to get romantically involved again. The movie is silly but embarrassingly seductive, because Roberts at her most vulnerable is so irresistible. She tries on various stage costumes, hats, and wigs (her new love interest is a theater teacher and they are backstage) and starts flashing that trademark sunshine grin. The metaphor is obvious; she's shedding her own emotional disguise while trying on actual disguises. Critics, including me, are often annoyed by this montage technique in contemporary movies, but the audience tends to accept it at face value. It's lulling. The montage music is usually catchy, and in this impatient day and age, who really wants to watch the painstaking pace of actual progress in any real person's life?

My story of learning to swim, for instance, did not transform me overnight into a better person, willing to accept all challenges and embrace change. But I had to admit, if anyone could actually see a movie of my life—the kind that we unspool in our own heads—this made a logical montage. Replacing a weakness I'd lived with for decades in secret shame gave me the freedom to think about other alterations I could make in myself, including some I hadn't even considered yet. Through learning to put my head in the water, I realized I could open the locks on many prisons I'd devised, often unwittingly, for myself. Yet again, the key had been Dolan.

CHAPTER 15

Lessons in the Impermanence of Things

MATT AND I STOOD in the parking lot behind the Menlo Park apartment, looking at the navy blue Mercedes next to my Jetta, dwarfing it. My gaze was admiring, Matt's skeptical.

"What year is it again?" Matt asked.

"It's an '82," I said. "But supposedly these things go forever. Did you see the sheepskin seat covers?"

"Yeah," he said, without enthusiasm. "*How* many miles?"

"It's in kilometers," I said. "But pretty close to 400,000."

"That's a lot," Matt said.

I ignored him. "Here are your keys," I said.

I'd long been adamant that I wasn't going to break down and buy a car for Matt for fear that I would "enable" those slacker tendencies of his. But whenever I had broached the topic of his getting one, he'd shut it down. "I don't have any money. How would I even pay the insurance?" I'd come to the conclusion that waiting for him to get his act together was pointless. The fellowship was over, and Dolan and I were about to move back to Alameda. I was going to be teaching at Berkeley that fall. Between that class, working full-time at the paper, and the day care drop-off and pickup, I was sure I'd go mad trying to negotiate our lives with just one car.

The new me, the one who knew how to swim with her face in the water, had decided to take action to fix a problem. Why cling to my earlier pronouncement? If, by using some of the money my father had left me, I could simplify the complex dance of coordinating a family of three with two households and three different daily destinations, wasn't it worth it? I'd told Matt to ask his mother for half the money. I'd put up the rest, and I was adding him to my car insurance, which, given the age of the car, wouldn't cost too much.

The Mercedes had belonged to friends from the fellowship who were headed back to Germany, so for me it had sentimental value. Matt had no such connection. His ideal car would be one of those hulking pickup trucks that have two rows of seats and are named after some forgotten Native American tribe or a type of desert wind. But he'd have to buy that for himself someday.

"Isn't it nice?" I said. "Look at the sunroof."

"It's okay," Matt said. For a second, I felt like the mother who just bought her son sneakers that aren't cool enough. The quick heat of resentment passed through me. *Ingrate*, I thought. And then I reminded myself what the car would mean to me: *independence*.

THE MERCEDES WAS indeed a welcome addition to our lives. Matt no longer slept over on the nights I had to go to screenings; as soon as I'd get home, he'd get in the car and drive away. This made us both happy. I hadn't thought so much about the psychic toll it had taken on him, to always feel stuck at my place. We immediately started getting along better. When he announced that he was giving notice on his San Francisco apartment to look for a place in the East Bay, closer to us, I felt as though we were making real progress. I wanted us to have separate lives that worked together rather than whatever strange hybrid it was we'd concocted since Dolan's birth.

But his month's notice quickly passed and still Matt hadn't found a new place. I wanted him to have enough time to find something he really liked, where he'd have roommates who might become friends instead of just strangers sharing a shower and toilet. So I told him he could move in with us for a few weeks while he kept on searching.

I bought a trundle that slid under Dolan's big-boy bed—telling my-self, at least it's not the dreaded bunk bed—and cleared out a closet for Matt. At the end of August, I heard the steady throbbing of the Mercedes's diesel engine and looked out the front window to see him pulling up at the curb, the car stuffed with all his possessions in the world. His collection of lacrosse sticks lay across the pile of clothes in the backseat.

Dolan clambered into the armchair in front of the window and propped himself up on his elbows. "It's Daddy," he shouted. I got on my knees behind him and kissed his ear. "That's right," I said. "But he's just going to stay for a few weeks. It's a visit."

This wasn't the first time I had extended an offer to Matt to stay with us while he saved money for a security deposit and looked for a new place. After all, it wasn't so long ago that I was living in Kir and Sam's trailer, and I hadn't forgotten how hard it was to make a transition. But until now, Matt had always resisted. When he said he thought it would be hard for Dolan to have him there full-time, even short-term, and then gone, I knew he spoke from experience. We were being careful to let Dolan know this was temporary.

Dolan got down from the chair and went to the front door, which he'd recently figured out how to open. "Daddy." He beamed as Matt walked up the front steps with an armful of clothing. Matt's face in-stantly came alive with love.

Most of my friends were dubious about this arrangement—"He's never going to want to leave," Karen said—and part of me feared they were right. But on a lot of levels, I was looking forward to hav-ing him there. For those weeks, or that month, I wouldn't feel like a single mother calling to ask for help. I'd have a real co-parent. Also, my Florence Nightingale complex was working overtime. His colitis had responded to the steroids earlier that year, but now I worried that it was coming back. If I could feed him really healthy foods for a few weeks, maybe that would help. On the nights when he didn't eat at my place, Matt had a tendency to get himself a burrito or a vat of creamy tortellini at the corner pizzeria. He'd complain about the ensuing digestive discomfort to me, but be back there the next week doing the same thing. I was plotting all the healthy chicken and fish dishes I'd make for him in the course of September.

My fantasy life was also rich enough to imagine us settling in together for some *What Color Is Your Parachute*-style counseling sessions during which I'd encourage him to start thinking in broader terms about his career. The file clerk job had not led to more opportunities at the bond trader. Matt would tell me about other people who had been promoted, and I'd think, *If you were more assertive, that could be you*. Every time I asked him how work was, his answer was always the same: "Boring." Occasionally he'd say: "*So* boring."

So one evening, after a fish dinner that involved no butter or cream, I took a deep breath and launched into it.

"You keep saying how bored you are at work," I said. "Don't you think it's time you either ask for different responsibilities there or start looking for a new job? Something you might find more stimulating."

"I can't until I find a place to live," he said.

"Why not?" I said.

"You told me you didn't want me bringing my computer in and setting it up in your house," he said. "I can't look for a job without having my computer set up."

So it was *my* fault?

"Oh, don't give me that," I said. "You tell me you spend all this time at the office playing fantasy baseball or whatever it is. Certainly you could be browsing job sites then. You could at least get some ideas."

How was it that I could go from maternal to annoyed with him in five seconds flat? Sometimes I was too mercurial for even me to understand. I wanted to help, but I slipped into scolding mode so easily.

"I guess," he said.

"What is it you want to do with your life?" I asked. "I don't even know. You used to talk about business school, but you took that class at Stanford and then seemed to lose interest."

"The class was okay," he said. "Not really what I expected, though."

He put his head in his hands.

"Why is it you're interested in the financial world?" I said.

"I just need to do something fast-paced," he said. "Otherwise I get bored."

It takes Matt at least seven minutes to open a can of cat food and divide it between Casco and McGee's dishes, a task I think should take forty-five seconds. He does wash their dishes, and freshen up their water bowl, which is nice. However, since he is often doing this while I'm trying to prepare dinner on the approximately two square feet of counter space in my kitchen, I am acutely aware of how long it takes him. I wouldn't call him fast-paced by nature.

"Do you have a larger game plan?" I asked. "One I just don't know about?" I wanted so much for the answer to be yes, for him to have some secret ambition I could help him achieve.

"No," he said very quietly. "I don't. I don't have any idea what I want to do. I never have."

Well, there it was, the heartbreaking truth. Such an absence of aspirations was alien to me. Bouts of shyness and lack of self-confidence had occasionally waylaid me on my own path, but I'd known I wanted to be a writer since I was eight. However much I wanted to help Matt, desire and direction weren't seeds I could plant for him.

"I don't think you're going to be happy until you figure that out, Matt," I said. "I know you resent me pushing you, but I do want you to be happy."

"I know you do," he said. He sounded so defeated, I started to cry.

I don't think Matt knew how to hope. I remember a conversation I'd had with him when I was waiting to hear whether I'd gotten the fellowship. I'd been full of enthusiasm and "what ifs," prattling on about how cool it would be to spend a year at Stanford.

"Well, let's not get too excited about this," he'd said. I was cooking dinner and Dolan was sitting on his lap, turning the pages of a Curious George board book.

"I'm not saying it's guaranteed by any means," I'd said. "But I think they're down to like twenty-eight people for twenty spots. I've got a better than fifty-fifty chance of getting it."

"I just don't like to get too hopeful about things," he'd said.

"You don't like to be *hopeful*?" I'd asked.

"When I have hoped for things in the past it seems like it's never worked out. So I try to not get too worked up about things that might happen, so it's not so disappointing if they don't," he said.

I'd said nothing more. To know that this was the attitude Matt had gone through life with, or most of life with, was just overwhelmingly sad.

Now I walked over to my houseguest, who looked so bleak, and knelt down in front of him. "You need to start thinking about what you want," I said. "You need to hope more. It's good for you."

ONCE, when my siblings and I were all sitting around the dinner table bitching about some new development on a piece of coastal property, my father had looked up from his bowl of soup and said, "Let this be a lesson to you in the impermanence of all things." The room had gone dead quiet and we'd all stared at him. He was a philosopher, but he did not often share profundities at the dinner table. He calmly dipped his spoon into the soup and went back to eating.

I had no idea at the time that my father was quoting Buddhist wisdom, but the phrase became a part of my thinking. "Let this be a lesson to you," I'd said, watching a movie theater I'd liked being torn down. "Another lesson," I'd said, coming upon a freshly paved road through woods previously unsullied by tar. Picking up the pieces of a vase I'd loved, knocked over by McGee's tail, I'd remind myself, ". . . in the impermanence of all things."

Still, I was not prepared for the reminder I got about impermanence two weeks later. After breakfast Matt had headed off to his weekly softball game, and Dolan and I had settled into a morning of playing with his railroad set. My cell phone rang just as I'd finally figured out how to reproduce the figure 8 on the box.

"Yeah, the car just died," Matt said. "I'm on Treasure Island, waiting for the tow truck. I'm thinking maybe it's the alternator."

I knew he knew nothing about cars. I'd watched him be completely flummoxed by opening the fuel tank cover on this one.

"Matt, you didn't let it run out of oil," I asked. "Did you?"

"No," he scoffed. "I'm sure it's not that. No lights have gone on or anything like that."

But when my mechanic called later to give me the verdict, it turned out that was exactly what Matt had done. He had driven it without oil and now it was a lump of useless metal. He had it towed in front of my apartment and it just sat there. I struggled mightily with the impermanence of this thing. There was nothing Zen-like about me when I confronted him. "Who did you expect to change the oil? Did you ever even check the oil?"

"No," he sniped back. "I didn't check the oil because I never wanted a car that was so old that you have to check the oil all the time."

"Three months you had it," I said. "You never thought about the oil once?"

The word "incompetent" hovered in my brain until I couldn't stand it anymore. After four days of the silent treatment, which he responded to with his own silence, rather than the abject apologies I wanted, I finally said it. We had put Dolan to bed and were sitting at the dinner table and I was grilling him about what he intended to do about getting another car. Then I said it. "Sometimes I think you are just incompetent." As the last word rang in the air, I felt like Jadis in C. S. Lewis's *The Magician's Nephew*, using the Deplorable Word, the word that ended a whole world. His jaw clenched and then pulsed, in that way that seems as unique to men as an Adam's apple. Then he went to bed. He had no other means of escaping me.

"Eesh," Liza said the next night. "You might as well have called him impotent." She was piloting her SUV through the Mission, looking for a parking space. We were going out to dinner. I had decided I needed to get away from my roommate.

"He *is* incompetent," I said. "He can't do anything. I asked him to peel potatoes the other day and you should have seen him, fumbling through it. It took him a half hour."

"He's probably scared he's doing it wrong," she said.

"He was! He left all the eyes in."

"I'm sure he's scared of you," she said. "You're scary. I'm scared of you. You're like a snapping turtle in that kitchen of yours. That's why I never offer to help."

We looked at each other and laughed.

"But one last thing," I said. "The other day he called me to ask if there was something wrong with the milk because there was all this goop on top."

Liza was trying to light a cigarette and make a left-hand turn at the same time. "Cream?" she asked.

"Exactly," I said.

I was conscious both that I needed to complain and that I *wanted* to complain. The source of this urge needled me, but for the time being, I wasn't going to let it stop me. Liza needed to hear each and every one of my grievances against Matt.

"Hugh called me the other night to ask me where Henry's baseball uniform was," she said as soon as she'd gotten the cigarette lit and exhaled long and hard. "At *his* house. I said, 'How should I know?' We're almost divorced and he still expects me to be his housekeeper."

"Let me have one of those," I said.

"No," she said.

"Liza, he's the nicest guy in the world but he let the car run out of oil," I said. "He's sleeping in the trundle bed I bought for him because he doesn't even have a futon. Give me one."

"You've got to just let him fail a few times and figure it out for himself," she said, handing me a cigarette. "If he's incompetent, it's not your problem. How many times have I said this to you?"

"But he keeps failing," I said. "And never seems to figure it out. How can it not be my problem? I don't want Dolan growing up with a father who expects the freaking Tooth Fairy to change his oil for him."

"You shouldn't have bought him a car," she said. "You should have made him buy it himself."

"I don't know how I could have done that," I said, exhaling out the window, guiltily imagining a dark future of breast cancer and premature death and Dolan without me. But these were dire times. "Short of taking him at gunpoint to a dealership. And cosigning his loan papers. And it did make my life easier. For a few months. Fuck. What am I going to do now?"

"You're going to tell him he has to get another car," she said. "On his own this time. No hand-holding. Tell him if he wants to see his son he has to get himself a means of transport."

"I don't want to threaten him with something I'd never do to him," I said. "Or to Dolan. Plus he's living with us, so it's not like that's a real threat."

"Well, you need to get him out of there anyway," she said. "You need to start charging him rent. And none of this has to be a threat. You just have to be firm: 'This is how it's going to be.'"

"I have no problem being firm," I said. "You know that."

"Firm without being critical," she said. "There's a difference. Firm doesn't have to be hurtful. Critical can be hurtful."

We both knew what she was talking about. Once we didn't speak for the better part of four months. She'd been angry with me for a perceived allegiance with Hugh—it was hard to stop being friends with someone you liked because a marriage was breaking up—and we'd gone back and forth in frustration with each other until I'd finally written her a scolding letter telling her exactly how unreasonable she was being. At the time I thought it was brutally honest and thus helpful. In retrospect, it was sanctimonious and unhelpful. For months there was nothing but awful silence between us, until her brother John brokered a reconciliation. I was lucky we were still friends.

"There's a spot," I said, pointing to a car that was about to vacate a parking place.

"Finally," she said, putting her blinker on. "Did you make dinner for them before you left?"

"Just some spaghetti," I said.

"I knew it," she said. "Enabler. Why are you still cooking for him anyway?"

"I don't know," I said, opening the car door. "Let's go to dinner and talk about anything but Matt. I feel like a broken record."

I DID KNOW. I started cooking for him because I wanted to make it easy for him to be there, for Dolan. He'd be that much more willing to babysit if he knew he'd get a nice hot meal. I guess it was a form of bribery, to entice him to be around for Dolan. Which was unnecessary, ultimately. I also thought it would make us feel more like a family. And it wasn't exactly agony, since I love to cook. But in all our time together, I had built up a lot of resentment over feeding Matt. And the food-related resentment was just part of the bigger resentment. The death of the Mercedes had drained my reserves of goodwill. Why did I have to do everything? Why had he never even attempted to cut Dolan's fingernails, for instance? Maybe this is how it was with husbands. But husbands could be counted on to make you feel good, at least occasionally, right?

"We need to talk," I said to him that weekend. Dolan was in his room, allegedly napping, but actually singing to himself and thumping his sippy cup of milk against the wall. Matt had taken my car to go look at two shared apartments that morning, but he hadn't been enthusiastic about either of them. His pace of apartment searching was such that I was getting worried my friends had been right.

"Okay," he said, folding himself into a chair, probably thinking, *Not again!* Casco immediately jumped up onto his lap and began licking herself. Through the window behind him, I could see the dead Mercedes. Leaves were piling up on its windshield.

"I need you to take more initiative around here," I said. "While you are living here, you need to cook at least twice a week."

"I will," he said. "I keep meaning to, but it's hard to plan for it."

This wasn't a good thing to say to me. Trips to the grocery store were hard to fit into my day, but they weren't something I could avoid. I had to feed my son. I had to pack him lunches. I made the time.

"Well, start planning," I said to Matt. "Start with thinking about what you're going to cook for dinner next Tuesday."

"I will," he said. "Maybe I'll make that chicken with papaya."

"That would be great," I told him. "And what are you going to do about the car? We can't go back to you not having one."

"I know," he said. "I guess I have to see if I can get a loan."

This is where it got hard for me. When I'd bought my Jetta, I had done a lot of research, about loans and the best way to buy a car. I'd ended up turning it into a story for the paper. I felt as though I knew a bit about the process, and I was sure I knew more than Matt. But this time it was all up to him. Liza's words rang in my head.

"Maybe you could call your dad to ask for some advice," I said neutrally.

"I think I'll call Charlie," Matt said. "He's pretty good at this stuff."

"Good," I said.

With the help of his stepfather, Matt was approved for a loan a few days later. I winced when he forgot to get approval from the credit union on the particular used car he'd picked out and they declined the loan, after he'd already driven the car off the lot. I waited to see what he would do, praying he wouldn't ask me to help. Again, thanks to Charlie, he figured it out. After the aborted effort with the Mercedes, phase one of my long-term plan to see him established in more of an adult life was complete, and I was pleased. Now on to phase two. We had reached the last weekend of the month and he still hadn't found an apartment.

"Starting October 1, you are going to have to start paying some rent," I told him over dinner. We were having pasta with shrimp, which meant that Dolan needed only minimal coaxing from both of us to eat. "Three hundred the first month. If you are still here in November, you'll have to pay $650."

He looked irritated. I remembered his mother telling me he'd been upset when she'd asked him to pay rent. But the very next day, he found an apartment in Oakland he could move into immediately.

The neighborhood wasn't what I would have picked out, and his roommates didn't seem like people he was thrilled to be living with, but as I kept telling myself, these were not my choices to make. At least I no longer had a roommate and Dolan had a father who lived close enough to come for dinner on short notice or pick him up from preschool when the need arose.

THERE IS SUCH A THING as an autumn chill in California, albeit not much of one. A few weeks after the death of the Mercedes, I turned the heat on for the first time. The smoke alarm went off within thirty minutes, and there was a vague burning smell coming from the furnace. I called the gas company, and they came out the next day.

"Just dust," the guy said cheerfully. "You've got a season's worth of lint and cat hair down there, and then you turn the thing on, and it just starts to burn off. I'll vacuum it out for you."

Matt was standing there with me. How I wish he had the gene that would make him able to diagnose the source of such a smell. I know this is sexist of me, but if I can, and do, make Thomas Keller's sautéed salmon with a beurre blanc and leeks, I would like the person who eats a dish like that in my home to just occasionally contribute something I *could* contribute but would rather not. I know I should just be grateful that he is better at brushing Dolan's teeth than I am.

The repairman suggested I move all the coats off the rack above the furnace.

"Could they catch fire?" I asked. I felt silly asking, but I've wondered. If I step out of the bathroom after a shower and shake a few drops of water down there accidentally, it sizzles.

"No," he said. "It'll just dry them out. But don't leave anything on top of the grate. And don't let your little boy play on top of it."

Dolan was peering around my leg at the time.

"That's a great old furnace," the guy said cheerily, on his way out the door. "Must be fifty years old, but it's in good shape."

"Well," I said, picking up my vacuum cleaner, which I had been storing on the grate. "I better move this."

The vacuum cleaner was the nicest thing I owned. I bought it shortly after becoming a mother. A freelance check had dropped from the sky, so I splurged. It was a Miele, a German brand Liza introduced me to a couple of years before. She has two. "Yes," she had told me. "They *are* worth $600. Worth every penny."

I treated mine with reverence. It skimmed across the floor, following me obediently like a very useful dog, reaching every nook and cranny, sucking up all the cat hair that had been resisting every previous vacuum I'd owned. As the gas man left, I put the Miele down in the living room, next to the bookcase. I loved it so much I could almost think of its shiny red body as decorative.

A week later, Matt and Dolan were watching a movie while I made dinner. "Can I turn on the heat?" he called out to me. "Sure," I said, slicing potatoes. I walked into the living room about half an hour later. The room was warm. "What's that terrible smell?" I said.

Matt looked up sleepily. He had his head on a pillow. Dolan's hand was affectionately slipped into his father's hair. "I don't smell anything." He had the least sensitive nose on the planet, but this was overwhelming. How could he not have noticed? But more important, what was burning? I went around the corner, to the hallway where the grate was. There was my Miele, splayed out on its back, its red plastic cover oozing all over the grate. The smoke alarm went off just as I was attempting to wrench the corpse free of its assailant. Its innards were exposed, and it looked as vulnerable and awkward as Kafka's cockroach.

"My beautiful vacuum cleaner," I wailed.

I had to go walk around the block, practically hyperventilating. It seemed he cost me money every time I turned around.

"Mummy, I sorry," Dolan said when I came back in the house, no calmer than before. He had his hands splayed out in his cute mime routine, the one that gets me every time. But usually he's using it because he actually did something naughty. "I sorry for the vacuum cleaner."

"You didn't do anything, honey," I said, rubbing his back.

In the other room I told Matt, stabbing at him with my finger, "You will go out this weekend and you will buy me another Miele. Just as nice as this one."

Then I had to leave. I got in the car and called Wib and told her how awful my life was, having this person around who ruins cars and melts vacuum cleaners.

"I'm just having trouble understanding," she said. "You have something on your floor that gets hot enough to destroy a vacuum cleaner?"

"Yes," I said. "It's a gas furnace. With a pilot light."

"Now, could Dolan burn himself on this?" she asked. "Because it seems to me if—"

"If Dolan sat on it for a half hour when it was turned up to seventy-five degrees and he was made of plastic, yes, he could hurt himself; in fact, he would melt," I said impatiently.

Why wasn't I getting the kind of sympathetic response from Wib that I wanted? Matt had launched an assault on two valuable possessions. (Both of German origin as it happened. Matt's heritage was Polish; was this a subconscious thing, a deep-seated resentment over World War II? What was next? Was he going to set fire to Dolan's Steiff teddy bear, the one I'd won at an auction?) Just as I had with Matilda, the romantically inclined couples' counselor, I was seeking allies. Wib disappointed me first by not indicting Matt and then suggesting that perhaps by constantly anticipating failures on his part, I'd made it hard for him to succeed.

I'd had enough lessons in the impermanence of things. I'll confess, on the day of the melted Miele, I wanted Matt gone. I wanted to be free of him. I didn't want to worry about his career. Or his living situation. Or his health. I didn't want to watch him eat ice cream and be itching to tell him not to because dairy could aggravate his colitis, all the while knowing that if I did say something, he'd be irritated and ignore me anyway. Mostly what I didn't want to feel was the sense that I was putting so much energy into caring for someone who didn't particularly seem to want me to care for him.

In truth, none of this actually had anything to do with the vacuum cleaner, but that's what I was fixated on. A few days later, I called Alison, hoping to chew over the Miele incident again.

"I'm thinking I'll have him split the cost of a new vacuum with me," I said. "Do you think that's okay?"

"No," she said.

"I should just pay for the whole thing?" I asked.

"Probably," she said, evenly. "Look, it's just an object. Don't get me wrong, when Katy used to break things, I'd get angry. But really, it is just an object, and in the long run, what does it matter? So he made a mistake. He didn't do it intentionally."

"I just feel as though he doesn't listen to me," I said. "I feel like he's turning me into this shrew."

"Maybe you're ordering him around too much," she said. "Maybe he's tuning you out because he can't handle all the orders."

I don't delegate many tasks, and I try to delegate only the ones I know should be easy for him. But when I do, my requests do sound like orders. This tendency stemmed from his passivity, and the fact that it often takes asking him three times to actually get something done, but now it's a pattern. When he does that prayer pose, the plea for protection from this nagging woman, it's usually accompanied by his saying, "Okay, okay, okay, *okaaay*." Lately, Dolan has begun saying it too. "It's dinnertime," I tell my child, and when he finally comes to the table, he's saying, "Okay, okay, okay, *okaaay*" in just the same tones of exasperation as his father.

"Look," Alison said. "We are controlling people and we tend to move very quickly. We process quickly. We get annoyed with people who don't move at our pace. Why do you think I get so irritable when everyone is milling around in my kitchen and I want to clean up? And I don't want anyone else to clean up, because they won't do the same kind of good job I would. This is not normal. This is hard for other people to be around."

"Matt definitely does not move at my pace," I said. "He's not stupid, by any means, but he's just kind of dreamy. I don't know, I just wish he were sharper by nature. Quicker to take the initiative."

Alison was kind enough to ignore the fact that I was essentially saying I wanted Matt to be more like me.

"You can't make him sharp," she continued. "Certainly not by snapping at him. The most important thing is Dolan. You've decided you want to have his daddy around, for his sake, so you just have to put up with melted Mieles." She laughed. "Sorry. I promise you it will seem funny someday. But did you really need a $600 vacuum?"

WITH MY PARENTS GONE, it made sense that I'd turn to my siblings in any crisis. But even had my father still been alive, I don't know that I would have shared the vacuum cleaner story with him. No matter whose fault it was, the fact that I'd possessed such an extravagant item wasn't the best illustration of fiscal responsibility. It was, I had to admit, similar to buying a $48 candle to remove the rat odor from the trailer you were living in because you didn't have the savings to move into a new apartment.

During one of our many bedside conversations during the last year of his life, my father offered to give me some money.

"A check for you and a check for Dolan," he'd said. "The maximum that the IRS allows as a gift. But I am thinking that I should perhaps put it in a trust, and put Benet in charge of it."

This sounded like a mild insult, but to complain seemed ungracious. I was the youngest and the only one of his offspring who didn't own her own home. I was certainly the least frugal and financially savvy of all my siblings (unless you count Wib, whose old habit of tossing unopened bills in a drawer had long ago convinced Sean that he should handle their money). I still wasn't saving, beyond what went into my 401(k), and I hadn't gotten rid of my debt. A part of me wouldn't mind if Benet did handle my money for me.

But I didn't want my father to depart this world thinking so little of me.

"I think Benet has his hands full without having to deal with my money," I told him.

"Perhaps Sean then," he said.

"I suppose," I said. I was grateful when Dolan woke up and immediately began banging his calves against the stroller, a prisoner wanting to escape, giving me an excuse to escape myself.

Later that day, Benet and I were in the kitchen cleaning up the dinner mess.

"Does he really think I'm that much of a loser that he has to create a trust for me?" I said, scrubbing a pot. "I'm forty years old."

"Scallops," he answered.

"Excuse me?"

"I think he thinks you'll spend it all on scallops and such," he explained, stacking dishes meticulously, the saucers here, not *there*. I stopped my scrubbing and scrutinized Benet's face, looking for the joke.

"What do you mean, scallops?" I said.

"Well, this summer, when you made scallops and pasta for everybody, you must have bought three pounds of scallops," he said. "He noticed."

"There were seven of us eating!" I protested.

"They're rich," he said. "And expensive. When Beth and I eat scallops, I buy four for each of us."

I turned the water back on and scrubbed the pot harder. I knew I tended to over-serve my dinner guests in general, a culinary retort to all those times when my mother, unable to shake her Depression-era upbringing, cooked only enough pasta for one portion each. But it never occurred to me that this tendency would lead to a greater judgment about me and money. Nor was this an unfair judgment. In the wake of the Miele disaster, I couldn't get that scallop conversation out of my head. The way it was nagging at me meant something, but I wasn't sure what.

MEANWHILE, my professional responsibilities were weighing heavily on me, and so was the feeling that I needed to step it up on the mothering front. Potty training was the next major hurdle. I longed to be done with diapers, which cost me more each month than electricity. At two and a half, Dolan was generally willing to pee in the miniature, throne-shaped potty I'd placed next to the toilet. But when it came to pooping, he preferred to go off in a corner when I wasn't looking, do it in privacy, and then find me and demand a fresh diaper. If I was attentive to the warning signs, I might be able to catch him before he started.

One morning that fall I noticed an ominous silence from the living room and scurried out of the kitchen to find him standing behind a chair, wearing a telltale expression of pained concern. "Let's poop on the potty," I said with false cheerfulness as I scooped him up under the arms and went running for the bathroom.

By the time I got him seated on his potty, he'd hit his internal pause button. He asked me to read him a book. And then another. And then a third. I used up another diaper in the process of giving up and then going back to deciding I had to be firm about this poop being done in the potty.

"It's hard," he told me. "Poop's not coming out today."

He asked for another book. Then he peed. "I did it," he said triumphantly. "That's just pee," I said, pressing him gently back onto the seat. My mind was busy thinking of the writing I had to do today. And the milk I had to buy. The life insurance I should get. And the fact that I'd once again be late to day care, trailing in well after everyone else was settled in for the morning, Dolan still sporting his breakfast egg on his face, me in yoga pants and woolen clogs, attempting to masquerade as a person not in pajamas. Small picture, big picture, back and forth. I was anxious to get to the computer, where I think best.

Maybe Dolan *didn't* have to poop. Maybe I was just wasting both of our time. "Let's go," I said.

"No, I pooping," he said. "Read another book." He looked like a little bird. I had put him to bed the night before without a bath, after we had been out having a windblown walk on the Bay, and now his hair was sticking out in every direction. Suddenly I was hugely annoyed with him. I had spent five straight days with him by myself. We went on two playdates that involved mostly negotiating for sharing, mopping up of tears, and threats that we would leave immediately if he didn't shape up. On the third day, I discovered he had broken the CD player. On the fourth day, I took him into a public bathroom with me and cautioned him not to touch anything. He promptly licked the wall.

"Time for school," I said, picking him up under the armpits. He shouted, "No," and kicked madly at my arms, my belly, my hips. He connected with my nose, hard. How much longer will I be able to control this strong little body, I wondered, picturing him as a teenager, slapping me aside as I try to flush his heroin down the toilet. He thrashed while I dressed him, and I stayed calm. Then I carried him, crying, out to the couch and attempted to put shoes on his wildly kicking feet. "I don't want to go to school" was muffled by his tears, but I heard it.

Then I screamed. All the frustrations of the last few months emerged in that one scream: the damn impermanence of things, the permanence of Matt and me, stuck with each other, the sense that I was doing too many things and none of them well. Dolan stopped crying. I carried him to the car without saying a word and stuffed him, like a sack of potatoes, into his car seat, while he sniffled. I was already ashamed, but I didn't apologize to him yet, because I was still angry. I said nothing to him in the car. I didn't slide open the mirror on my visor, which I usually use to watch him watching the world. A few blocks from his school, he pointed out the fire station to me. He sounded cheerful. He sounded as though he had just decided to let my insanity pass. I was amazed when he leaned against my legs in his classroom, reluctant to let me go. How could he not fear the crazy woman? I did.

As I drove home, I remembered myself at ten, lying on my bed, screaming into my pillow. In my memory, I'd cried so much that for a minute or two, there was a cascade of snot and salt water on my face so monumental, I was almost proud of the force of my own drama. Recovering, I heard steps on the staircase. He wasn't moving fast, but I knew his footfall, light and springy even when he wasn't in a hurry. He was always an energetic man. When we made pit stops on long drives, he mortified us all by standing in front of the car, kicking his legs into right angles and swinging his arms. I craned up from my pillow to look at the door, checking to make sure that the key was turned.

He knocked, softly. "Buglet?"

I ignored him.

"Mare-fare?"

"Go away," I told him.

"I'd like to have a word with you, dearie," he said, his voice conciliatory.

He was sorry. I had won. I went to the door and unlocked it. He was wearing a blue oxford shirt and chinos, his daily uniform in warm weather. In winter, he added a crewneck sweater, although never one with raglan sleeves. He was vehemently opposed to raglan sleeves, as if wearing them could diminish a man. His eyes had been full of rage just fifteen minutes ago. We had fought over the proper method of crabgrass eradication. For almost twenty-five years, this crabgrass has returned to haunt him. He suspected seeds carried on neighborhood cats or perhaps the same heavy spring winds that took down a branch of the best apple tree. The seeds could have been blown over from Mrs. Hessel's. She was not as diligent at lawn work as he was. He also suspected blue jays, those menaces of the avian world.

The crabgrass was tough. The grass around it gave way before it did, which is why my father wanted it removed very carefully. I had grown frustrated with trying to dig up each patch and had tried yanking it. He'd inspected my pile of sundered grass and cried out in vexation when he'd found rootless pieces. I'd told him that it was hard, and it hurt my hands, and the tool he'd given me, a sort of long fork without a middle tine, didn't work very well anyway. Then he'd seen remnants of feathery seedpods clinging to the reddened pad of my index finger, further evidence I was doing it wrong. Hadn't I listened? he'd stormed. And then I'd stormed back, about how he'd had six children purely to have a full workforce at all times. In short order, his eyes blazing, he'd threatened to crack me across my bottom. This was not unusual, but increasingly it was an affront to my all-important dignity.

But once he came to me, apologetic, I became the victor. The tool was not adequate, the work was too hard, the crabgrass should be disposed of by some other means. I was right. He was wrong.

More than thirty years later, I realize I never triumphed. He must have been regretting his loss of self-control, his own irrational rage. He felt guilty. He felt the way I felt, driving home from day care with an empty car and the mournful feeling that I could have just damaged my sunny child, whom I knew to be angelic in comparison with many two-year-olds.

If I wanted to, I could talk myself out of feeling too bad; I feared my father's wrath when I was growing up, but I never feared him, never doubted his love. Maybe Dolan and I will be like that, I could tell myself. There was nothing wrong with my relationship with my father. Except of course that I never felt I could possibly do everything right enough to really impress him. And that as an adult, I cared far too much about being right.

I WAS AWARE OF AND contemplating my urges to be right, but that didn't necessarily mean I was about to abdicate all claims to certainty. There were things I was, in fact, very right about. Matt's medical situation for one. I wanted him to find a new doctor to treat his colitis. I wanted him to see someone who would suggest a more holistic approach, who would encourage him to try acupuncture—he met such suggestions from me with disdain—and make real dietary changes. That person would change everything, I believed, get him on the track back to good health and teach him how to manage his illness. When he told me he'd made an appointment to see someone new, someone whom he'd researched and who had a good reputation, I felt like falling to my knees to cry hallelujah.

Because I am his family, his "she," at least for the time being, I went to pick him up at the hospital after his latest colonoscopy.

"Are you here for Matthew?" his new doctor asked. I nodded.

She looked competent and alert, neat and tidy under her white jacket. She was probably first in her class at medical school. She was young enough to appreciate the usefulness of acupuncture and yoga in treating a stress-related illness. She would make him better. "Will you be driving him home?"

"Yes I will," I said. Matt had told me to come an hour after the procedure.

"We're going to let him sleep for another hour at least," she said. "He's had a rough time. I stopped the procedure halfway through because I didn't want to hurt him."

Matt had been telling me, as usual, that his colitis wasn't that bad, that he wasn't in what they call a flare-up. I had doubted him, but he kept insisting that he knew what he was talking about.

"His colitis is very severe," she said.

I had been smiling at her, the obsequious curl of my lips intended to let her know that she and I would be a team in restoring Matt to his former self. I stood there stupidly, the smile now frozen.

"I want to put him on some much stronger medications and up his steroids," she said. "If he doesn't respond to that, I'm going to have to recommend surgery."

I started to cry. Surgery meant he'd have his colon removed, that he'd shit in a bag for the rest of his life. Even the most confident young man in the world would have trouble adjusting to that life. The thought of Matt's beautiful young body torn apart was too awful. And this all started right after our son was born. What a toll our mistake had taken on Matt, even if he didn't admit it. He'd gotten so used to his disease that he wasn't even able to see how serious it was. I put my sunglasses on and walked around the neighborhood, crying for him.

I wore my own stress like a big black cape, flapping it in the face of anyone unlucky enough to cross my path. Matt wore his tucked away on the inside and it was literally eating away at his core. How much of this was my fault? How much had my badgering about everything from careers to trivial things like how he did the dishes contributed to his internal misery? I was so busy thinking about the stress of being stuck with him that I wasn't thinking about his stress over being stuck with me.

When I returned an hour later I found Matt groggily walking the halls, looking for me. I took his hand and led him to the car. As I settled him on my couch to sleep the afternoon away, I found myself treating him as tenderly as I treat Dolan whenever he's sick. I realized how much more elusive a solution was than I had thought, and how little my impatience was helping matters. On that day, I watched him eat the chicken broth I'd put in front of him and thought about what it would be like for Matt to get sicker. I told myself I would never again even *think* that I wanted Matt gone.

I WAS DRIVING Dolan to preschool a few weeks later when he asked from the backseat, "Daddy going to pick me up?"

"Yes he is," I said, looking up to the mirror so I could see his face. "Mummy has to go to a movie tonight for work. You guys are going to have dinner together. Daddy is going to make you something nice."

Matt was finally making some real headway through the Marcella Hazan cookbook I'd gotten him the previous Christmas. He was eager and careful in the kitchen, and I could see his confidence building. He'd announced to me the week before that he thought he'd made the best puttanesca he'd ever had. "Better than mine?" I'd said, raising my eyebrows at this new cockiness.

We drove on, turning onto the road that ran next to San Francisco Bay, where we frequently saw pelicans and hawks.

"I'm going to be a daddy someday," Dolan announced.

He sounded the way some kids do when they talk about being a ball player or a fireman. Like being a Daddy was a Big Deal.

"Really," I said.

"Yep," he said. "I'm going to be a daddy, just like Daddy."

Now I *knew* the significance of fathers—I was still weeping over the loss of my own—but why wasn't I acknowledging deep, deep in my heart, how important not just "a father" was to Dolan, but this particular father? This man, who had never once said "No" when I'd asked him if he could take care of Dolan?

"That's great," I said. "Then I can be a grandmother."

I watched his face in the mirror. He looked content, gazing out at the water, thinking about his daddy. To him, his parents were equals. He saw no incompetence or competence. He measured in love. Both of us gave it to him; both of us deserved it in return.

When people ask me to describe Dolan, I usually struggle for a minute, trying to sum him up. Should I detail his insane passion for baseball? Should I talk about his sense of humor, or the way he makes me feel? Invariably what I say is, "He's just really *nice*," which is so wonderfully true. Moreover, every time I say it, I think, *He's nice like his daddy.* I observe that one niceness is the emulation of another, but I don't think I've been grateful enough to the source.

When we are cuddling at bedtime Dolan says, "I like you forever."

"And I love you," I say back.

"I love you too," he says. I kiss him ferociously, on his forehead, on his cheeks, again on his forehead. He kisses me back, the same way.

"I have to go," I tell him.

"No," he says. "I'm keeping you."

I soften. "One more minute," I tell him.

"Two minutes," he tells me. And so I relent.

He snuggles into me, stroking my hair. "I like your hair," he says. "It's like chocolate." His round little face is pressed up against mine, his eyes open, his smile enchanting. His combination of innocence and beauty is almost too much to be believed. In the softest voice I could possibly imagine he says, "I'm petting you." He makes me so happy I can hardly stand it.

AS I WAS BRUSHING my teeth that night, I thought about what Dolan had said. "I want to be a daddy, just like Daddy." I looked in the bathroom mirror. In the time since the end of the fellowship, something new had appeared on my forehead, a lump where I had been knitting my brows together. I realized that I looked peeved so much of the time that it was ceasing to be an expression and starting to just be my face. I rubbed the lump, but couldn't get it to go away.

Had I assigned myself the role of shrew?

There's a line in *The Philadelphia Story* I keep thinking about (that Katharine Hepburn, she *haunts* me). Hepburn, as society belle Tracy Lord, tells Mike, the journalist played by Jimmy Stewart, "The time to make up your mind about people is never."

When had I made up my mind about Matt? Was it when he'd made the crack about not cleaning my cat litter? The first time he'd said "her and I" instead of "she and I"? Or even earlier, on that first night, when he'd confessed to needing a J-O-B? My objective in maintaining a good relationship with Matt had been on behalf of Dolan, who I thought would do better with a father who was around. But somewhere in there I'd also made a judgment about Matt. I'd scrutinized him in those first months of knowing him, and I'd found him lacking. I disapproved of him. I disapproved of everything about him that was not like me, and not like the man I thought I might end up with. I'd felt it was up to me to make him *better*. And when I wasn't trying to figure out how to make him better, I was chafing against the fact—or rather, my perception—that this was my job.

It probably would have taken a psychologist only five minutes to determine that the disapproval that came so easily to me was a direct result of having a father who disapproved of everything from raglan sleeves to children who weeded crabgrass the wrong way. But wherever it came from, holding on to it was not doing me any good. If this disapproval campaign I was running succeeded, the end result would be Matt completely undermined. He was not some movie I was trying to persuade paying audiences to stay away from. He was the father of my child, and my child thought he was perfect.

There I was in the mirror, lumpy brow and all. Far from perfect myself. For instance, I'd been so furious with Matt for letting the car run out of oil, but the truth was, seven years before, I had done the exact same thing to my trusty old Volvo, which my dad had bought for me when I got out of graduate school. It had seized up in the middle of a tunnel. I even knew how to change that car's oil, part of a female empowerment tutorial I'd given myself, but I'd gotten busy and distracted and ignored my old girl's needs. What was the difference between Matt's not checking the Mercedes's oil and what I had done?

As for the Miele, yes, I had made a production about moving the vacuum cleaner off the grate. But I'd recently used some of my inherited money to hire some housecleaners to come twice a month. They hadn't been there for the ceremonial move of vacuum from furnace to living room; maybe they had innocently put it on the grate after using it. Maybe I'd forgotten and put it there myself. All Matt had done was turn on the heat. Yet my first instinct had been, on seeing my roasted appliance, to hang *him* over the fire. I realized how much I *wanted* to blame him for any and all mishaps, particularly ones that involved money.

I had to look away from myself at that moment, and as I did so, I caught a glimpse of a photograph of me with friends at an oyster bake in Pt. Reyes fifteen years ago. Was it a Proustian leap that made my mind go from oysters to another shellfish, scallops? Or had the events of the last few weeks just been leading me to this moment? Because what about those three pounds of scallops I'd purchased for a family dinner that summer? Never the sensible choice for me, always the indulgent one. Again, who was I to cast stones? Was Matt so different from how I had been at his age? Were the things about him that struck fear into my heart fears about his lacks, or my own?

I remembered what Liza had said to me, *kept* saying to me, every time there was a fresh disaster. "Let it go." Whenever she said it, the words bounced off me, barely registering, an impossibility, as impossible as learning how to swim properly or accepting that I would never get to speak to my parents again. Could I let go? I was in charge, steering what I perceived as a fragile ship of a family forward.

If I let go, things would fall apart. Or maybe not. Maybe they would reshape themselves. Maybe my brows would unknit.

"Let it go," I told my reflection. "Just let it go."

MANY YEARS AGO, when Kir and Sam were first settling into marriage and establishing a home together, I went over to their new apartment to see a couch and chair they'd gotten at a thrift store. It was a matching set, upholstered with emerald green velvet. The legs were dainty, the wood frame nicely carved. It was a sweet set, and I'd have bought it too. But it wasn't exactly masculine.

"I love it," I said. "But I'm surprised Sam went for it."

"Well, I had to let him think it was his idea," Kir said.

I looked at her with bafflement.

"I showed it to him and said I thought I liked it," she explained. "Then I started looking at some other ones, none of which I liked at all. I wanted this one. But I had to play it cool, tell him, I don't know, do we really want something so green? Then he got on the couch's side and started defending it and here we are."

"Huh," I said. "That's some strategy."

"You've got to do that with men sometimes," Kir said. "They need to feel like they're in charge."

Fine for you, I thought, but I'm never going to cater to a man's ego that way. Isn't it kind of disingenuous? Don't I have to stand up for my voice as a woman with just as much right to make decisions as a man?

Twelve years later, I stood in my kitchen, and as Matt asked whether I wanted the Pinot Noir or the Merlot with my pork chops, I remembered Kir's green velvet couch. I could continue to coast on the scraps of wine knowledge I'd retained from waitressing days, or I could let it go. Matt had been reading the wine book his father had sent him. He'd already come a very long way from the boy who believed Safeway's bargains were not to be passed up. "You decide," I said. It was easy. And every little thing I let go of made the bigger ones seem easier as well.

Habits aren't broken overnight, of course. I think back to the first half of my pregnancy, when I could still catch myself calculating my years of fertility and daydreaming about whether I'd ever get to be a wife and mother. I was so used to the absence of these things in my life that I could, for a few minutes, forget that the baby, at least, was right there, in my belly, and this was no longer something to fret about. The same was true of my new attitude toward Matt. Even after the final results of those lessons in impermanence—recognition of reason as it were—I still had to fight to remember to keep those old, familiar frustrations in check. I had to focus not on being Matt's boss, but rather his partner in co-parenting.

As I tried to be gentle where once I was sharp, I found that it not only helped in the way Matt and I got along, it brought me peace. Letting go felt good, like putting my face in the water when I swam.

Around that time, Matt started changing aspects of his life. What came first, the chicken or the egg, I don't know. I only know that when I was no longer anxiously hanging over his shoulder, he very quietly went out and got a new, better-paying job at a good company, without ever so much as telling me he'd interviewed for the job. He bought a fat stack of books about coping with colitis and began quoting them to me. It seemed to me that his self-confidence grew. Or maybe it was just that without me squashing it, it had room to breathe.

I knew things were truly different when it came time to move Dolan to a new preschool. I'd gone by myself to have a tour of a nearby Montessori school, planning to make that decision as I had all the others, without him. I liked what I saw, but I wasn't sure my instinct was right. I realized I wanted Matt's input. So I asked him to come with me on a second tour.

"What'd you think?" I asked him as we stood on the sidewalk afterward.

"It's great," he said. "We should absolutely send him here."

And just like that, my doubts were gone.

When I went to see the movie *Knocked Up*, I laughed so hard I could barely hear some of the dialogue. It was our story in so many ways, except that Katherine Heigl was way prettier than I and Matt was way cuter than Seth Rogen. Also, we didn't fall in love the way they did, which would have made everything so much easier. We were messier because we were real. And our story didn't end on the day our baby was born. Our story goes on, but one part of the story, the part where I am at war with the circumstances that brought me my son, is over.

Dolan has given both of his parents a purpose in life. Together, he and Matt have taught me about the limitations of all my old expectations. Where or how your child comes to you doesn't matter. How you feel about the résumé of the father of your child should not matter at all. All that's relevant is what's written on his face when he looks at his son. I do know what color Matt's bones are.

Now

WIB IS IN TOWN, getting groceries for dinner, and Dolan and I are alone at the Boathouse. After readings of *Lilly's Purple Plastic Purse*, his current favorite, and *The Tale of Benjamin Bunny*, my current favorite, he has been persuaded to nap. As I luxuriate in the hammock on the screened-in porch, I amuse myself thinking of the way Old Mr. Benjamin Bunny—who had no opinion whatever of cats—wallops Mr. McGregor's unfortunate cat. I watch as Mr. Bigelow comes down to the dock. He rows to his motorboat to bail it out. He spends fifteen minutes getting everything shipshape, and then returns, carefully tying up his dinghy and disappearing up the ramp with his oars on his shoulder. This is about as exciting as it gets in an afternoon in the Cove.

I go downstairs, into the dark room that I'd always imagined would be my wedding chapel. The floorboards creak. Wib was right; this is no place for the old and infirm. Of course, they are both gone now, our old ones, our infirm ones. But even still, there'd be no way of airing out the damp, or warming up the constant chill. This was an impractical place for a wedding. I slide the heavy door open. The old ramp is just a few jagged pieces of wood sticking out of the water. Another couple of winters and it would be gone altogether.

I watch as a lobsterman pulls traps out in the deeper water. I remember my younger self, so desperate for answers, so ready to blame myself, and feel both fond of and sorry for her, for all the time she spent fearful her future would not be the right one.

I suppose I would like to have a man in my life. But because I've beaten the biological clock, on my own terms, the pressure is off, and with it, the inclination to put myself out there. Something easy, something fun, something natural may come my way in the future. In the meantime, it no longer feels as though anything is missing. I have never been so productive, or fulfilled. All the energy that I used to waste on my love life is channeled into the life Dolan and I have together.

Out in the Cove, the sandbar is growing. I hear a shout from upstairs. Naps, even short ones, will soon be a thing of the past.

"Mommy," Dolan yells. "Come get me. I need you."

I find him on the bed, trying to peel off his diaper.

"I want to go see the ocean," Dolan tells me.

"Sure," I say. "You've got to wear your Tevas, though."

"No Tevas," he says knowingly, as if he were trying to correct a misstatement on my part.

"Yes, Tevas," I say, firmly.

I carry him down the steps to the Cove. The water is only up to my ankles when I step off the last step. At high tide, the last nine steps are usually under water.

"Almost warm," I tell Dolan.

"Let's go to *KoHo*," he says.

KoHo is Sean's little day sailer. She is drifting at anchor, out in the shallows. I wade toward her, pointing out the hermit crabs to Dolan on the way. They scuttle away from my feet as fast as they can go, and Dolan laughs. "They're going to bite us," he says gleefully, gnashing his teeth next to my nose.

At moments like this, I ache for my parents, for my mother particularly, who would have gotten such a kick out of the clever, funny grandson she never got to know. Then I look into his merry face, and inside his eyes, so much like hers, I find my memories of her, laughing at Benet's and my antics, poring over some battered old Michelin guide, tearing up at an old movie, lifting her face to the sun. *She has not left me entirely,* I think. And as I smile back at him, I feel her within myself—and him, my Babbo, my Grinch, my father—reproduced in the act of loving a child. When I am holding Dolan's hand, I often realize that my thumb is idly stroking his soft skin in exactly the same gesture she used to use on my small hand. The sensory memory has been retained and is now cast back, a mirror reversed. She is in my body.

My father is in the winter sky, in the Winter Hexagon, which, anchored on Orion's shoulder, reminds me of his poetry and of the last words he heard in this world. I see him in other faces, faces I don't even know. I saw an old man in a blue blazer on a train platform where I waited with the other passengers, pressed up against the edge, guarding our right to claim seats. He looked anxious. Though he looked nothing like my father, I could suddenly see my father in *his* blue blazer. He too would be anxious, in that way that the elderly so often look anxious about the complications of moving through the world when you are no longer strong. In the face of a stranger, I see my father's eyes, his brow, and think of the way he loved our foreheads.

"It's the most beautiful part of a woman's face," he pleaded once, in the midst of an attempt to convince me against bangs. His hand was laid sideways on my forehead, as if he were checking for my temperature. Now that I am a mother, a mother who pushes back her son's hair to place her whole palm on his forehead, I imagine that he was remembering, in that anti-bang gesture, what it was like to hold that forehead in his hand when I was small. I scoffed and pulled away from him. I was nineteen. I went and got bangs, which never looked right. As I stood on the platform trying not to stare with longing at the old man in the blue blazer, my eyes welled up. All I want is to leave a legacy of love on this earth as true and as deep as the one my parents left.

I fell in love with Dolan unconditionally, and only later did I begin to see pieces of myself in him. That reflection has made it so much easier to love myself. I think the same is true for Matt. I think of my parents, seeing themselves reflected in six young faces over so many years, and I hope that it was true for both of them as well, that their children gave them the gift of self-love.

I put Dolan in the boat first, and then clamber on myself, settling against the warmth of the boat's white bottom, heated by the sun. Sean has already taken us sailing a couple of times, and Dolan liked it very much. But he almost seems to like sitting at anchor in waist-high water better. He rocks us. Then he pretends to fish off the side, using one of Sean's ropes.

"Where did water go?" he says suddenly. The rock wall nearby looms above our heads. At high tide, only the top few inches of it will show above the water.

I squint at him. "It went out to the rest of the ocean," I explain. "It will come back later. This is low tide."

"I *like* it," he says enthusiastically.

"Me too," I tell him.

Acknowledgments

FIRST AND FOREMOST, the greatest of thanks to Matt, who made everything possible. I aspire to be as loyal and kind to you as you have been to me.

A sincere thank-you to my editor, Lee Boudreaux, whose diligence and intelligence are matched only by her enthusiasm and patience, and to the ever-helpful Abigail Holstein at Ecco. And also to my agent, Henry Dunow, who made me laugh even while delivering merciless editorial comments.

My sister Elizabeth was with me every step of the way and deserves special thanks for fielding and enduring many neurotic phone calls and e-mails. Other thanks go to Adrian and Sean, particularly for refraining (mostly) from big-brother ribbing; Benet, in particular, for his poetry knowledge and photographic skills; Katy for allowing me to call her "an insomniac stoner"; and Alison for her sense and sensibility. And to Beth Pols and Karen Totman for stepping in with advice and help whenever needed. Also, Aunt Elizabeth and Kesiah Scully.

For professional advice, inspiration, and often plain old comfort: Anita Amirrezvani, Sylvia Brownrigg, Sara Catania and Mark Nollinger, Stacy Finz, Heidi Julavits, Peggy Orenstein, Tom McNeely, Kate Moses, Bernard Taper and Gwen Head, Eric Wahlgren and Ayelet Waldman. And Karen Hershenson, who steered me to my title and brainstormed with abandon.

Mary Fernald, friend for twenty-five years, thank you.

Also to: Julie Fields, who is just the kind of reader this book is intended for and therefore had to suffer through a painfully rough first draft; Joe Garofoli, for an evening of drunken artistic advice; and to the best trailer park managers in the West, Kirsten Jones Neff and Sam Neff.

To those who lent me writing spaces, you have no idea how much that meant. April Lynch, Colin Johnson, and Jason Stone, who sent me to hotels. John Bigelow, Leda Olinger, and Tom Fernald, who opened up their homes to me and did not complain when I left their cupboards bare of the sugary and the salty. For Grotto hospitality: Susan Gerhard, Ethan Watters, Xandra Castleton, and David Munro. Also Java Rama in Alameda and the Alameda Free Library. A nod to the late great Johnny Cash, whose version of "Ring of Fire" jump-started many a writing session.

At the *Contra Costa Times*, I owe much to the gracious, forgiving, and talented features staff, particularly Lisa Wrenn, Lynn Carey, and Anne Chalfant. John Armstrong, thank you for being such a movie buff that you continue to employ a local critic during the dark days of journalism.

I owe the astounding gift of time, space, and a life-altering experience to the John S. Knight Fellowship for Professional Journalists at Stanford University, particularly Jim Bettinger and Dawn Garcia.

My Knights, I'm forever grateful for your fellowship, encouragement, and friendship: Jo-Ann Armao, Karen de Sa, Daniel and Maria Cristina Coronell, Artur and Gosia Domoslawski, Inday Espina-Varona, Carola Fuentes and Rafael Valdeavellano, Emily and Collin Harris, Chi-Young and Young-Joo Shin, Guillermo Lopez Portillo and Karla Iberia Sanchez, Allan Au and Tongwa, Pam Maples, Maria Martin, Tom and Gretchen Meyer, Suman and Purnima Pradhan, Ivan and September Penn, Janet Rae-Dupree, Laura Rauch, Mike Swift and Deb Petersen, Martin Turner and Carolyn Gilbey, Gary Wolf and Christa Aboitiz.

Finally, Dols Pols, my little one, when you grow up and are ready for this, know that no one has ever made me as happy as you.